The Dutch East India Company
in Early Modern Japan

The Dutch East India Company in Early Modern Japan

Gift Giving and Diplomacy

Michael Laver

BLOOMSBURY ACADEMIC
LONDON • NEW YORK • OXFORD • NEW DELHI • SYDNEY

BLOOMSBURY ACADEMIC
Bloomsbury Publishing Plc
50 Bedford Square, London, WC1B 3DP, UK
1385 Broadway, New York, NY 10018, USA
29 Earlsfort Terrace, Dublin 2, Ireland

BLOOMSBURY, BLOOMSBURY ACADEMIC and the Diana logo are trademarks of
Bloomsbury Publishing Plc

First published in Great Britain 2020
This paperback edition published in 2021

Copyright © Michael Laver, 2020

Michael Laver has asserted his right under the Copyright, Designs and
Patents Act, 1988, to be identified as Author of this work.

Cover image: Camels with Dutch Handlers, ca. 1821. Purchase, Sue Cassidy Clark Gift,
in honor of John T. Carpenter, 2012 (© Unidentified Artist / THE MET)

All rights reserved. No part of this publication may be reproduced or transmitted
in any form or by any means, electronic or mechanical, including photocopying,
recording, or any information storage or retrieval system, without prior
permission in writing from the publishers.

Bloomsbury Publishing Plc does not have any control over, or responsibility for, any
third-party websites referred to or in this book. All internet addresses given in this
book were correct at the time of going to press. The author and publisher regret any
inconvenience caused if addresses have changed or sites have ceased to exist,
but can accept no responsibility for any such changes.

A catalogue record for this book is available from the British Library.

A catalog record for this book is available from the Library of Congress.

ISBN: HB: 978-1-3501-2603-9
PB: 978-1-3502-4681-2
ePDF: 978-1-3501-2604-6
eBook: 978-1-3501-2605-3

Typeset by Deanta Global Publishing Services, Chennai, India

To find out more about our authors and books visit www.bloomsbury.com and
sign up for our newsletters.

Contents

Preface	vi
Acknowledgments	x
Introduction: The Dutch East India Company and the Rhythm of Life in Japan	1
1 Gift-Giving and the Early Modern Web of Diplomacy	19
2 Horses and Camels and Birds of Paradise, Oh My: Exotic Animals as Gifts	37
3 Most Exquisite Curiosities of Nature and Art	55
4 Rarities and Curiosos: Scientific Paraphernalia as Gifts	77
5 A Taste of the Exotic: Food and Drink as Social Lubricant in Early Modern Japanese-Dutch Interactions	97
Epilogue: Gifts and the Coming of the Americans	115
Notes	123
Bibliography	153
Index	166

Preface

While the majority of scholarship on gift-giving in Japan has concentrated on the modern era, and has often been sociological or anthropological in nature, gift-giving has been a feature of life in Japan for centuries, and probably has been a fundamental part of life in general since ancient times. Anyone who has lived and worked in Japan knows that one cannot go on holiday without bringing back to the office the obligatory *omiyage*, or small gifts, often of sweets native to the region one visited.[1] One study of Japanese consumer behavior while on vacation in the United States determined that tourists spent about the same amount of time and energy buying *omiyage* for their friends, family, and co-workers back in Japan as they did on all of their personal shopping.[2] The present work will focus primarily on the early modern period, which in Japan is roughly from the 1600s through to the mid-nineteenth century, corresponding approximately to the period of the Tokugawa shogunate (1603–1868), although to be sure historians will rightly argue that many aspects of the early modern era, including institutionalized gift-giving by Japanese and foreigners, were in place before this period. The focus will furthermore be on the gifts that were given between the officials of the Dutch East India Company and the shogunal court and other high-ranking personages in Japan with whom the Dutch interacted.

While the present study will concentrate on the VOC[3] activity specifically in Japan, Dutch gift-giving was a prevalent part of the Company activities in many, if not all, parts of Asia. Claudia Swan states that "early modern encounters among foreign potentates and their emissaries almost always involved the exchange of valuable goods as gifts. Most of these presentations were aligned with trade interests or practices: these gifts were nearly always related to negotiations concerning trade, which in turn were the negotiations through which international relations were forged."[4] Markus Vink, for example, has highlighted the role of gift-giving in several Dutch embassies to the Nayaka state of Madurai in the seventeenth century. Vink lists the many exotic and costly gifts brought to the court, including elephants, horses, and high-quality cloth, as well as European manufactured goods.[5] Similarly, Bhawan Ruangsilp has detailed Dutch relations with the court at Ayutthaya, including the regular giving and receiving of sometimes costly gifts, some presented as gifts from local Company officials and some presented as official gifts from the House of Orange in The Netherlands.⁶ John Wills recounts how Dutch gifts played a central part in the VOC's attempt to open up trade with the Qing court in China; although the gifts were carefully selected, the Dutch were ultimately rebuffed by the Chinese emperor at every turn and were obliged to trade at Canton along with the other Western powers of the time.⁷ Many other scholars have written about the exotic gifts given to Asian potentates from the Shahs of Persia in the West to the emperor of China in the East. In fact, just as there was a vast network of VOC trade spanning Asia, so also there was a parallel network of gifts that flowed from the Netherlands to Batavia and onwards to the various factories across Asia. In this regard, then, Japan was certainly not unique, although the scale of the gifts, offered year after year for over two hundred years, as well as the vast range of gifts, was probably unmatched in other Dutch trading factories in Asia.

Studying Dutch gift-giving in Japan affords us a detailed and comprehensive view of how diplomacy and foreign trade in early modern Japan was facilitated. Through a study of gift-giving, we are able to see how the Dutch tapped into an already existing pattern of intra- and cross-cultural interaction to further their commercial goals in Japan. Very quickly the Dutch realized that plying the Shogun and his officials with gifts, as well as the myriad smaller gifts showered upon local hosts, was not only indispensable to gaining an audience in the former case, or in moving along the machinery of everyday life in the latter, but was also, in fact, the cost of doing business. The Dutch were in an excellent position to do this since they had a far-flung trading network in Asia and beyond from which they could draw much of the exotica used as gifts. Horses from Persia, fine woven cloth from Southeast Asia and Bengal, exotic birds from the hinterlands of Java and Borneo, and manufactured goods from Batavia and the Netherlands were all shipped across Asia to be used as gifts in various factories, and the Dutch settlement at Deshima was no exception. One is able to trace through the communications sent to the Company headquarters in Batavia (present-day Jakarta) the array of gifts requested for the Japanese.

Much more than this, however, the study of gift-giving affords us a detailed view of everyday life for the Dutch in the port city of Nagasaki as well as in the Shogun's capital city of Edo. We are able to see, for example, how the use of gifts served as a social lubricant between the VOC merchants and the bureaucracy with which they were obliged to interact on a daily basis. We are able to see how gift-giving helped the Dutch to navigate the tricky web of power and prestige that confronted them at almost every turn in Japan, from visits from high-ranking daimyo to the bewildering array of requests that arrived routinely from local officialdom in Nagasaki. And we are able to see how providing Japanese men of influence with the curiosities they craved, as well as the prestige that was essential for maintaining their social position, was a fundamental part of the Dutch strategy in Japan, which is why the giving of gifts was so meticulously attended to and why they play such an outsized role in the diaries kept by the chief merchants on their contrived island home.

Perhaps the most useful aspect of gift-giving in early modern Japan is that it allowed both sides, the Japanese and the Dutch, to use the giving and receiving of gifts for their own political and economic ends, even when those ends were radically different. An example of this is illustrated in a diary entry of the chief merchant for March 20, 1650, which states categorically that the Dutch sent a special ambassador to Edo loaded with gifts not for filthy lucre (despite the ambassador's ship being stuffed with merchandise), but solely to pay respects to the Shogun.[8] Of course we know that the primary reason why the Dutch sent the envoy and the gifts was because the Shogun continually demanded it, and so the VOC finally complied after many years in order to preserve the trading privileges the Dutch enjoyed in Japan. After all, just as with tips on gift-giving offered to business executives doing business in modern-day Japan, so too with Dutch gift-giving: it was the ritual and social form of the gift and its presentation that really mattered, not the ultimate intention behind it.[9] For their part, the shogunate used the highly ritualized presentation of Dutch gifts to demonstrate to their vassals that it was the uncontested arbiter of foreign relations in Japan, and it did this by highly organized spectacles of tribute-like visits to court, complete with public displays of submission and lavish exotic gifts. In the earlier example of the special ambassador, the Dutch motive was to ensure that the commerce they enjoyed for the past forty years in Japan continued, and to that end, the Company was willing to engage in the pageantry of what amounted to a more or less ad hoc "official" embassy. Gifts were a way for the Dutch to continue enjoying their privileged position in Japan, both for the good of the Company, and also, it must be said, for the (semilegal at best) personal enrichment of the higher-ranking Company merchants, certainly among the worst kept secrets in the Dutch East India Company.[10]

Gift-giving was not simply a social nicety that was incidental to Dutch trade in Japan; rather the performance of shogunal power and the yearly reenactment of Dutch servitude was a central aspect of the Dutch presence in the country. This is clearly seen in the Dutch diaries as the chief merchant meticulously recorded all of the items sent to the Shogun and his officials, along with the painstaking and laborious process of packing and transporting them. Recorded for posterity are even seemingly trivial instances of gift-giving, a bottle of wine here, a few almonds there, and who doesn't like a jar of elephant fat now and again. In short, the VOC archives reveal the minutiae of gift-giving in Japan, year after year, decade after decade, in exacting precision. We are able to see what gifts were brought for the year; we are told when the official inspection occurred and what worthies came round to have a gander at the exotica; we are told if the gifts happened to be too lavish or not lavish enough; we are told when the gifts were loaded on the special barges to be sent ahead to Edo; and we are often even told how much European wine was ladled out into bottles, and when the Nagasaki *bugyō* would sample it to make sure it was fit to be used as presents (surely a perk of office if there ever was one). This is all quite aside from the actual presentation of the gifts, laid out in Edo on specially made presentation trays for the upper echelon of society to behold. We are told about the lesser, but no less exotic, gifts given to the officials in Nagasaki, the shogunal officials in Osaka and Miyako, and the highest ranking shogunal officials in Edo.[11] We are told in often exacting detail about the many personal gifts that were given, from bottles of wine to several pounds of butter to European manufactured goods. We are able to see the "return gifts" either given to the Dutch after their audience with the Shogun or more personal items given in return for an ad-hoc Dutch gift. And finally, we are often told what items the Shogun and his officials desired for the following year before the process began all over again with the arrival of the next season's trading ships. In short, the giving and receiving of gifts is a pervasive topic in the Dutch diaries every year for roughly two hundred years.

This book will examine gift-giving between the Japanese and the Dutch through two lenses. After situating the Dutch presence in Japan from the early seventeenth century onwards, we will examine the theoretical framework of the institutional giving and receiving of gifts: from Mauss' and others' assertion that the giving of gifts created a binding web of reciprocity from ancient times; to Constantine Vaporis's intimation that gift-giving, subsumed in the larger phenomenon of the court journey, was a version of the alternate attendance system (*sankin kōtai*) that institutionalized a system of service obligation on daimyo; to Ronald Toby's work in identifying the Tokugawa desire to use foreign embassies to Edo, including ritualized displays of submission, as a way of creating a new Japanese-centered tribute system, as opposed to the traditional Sino-centric worldview based on the Chinese Son of Heaven. In all of these theoretical constructs, gift-giving plays a central role, which is certainly no surprise given the pervasive and ubiquitous nature of gifts in the Dutch-Japanese relationship over the centuries and, indeed, in virtually every facet of social and political life even in our own times.

Acknowledgments

This book has been years in the making. As anyone who has fallen victim to the double-edged sword of academic administration knows, and as the renowned academic Yoda once observed, "If once you start down the dark path, forever will it dominate your destiny. Consume you it will." Because this has been a decade-long process, the number of people to thank has grown to inordinate lengths. I first conceived of this project while spending the summer of 2007 at the Center for Nonwestern Studies at Leiden University where I was mentored by Dr. Willem Boot and Dr. Leonard Blussé. It was while at Leiden that I discovered the wonders of the Dutch East India Company archives at the National Archives in The Hague and the Museum Volkenkunde (National Museum of Ethnology) in Leiden. The staff at the archives were always quick to lend a hand, or several hands, and were always responsive to what must surely have been my litany of annoying and repeated requests. Similar thanks are due to the staff of the Leiden University Library, and in particular to the library staff at the Institute for Area Studies. Over the course of the summer, I spent many, many hours in these libraries scanning primary source documents and learning from the many researchers whom it was my great pleasure to meet. It is not too much to say that the course of my entire academic career has been shaped by my experiences in the Netherlands and at Leiden University in particular.

I would be remiss if I did not acknowledge the support of my own institution, the Rochester Institute of Technology, for providing resources to complete this manuscript, and in particular the College of Liberal Arts for financial support for a series of research trips over the years that have contributed to this book.

I am grateful for the support of Bloomsbury Press as this book progressed from concept, to refined concept, to project proposal and sample chapters, and to, at long last, finished manuscript. I deeply appreciate the professionalism and enthusiasm the editors at Bloomsbury have demonstrated every step of the way. My gratitude also extends to the anonymous reviewers who provided helpful and insightful comments that have made this work much better than it would otherwise have been.

I am grateful for the many scholars whose work has influenced my own. In particular I have long admired the work of Martha Chaiklin, Adam Clulow,

Leonard Blussé, Cynthia Viallé, Suzuki Yasuko, and many others. Over the years, I have had the privilege of interacting with these giants of the field at conferences, and their work has given me a standard to which I can only aspire.

And finally, this book is dedicated to Dr. Denis Gainty, an eclectic scholar of modern Japan who taught for several years in the History Department at Georgia State University. Denis was a true friend and confidant who continually provided me encouragement and support, and who was always available to laugh, and to share whatever happened to be going on in our increasingly complex lives.

I met Denis when we were both graduate students, making our way through premodern Japanese language with luminaries such as Dr. G. Cameron Hurst of blessed memory and Dr. Linda Chance. After graduation, Denis and I would make a point of seeing each other at least once a year at various conferences where we would immediately pick up right where we left off. Denis passed away tragically at much too young an age in 2017, and while there have been many moving tributes to this beautiful father, teacher, scholar, and friend, they will never be enough to truly convey how much Denis meant to so many around him. He will forever be missed, and no matter how many years may pass, there will always be a gap in my life. This book is dedicated to you, my friend, with much love and respect.

Introduction:
The Dutch East India Company and the Rhythm of Life in Japan

In July 1654, the chief merchant of the Dutch East India Company in Japan noted in his diary that the *bugyō* (governor) of the city of Nagasaki was pleased with the presents that were given to him for that year. He continued on, in what can plausibly be construed as a piece of advice for his successors who would no doubt look back at the diary, stating, "You can see how one could capture and retain favors here with trifles."[1] In a similar piece of advice offered a few years earlier, a previous chief merchant had noted in a similar tone of political calculation, "I think that this stratagem should be pursued in future, for it only costs the company a handful of spectacles, some telescopes, butter, tent wine, almonds, cheese, and other such trifles."[2] While the gifts on these particular occasions might have been thought of as mere trifles to the merchants who wrote this sage advice, the VOC went to great lengths, almost extraordinary lengths, to ply Japanese officialdom with a variety of gifts, some anything but trifling. The Company brought to Japan large animals both tame and wild, including Persian horses, buffalo, elephants, camels, and exotic birds. While most gifts took the form of various types of fine woven goods such as silk, Company servants also brought to Japan a wide variety of European manufactured goods, including telescopes, globes, spectacles, and weapons—most commonly pistols, but also cannons, grenades, and mortars.[3] Many of these gifts, especially the smaller manufactured goods, were lumped together in what the Dutch called "*curiosos*," or "*rariteyten*," and all of these gifts were, in one way or another, used to maintain the cordial relations with Japanese officialdom that prevailed, with the odd exception, for the better part of two centuries. It has been well established that gifts play an important part in trade and diplomacy, and the history of presenting gifts for political or economic gain is probably as old as civilization itself.[4] I don't think it too far-fetched to say that gift-giving is a fundamental part of what it is to be human and to live in human society. How one conceives of a gift, however, varies widely from era to era and is dependent on the circumstances in which the gift is offered and received. In this book we will examine the situations in which gifts were given—from the personal gifts exchanged between VOC merchants and Japanese officialdom to the gifts that were largely predetermined by tradition and convention and were exchanged formally between the Company and the shogunal court in Edo.[5] We will detail the many exotic and bizarre gifts that were brought to Japan by the Dutch over the course of the seventeenth and eighteenth centuries; we will have occasion to examine the meticulously detailed procedures and rituals that accompanied the presentation of gifts; we will examine the yearly journey to the shogun's court in the city of Edo, a central aspect of which was the formal presentation of the gifts; and finally we'll be able to glimpse gift-giving in the context of daily life for the handful of Dutch merchants who lived on their tiny man-made island in what must have seemed to them the very end of the Earth. Before we can fully understand these gifts and their presentation and reception, however, it is necessary to have a rudimentary understanding of the fascinating historical background to Dutch trade in Japan.

The Dutch in Japan

In 1600, a Dutch ship by the name of *De Liefde* limped into harbor in western Japan, its original crew of around one hundred reduced to about twenty bedraggled men, most of whom were unable to walk and on the verge of death.[6] This harrowing journey that originated more than a year and a half earlier from Rotterdam had as its goal the increasingly lucrative Japanese trade in precious metals, mainly silver. If the Dutch could tap into this trade, they could in turn obtain a cargo of spices from Indian Ocean ports that would, if all went well, make the ship's owners fabulously wealthy. The Dutch had heard reports from countrymen who had served with the Portuguese of fantastic riches the Japanese islands could offer in exchange for high-quality silks that were in such demand in Japan.[7] The Portuguese used their trading post on Macau to obtain Chinese silks and soon learned that by shipping them to Japan, they could sell them for a great profit in precious metals. Before long, enormous Portuguese carracks were leaving Japan fully laden with silver, and the captaincy of these Portuguese missions naturally became a source of great wealth, and thus great competition, among the Portuguese gentlemen in Macau.

This fabled wealth, combined with the fact that the Dutch and the Portuguese were constantly at war, led the Dutch to undertake voyages to the East Indies in order to try to tap into the riches that the Portuguese and Spanish had hitherto monopolized. This was the impetus behind the voyage of the fleet of which *De Liefde* was a part. In the event, the *Liefde* was the only ship to arrive in Japan, the wretched crew undoubtedly thanking God for delivering them from the ghastly voyage of death. It's a historical irony that the best-known sailor on the ship was not Dutch at all, but an Englishman by the name of William Adams.[8] Adams would go on to become a trusted adviser to the first Tokugawa Shogun, Ieyasu, and would spend the rest of his life as a successful merchant in Japan (and most impressively would be played by Richard Chamberlain in the 1975 screenplay based on James Clavell's novel *Shogun*). The ship, however, was Dutch, as were the few survivors who made landfall with Adams, many of whom remained in Japan for at least the next few decades. Adams is the most well known, but other sailors, among them Jan Joosten van Loodensteyn, Jacob Quackernaeck, and Melchior van Santvoort, played a role in helping to establish the Dutch presence in Japan. These latter two were allowed to leave Japan in 1604 and journeyed to Patani, in modern-day southern Thailand, where they alerted their Dutch compatriots, employees of the VOC that had been founded only two years prior, to the trade possibilities in Japan.[9] Adams likewise alerted his own countrymen to the possibilities of trade with Japan, and in 1613, an English ship captained by John Saris arrived to set up the furthest flung outpost of the English East India Company.[10]

Nine years would pass between the arrival of the *Liefde* and the establishment of the first Dutch trading post in 1609. In that year, the Company finally got around to sending a contingent of VOC merchants to establish a trading post in the western port city of Hirado, a territory controlled by the Matsura family. As soon as the VOC arrived, Abraham van den Broeck and Nicholaas Puyck made the long journey to visit Tokugawa Ieyasu, the first Shogun of the Tokugawa *bakufu*, and were accompanied by an interpreter, Melchior van Santvoort, one of the survivors of the ill-fated *Liefde*.[11] It is notable for our purposes that on this very first mission to the shogunal court, the Dutch brought presents for the Shogun along with an official letter from Prince Maurice of Nassau.[12] With support from William Adams, Ieyasu granted the Dutch wide-ranging rights to trade throughout Japan, granting them a *shuinjo*, or red-seal letter, so called because of the official vermillion seal of the Shogun.[13] Armed with this important document, the Dutch journeyed back to western Japan and arranged for their trading post, or "factory," to be set up in Hirado, whose daimyo was on friendly terms with the Europeans, and who had a long history with maritime trade and its close relative, piracy.

As mentioned before, as part of this initial journey to the court of Ieyasu (at the city of Sunpu rather than Edo, as Ieyasu had in theory retired in favor of his son Hidetada), the Dutch took gifts to the Shogun, no doubt on the advice of William Adams. Included was porcelain from Southeast Asia, ivory tusks, and Persian carpets.[14] The English as well, when they visited the court of Ieyasu a couple years later, took along presents, including a "Turkish carpet." The English were given in return ten folding screens "to hang a chamber with" and a suit of armor which today stands in the Tower of London.[15] From the very earliest moments of Dutch and English interactions with the Japanese, they were employing the age-old political strategy of plying the authorities with gifts, and receiving gifts in return.

The initial Dutch presence in Japan was not particularly profitable, despite the fact that as several scholars have noted, Japan was at that time producing as much as one-third of the world's silver, even taking into account the enormous silver mines of the Spanish "New World."[16] The challenge the VOC faced was that they could not bring to Japan a consistent or large enough supply of raw silk, the commodity in greatest demand.[17] The Portuguese were able to obtain Chinese silk at Macau, the Spanish were able to trade with Chinese merchants in the Philippines using New World silver shipped from Acapulco, and the Japanese were traveling to several destinations in Southeast Asia in junks full of silver. The Dutch, with no steady supply of Chinese silk, had to resort to the vicissitudes of capturing Portuguese and Chinese ships, a practice that led the Company to be accused of piracy, a reputation that it was not totally able to shed even decades later.[18] Only with the establishment of a VOC factory on the island of Taiwan in the 1620s was the Company able to secure a somewhat consistent supply.[19] Even then, it was not really until the 1630s, when the Shogun forbade all Japanese from traveling abroad on pain of death, and in 1639, when the Portuguese were kicked out of Japan, that Dutch trade would reach its zenith.[20] For a few decades beginning in the 1630s, the VOC factory in Japan was the most profitable of all its trading posts in Asia.[21] It is in the context of this enormously profitable trade in precious metals that the Dutch gifts to the Shogun and his officials should be viewed.

In exchange for bringing a wide variety of silk to Japan from places as varied as Taiwan, Tonkin, Persia, and Bengal, the Dutch took away an enormous amount of silver, literally tons each year, enough to finance a fair amount of VOC commercial activity in Asia.[22] Later, the VOC would be able to obtain gold in significant quantities, and finally copper, after silver and gold exports were severely curtailed in the later seventeenth century because of Japanese concerns over precious metals drains from the country.²³ Japanese silver, gold, and copper, therefore, was the impetus for trade in Japan, and because this trade was so valuable to overall Company profits, the VOC went to extraordinary lengths, including gift-giving, to ensure continuous, smooth trade. When we read of the yearly visit to the shogunal court (in Dutch the *hofreis*, or literally "court journey"), the sheer logistics of transporting the Dutch merchants, their interpreters and minders, their luggage, the trade items, and finally the huge amount of gifts that were sent ahead on barges, it is quite remarkable that this journey occurred year after year, decade after decade for well over 150 years, until Company finances made such yearly visits prohibitive and they were allowed to make the journey only once every four years. Even then, VOC gifts were still required to be sent to Edo in "off years," although without the extravagant arrangements and the expense of making the actual journey.

Tokugawa Japan

The Tokugawa family was one of a number of powerful warrior families that competed for power both regionally and nationally in the "Warring States Period" from roughly 1467 to 1600.²⁴ Originally a small daimyo family in central Japan, the Tokugawa allied itself to the rising Oda clan, led by the ruthless warlord Nobunaga. After Nobunaga's death, Tokugawa Ieyasu and Oda's capable general Toyotomi Hideyoshi fought a series of battles to a draw, and when it became apparent that the two families would weaken each other by continuing to fight, Ieyasu agreed to become Hideyoshi's vassal and was awarded with an enormous grant of land in eastern Japan, centered around modern-day Tokyo. The Tokugawa thrived as Japan was pacified under the Toyotomi clan so that when Hideyoshi died in 1597, Ieyasu was one of the most powerful warlords in the country. Ieyasu, along with four other Toyotomi vassals, were made regents of Hideyoshi's young son, Hideyori, until the minor could attain his adulthood and rule in his own right. Such an eventuality never happened, however, as the regency split into two competing factions and it became clear that warfare would result.

Ieyasu and his allies met the competing faction, led by Ishida Mitsunari, at Sekigahara in eastern Japan in October 1600. A timely defection to Ieyasu's side helped ensure that the Tokugawa and their allies were victorious in this enormous and epic battle. Clearly, the Tokugawa had become the paramount military force in the land, although it would be several decades before the complete machinery of Tokugawa rule was set firmly in place.

After arranging for the emperor to bestow the martial title of "shogun" on Ieyasu, and after retiring to arrange for his son, Hidetada, to ensconce himself firmly in the line of succession, Ieyasu spent his remaining days shoring up his family's power. He took into direct Tokugawa control all of the silver, gold, and copper mines;[25] he arranged for his erstwhile enemies to be either stripped of their domains, moved to other, smaller domains, or simply have their domains dramatically reduced in size; and, significantly for our purposes, he arranged to have all foreign affairs put under his government's direct supervision.[26] The city of Nagasaki, for example, even though nowhere near adjacent to Tokugawa lands, was nevertheless directly controlled by the shogunate, so when the Dutch were moved to Nagasaki from their original factory in Hirado, it was so that the Tokugawa could not only consolidate Chinese and European trade in one location but also directly oversee the last remaining European presence in Japan.[27] This latter move is easily understandable since the majority of foreign activity happened mainly on the island of Kyushu, home to some of Ieyasu's most powerful enemies, including the Shimazu family of Satsuma domain.[28] In other words, control over foreign trade was not so much driven by fear of foreigners, but rather a desire to limit the potential for domestic rivals to use foreigners, or the wealth from foreign trade, against the Tokugawa. This was not simply paranoia on the part of the shogunate, for when the Tokugawa regime finally met its end in the nineteenth century, it was at the hands of these very western domains, and in the context of foreign incursions.

We can conceive of foreign affairs in Tokugawa Japan as falling under three categories: foreigners arriving in Japan and perhaps residing either permanently or temporarily; Japanese traveling abroad and again, residing abroad either permanently or temporarily; and, finally, foreign goods and/or ideas circulating in Japan. The Tokugawa, as we'll see further, instituted various mechanisms to control all three categories.

The Tokugawa instituted control over the country in a variety of ways, including issuing regulations for all classes of people, from high to low, including the peasantry, the nobility, the religious officials, the warriors, and the so-called outcastes (*eta* or *hinin*). But it is in the area of foreign affairs that we see the most dramatic usurpation of power. Like many aspects of the social, economic, and political changes of the early seventeenth century, many Tokugawa innovations were extensions of polices that Hideyoshi had begun to institute. For example, Hideyoshi confiscated the commercial city of Nagasaki from the local daimyo, who had given the Portuguese Jesuits extraordinary privileges in the city, and put it under direct control.[29] Similarly, Hideyoshi officially banned the practice of the

Catholic faith and ordered that all foreign priests leave the country immediately, going so far as to execute twenty-six Christians in 1597, including six priests.[30]

The first third of the seventeenth century was a formative period for the shogunate, and saw a gradual and incremental adoption of policies designed to enhance Tokugawa control throughout Japan at the expense of the daimyo. The restrictions on foreign affairs were designed largely to exercise greater control over the powerful domains of western Japan that represented real threats to the Tokugawa and that had traditionally benefited from foreign trade. The Tokugawa gradually curtailed the vibrant overseas Japanese trade by first restricting foreign travel to a select group of families and then, by the 1630s, forbidding all Japanese from traveling overseas whatsoever.[31] These restrictions were codified in a series of seventeen edicts that have come to be known as the *sakoku* edicts, the final version of which was promulgated in 1635.[32] The first several edicts essentially ban Japanese from traveling abroad, and also ban those Japanese who were already abroad from returning home under pain of execution. Prior to this ban, several Japanese had travelled quite regularly abroad to places as far afield as Siam and the Philippines, places that boasted rather large settlements of Japanese who made their living trading with the local merchants, and who at times became embroiled in local politics.[33]

The Tokugawa also took great pains to regulate exactly who was able to come to Japan. In the early seventeenth century, a large number of Chinese lived in various ports in western Japan; Portuguese and Spanish merchants and priests lived, traded, and preached in various places, mostly in western port cities; and English and Dutch merchants began to trade in Hirado in competition with their Iberian rivals. Over the course of several decades, the Tokugawa began to slowly but inexorably curtail this foreign activity. The first restriction was to limit foreign trade to either Hirado or Nagasaki—the English and Dutch in Hirado, and the Portuguese, Spanish, and Chinese in Nagasaki. The Spanish were the first Europeans to be explicitly banned from Japan for fear that they had imperialist designs, a fear reinforced in Edo by the Spanish conquest of the Philippines.[34] The English then departed Japan in 1623 as they were simply not able to obtain a supply of Chinese silk, the only way to really turn a profit in Japan. The Portuguese were banned from Japan after the Shimabara Rebellion of 1639 was interpreted by the Tokugawa to be a Christian revolt and was savagely suppressed.[35] The authorities reasoned that the Portuguese would never be willing simply to trade without also trying to proselytize, and they thus took the fateful and definitive decision to ban their trade. Japanese resolve was tested the following year when the Portuguese sent an embassy to try to restore trade; this was a severe miscalculation as the embassy was not only rebuffed but all Portuguese with the exception of thirteen servants were also executed for defying the shogun's order of expulsion. With this dramatic act, the Dutch became the sole Europeans allowed to trade in Japan, a position they would jealously maintain for over two hundred years.[36]

The Dutch believed that with much of their competition gone, and with the Japanese unable to travel abroad, they would reap immense profits from the Japan trade, and they were partially right, although little could they know that almost immediately their own trade (and freedom of movement) would be restricted.[37] To be sure, a few years earlier the Dutch were restricted to trading only in Hirado, which elicited page after page of frustration in both the Dutch and the English diaries, including prognostications of gloom and doom.[38] In the event, the Dutch trade was not effected all that much, yet now they faced a more serious restriction: the removal of their entire factory from the private domain of Hirado to the shogunal controlled city of Nagasaki. What was worse, the Dutch were now required to live in a secluded, heavily guarded man-made island called Deshima, originally constructed for the Portuguese before they were unceremoniously booted from the country. Deshima was an artificial, fan-shaped, island (indeed, sometimes called *tsukijima*, or "moon island" because of its crescent shape) built specifically to house European merchants. Measuring 600 feet by 200 feet, it was not a large place, and one can imagine that privacy must have been at a premium.[39] At any given time there were about a dozen Dutchmen on the island, as well as a phalanx of people tasked with "guarding" the small bridge that separated the island from the mainland, and, naturally, the legion of interpreters who came and went constantly.[40] Women were technically not permitted to live on the island, although the Dutch were allowed to visit prostitutes in the Maruyama District of Nagasaki, and prostitutes, euphemistically referred to as housekeepers, were allowed short-term stays, although later the terminology changed to that of "temporary marriages."[41] Engelbert Kaempfer is somewhat dismissive of the prostitutes in Nagasaki, writing, "Truly our young sailors, unacquainted as they commonly are with the virtues of temperance, are not ashamed to spend five *rixdollars* for one night's pleasure, and with such wenches too, whom a native of Nagasaki could have for about two or three *maas*, they being none of the best and handsomest."[42]

At any rate, in the months preceding the transfer in 1640, the Dutch mocked the Portuguese for having to live on what they delightedly called a prison, so it is deliciously ironic that soon after the Dutch themselves would be "sentenced" to the prison of Deshima.[43] More onerous to the Dutch, however, was the fact that Dutch silk imports were now to be subjected to what was known as the *Itowappa Nakama*, or the "silk cartel."[44] In this system, the price of Chinese silk imports were subjected to a price set by officially designated silk merchants depending on the quality of the silk: high grade, low grade, and medium grade. The Dutch seemed to think that such a cartel, made up of merchants from the largest commercial cities in Japan, would ruin their trade, although in the event, Dutch trade actually took off and became more profitable than at any time previously.[45]

This increased prosperity, however, was at the expense of Dutch freedom of movement. The removal of the Dutch to Deshima was arguably the final piece of the "*sakoku* edicts."[46] The move, although certainly shocking to the Dutch, makes a great deal of sense given the overall trend of Tokugawa control of foreign relations.[47] First, whereas Hirado was controlled by the Matsura family, Nagasaki was directly controlled by the Tokugawa through officials called *bugyō* (magistrates, or what the Dutch call "governors") who were appointed by the Shogun.[48] "Governor" is a misleading term because the role of the official was not necessarily to administer the government of Nagasaki, but rather to oversee and regulate the foreign trade of the city on behalf of the Tokugawa shogunate, and more broadly still, to implement the so-called *sakoku* edicts. The *bugyō* were also charged with managing the supply of silk imported into Japan, and it was easier to do this if all the silk came into a single port.[49] Like much of Tokugawa policy, the use of *bugyō* was inherited from the government of Hideyoshi, who appointed the first official in 1595 when he confiscated the city from the local daimyo in an effort to enforce his anti-Christian edicts. Later in the 1630s the Tokugawa increased the number to two, with the two *bugyō* alternating between Nagasaki and Edo.

Second, the silk cartel was much more than simply a set of licensed merchants, but was an entire mechanism to deal with Chinese silk imports. While the "*sakoku* edicts" are popularly associated with the proscription of Christianity and the banning of Japanese travel abroad, several edicts were designed to ensure an equitable distribution of silk throughout the country.[50] By moving the Dutch to Nagasaki, the silk cartel was able to exercise a measure of direct control over silk imports, especially given the fact that the Chinese were also confined to Nagasaki. Despite this logic, the Dutch were not at all pleased to be confined to their island, in particular because their every movement would now be scrutinized by an army of officials, and, as they were soon to discover, they would be obliged to host a continuous carousel of guests, all requiring a measure of hospitality.

The final way in which the Tokugawa attempted to control foreign affairs was by closely regulating the goods and the ideas that were imported into the country. The Tokugawa took great pains to establish control, either direct or indirect, over all Japanese points of contact with the wider world. Three of these "windows," as they are sometimes called, were farmed out to Tokugawa vassals, and the other window was directly controlled by the shogunate.[51] Japanese contact with the Koreans was regulated by the So family on the island of Tsushima; contact with the Kingdom of Ryūkaya, today the prefecture of Okinawa, was controlled by the Shimazu family of Satsuma domain; and contact with the indigenous Ainu peoples of the northern island of Ezo, known today as Hokkaido, was controlled by the Mastsumae family. Although contact with these three groups of people was regulated by non-Tokugawa families, the *bakufu* took a close interest in making sure that all foreign contact through these three "windows" was conducted properly and according to shogunal wishes. In fact, on the few occasions in which an impropriety cropped up, the *bakufu* was quite willing and able to intervene.[52]

The other "window" was regulated directly by *bakufu* officials, namely, Chinese and Dutch trade at the western port city of Nagasaki. The Dutch were corralled onto the island of Deshima and "cared for" by a gaggle of officials, while the Chinese were likewise eventually confined to a compound near Deshima called the *Tojin Yashiki*, although the Chinese were not guarded as heavily or as strictly as the Dutch.[53] The Japanese officials responsible for the Dutch established an elaborate procedure for receiving incoming ships, processing the goods and people on those ships, and regulating the movement of the foreigners once they were in Japan.[54] One such procedure was the yearly collection of what the Dutch called the "news of the world," or in Japanese, *fūsetsugaki*.[55] These documents were immediately collected from arriving ships, both Chinese and Dutch, translated into Japanese, and forwarded to the shogunal court for review. In this way the Japanese managed to stay abreast of major world events despite the ban on Japanese travel abroad.[56]

The Japanese were keen to know, as much as possible, exactly what goods were coming into the country from abroad, but they were also keen to make sure that nothing that could even remotely be conceived of as Christian paraphernalia made its way into the country. To this end, the officials in Nagasaki instituted an elaborate procedure of inspecting incoming Dutch ships that entailed mustering the crew, searching the ship and all cargo, and reading to the crew the shogunal ban on Catholicism.[57] All books were confiscated in order to be inspected, and even the most oblique reference to Christianity would be met with official opprobrium, if not harsh punishment (and indeed the import of books was banned for decades). In fact, the official reason for the Dutch removal to Nagasaki from their trading post in Hirado was that the Company had constructed a new stone warehouse and inscribed on it the date using the phrase *Anno Domini*, which the Japanese found to be an unacceptably overt expression of Christianity.[58] Likewise, English ships, when they arrived at Hirado were not allowed to fly the English flag as the Cross of Saint George was too blatant a reference to Christianity.

After a brief lull in persecutions after the death of Hideyoshi, Tokugawa Ieyasu began to clamp down again on Catholicism in 1614 when his government passed a strict law that forbade the propagation or even the practice of the faith. After this date, a steady series of investigations led to the gradual eradication of the faith, including large-scale pogroms in places such as Edo and Nagasaki. Anti-Christian zeal reached new heights under the third Shogun, Iemitsu (1604–51), who instituted a comprehensive mechanism for rooting out Christians, including cash rewards for informants, brutal torture of suspects, and a nationwide system of domestic surveillance headed up by a new office called the *Shumon Aratame Yaku*, or inspectorate of religions.[59] The original head of this office was a man by the name of Inoue, Chikugo no Kami, Masashige, who turned out to be a great benefactor of the Dutch while at the same time a great scourge of captured Christians.[60] Inoue held the position of *ōmetsuke*, which can be translated in various ways, but perhaps in this context we might choose "inquisitor," or "chief inspector," although his remit extended beyond religion to the Dutch presence in Japan in general.[61] The *sakoku* decrees of the 1630s contain several definitive items proscribing the propagation and practice of Christianity, and a whole host of procedures were developed to ensure enforcement of the ban. Placards were posted in most public spots, especially in western Japan; a test was developed that entailed treading on images of Christ or the Virgin Mary to demonstrate one's aversion to the faith (the *fumi-e*); and all Japanese households were required to register at a local Buddhist temple.[62]

Tokugawa hysteria about the threat of Catholicism reached fever pitch after the Shimabara Rebellion of 1637–38. Although the rebellion—located on Kyushu, not too far from Nagasaki—came to be regarded as primarily a religious movement, it was probably more a protest against local misrule and oppression, including exceptionally harsh taxation.[63] The *bakufu* chose to interpret the affair as a religious uprising (in point of fact, many of the leaders were Christians), and after quelling the uprising with great effort and great loss of life, stepped up its anti-Christian pogroms to the extent that within a decade, Christianity, or at least institutionalized Christianity, was all but eradicated from Japan.[64] At first, the method of ridding the country of the faith was simply to execute Christians, often in large numbers by a variety of methods. Afterward, the focus shifted to making captives renounce their faith with a number of exquisitely designed tortures, including a torture called the *ana-tsurushi*, often translated as the "pit torture."[65] Captives would be tightly bound, and hung upside down in a dark pit, often with excrement or other filth at the bottom of the pit. A small cut would be made in the forehead to prevent the captive from passing out from blood pooling in the head. This torture on the surface perhaps seems not as gruesome as others that humans in their ingenuity have dreamed up, but apparently it was unbearable for most people, and even foreign priests who came to Japan fully prepared to face martyrdom recanted their faith.[66]

By 1640, the Tokugawa *bakufu* had effectively established its control over the country. All foreign affairs were either directly or indirectly controlled from Edo, although local domains such as Satsuma, Tsushima, and Matsumae certainly had a modicum of leeway in conducting relations with the Ryūkayan Kingdom, Korea, and Ezo, respectively. A rather comprehensive set of regulations for every social class were promulgated, and daimyo were required to spend half of their time at the shogunal court (the *sankin kōtai* system that served not only to keep potential enemies close but also to drain daimyo resources). And finally, the Tokugawa established a Japan-centered system of foreign relations in which Korean and Ryūkayan Island embassies paid their respects to the Shogun, The Dutch came yearly to present lavish gifts to the Shogun, and the Japanese managed to establish significant Chinese trade without having to send tribute embassies to China.

The *Hofreis* (Court Journey)

It is within this context that the yearly Dutch visits to Edo should be examined.[67] The journey itself took up several months, beginning in February and ending in mid-spring, and was the single biggest expense of the Company in Japan. This was because the Dutch were obliged to pay not only for the gifts for the myriad officials but also for the legion of porters to carry the Dutch and their belongings, the lodging on the journey to and from Edo, and the rent for the Dutch residence in the capital.[68] The Dutch spent the days before the journey carefully packing the gifts for the Shogun and his officials in crates before they were loaded on special boats (the *hofreisbark*) and sent ahead of the Dutch and their porters.[69]

The journey was a combination of trips made by sea and overland and went through many of the major cities: Shimonoseki, Osaka, Miyako (Kyoto), and finally Edo. The *bakufu* established officials to oversee the major urban centers of Nagasaki, Osaka, and Miyako, and each had a high-ranking official or, in the case of Nagasaki, two officials, who officially received the Dutch on their journey and were also presented with official gifts. These gifts, while often presented on the way to Edo, remained unopened in deference to the Shogun until the Dutch retraced their journey back to Deshima a couple months later.[70] Once in Edo, the Dutch were received in audience by the Shogun, although this could take quite a long time to arrange, and so the Dutch had lots of time to interact with the elite of Edo, including the giving and receiving of smaller, more informal gifts.

The audience itself was a ritualized affair, culminating with the chief merchant bowing before the Shogun and being announced as the "Oranda Kapitan." During the audience, that year's gifts were elaborately and ostentatiously displayed on specially made presentation trays. Once the audience was over, the shogunal counselors officially congratulated the Dutch on a successful audience and the Dutch were then able to commence the round of gift-giving to the various and sundry officials. Specially chosen gifts were sent to their residences where they were received by the officials' servants, or secretaries as they are called in the Dutch diaries. A few days later, the Shogun would send the Dutch the prescribed "return gift," consisting often of a quantity of silver and quite lavish Japanese kimono. The other officials who received gifts would then send their return gifts, again prescribed gifts that rarely changed. During this time, the Dutch received daily visits from curious Japanese officials and daimyo, whom they invariably entertained with food and drink. They were also able to do a certain amount of business in the capital, especially selling goods that the elite of Edo society had asked the Dutch to bring in previous court journeys. Finally, after a stay of roughly a month, the Dutch received permission to depart, whereupon they would begin the arduous journey back to Nagasaki traveling the same route by which they had come and being received by the same shogunal officials in Miyako and Osaka.

The court journey happened in this way every year until 1764 when the Shogun allowed the Dutch to make the journey every other year, in consideration that the volume of Dutch trade was not what it once was. However, the Dutch were still obliged to present the same amount of yearly gifts, but on these off years, they would give the gifts to the Nagasaki *bugyō* who would then forward them to Edo.[71] The journey was further reduced to once every four years from 1790, although, again, the Dutch were obliged to send yearly gifts through the *bugyō*.

Dutch visits to Edo served a variety of purposes, as did the gifts they lavishly bestowed. First and foremost, the ostensible reason for the journey was for the Dutch to "pay their respects" to the Shogun, essentially a highly visible and ritualistic act of submission that served to illustrate in no uncertain terms that "barbarians" from afar came to Edo to recognize the Shogun as not only the rightful ruler of Japan (on behalf of the emperor, of course) but also the political and military center of East Asia. In other words, Dutch visits to court, just as with Korean or Ryūkayan Islander visits, were physical manifestation of what Ronald Toby calls a Japan-centered worldview in contradistinction to the Sino-centric worldview that traditionally held in East Asia.[72] Grant Goodman and others equate Dutch visits with the tribute system, and cite as evidence for this the elaborate ceremony the ritualized aspect of the audience and the gifts that the Tokugawa gave the Dutch in return for their visit to Edo, which could at times be quite valuable.[73] There are other interpretations that we may give to these visits, however. For one, Dutch visits to the capital served to transfer Dutch knowledge directly to the political and military elite at the center. Early on, this knowledge mainly concerned martial skills, such as the working of artillery, as well as Dutch intelligence about the Catholic presence in Asia, especially the Portuguese, but it later began to take the form of scientific knowledge.

In the first couple of decades of court journeys, the Japanese officials asked the Dutch to bring a member of the Company who had knowledge of "pyrotechnics," and this person held demonstrations involving the firing of canons as well as sessions with shogunal military personnel who were instructed in the workings of Dutch weaponry.[74] Dutch gifts to the Shogun and his entourage often consisted of weaponry, both utile and decorative, artwork with martial motifs, and raw materials that could be used for military purposes such as lead and saltpeter. Gradually, however, the Dutch began to relate other types of knowledge to Edo, mainly medical and geopolitical knowledge. The "surgeon" became an indispensable member of the VOC party to Edo precisely because there was an enormous demand for imported medicine, Western medical skills, and medical knowledge in general. The surgeon was kept quite busy while in Edo, attending to the various ailments that afflicted the shogunal officials and daimyo. And of course, in the eighteenth century, Dutch medical knowledge and medical books would play an integral role in the propagation of *rangaku*, literally "Dutch studies," but more accurately translated as "Western studies."[75]

Just as the Japanese requested military personnel (including equestrian instructors) and surgeons, so they also requested an "herbalist." For years, the Japanese had asked the Dutch to import various kinds of medicines, along with their uses and descriptions translated into Japanese. To complement this, the Dutch brought an herbalist to Japan in 1669 to introduce the Japanese to scientific instruments, for which the Japanese were grateful, although immediately the Dutch were informed that they would prefer an herbalist that was a bit older and more experienced![76] Not even a year later we read that the Japanese were upset that a new herbalist had not yet come, to which the chief merchant wrote, clearly exasperated, "These people think that if Japan orders it, then they should be fetched from Holland willingly or unwillingly."[77]

Another reason the Dutch were made to visit the shogun's court yearly was to distribute curiosos and rarities to the Shogun and his officials, many of which came to be specially ordered. The clearest expression of this comes in a remark by a Japanese official recorded in the Dutch diaries in 1664: "The Dutchmen have many things in their country which were very rare here. If they knew these things and brought them here, the shogun would be pleased."[78] These gifts, far from mere trifles or eccentric requests, served to create a culture of goodwill between the Company and the Shogun that lasted for over two hundred years.

One aspect of gift-giving that needs to be addressed is the distinction between gifts that were more or less set in their quantity and value, mainly comprising cloth goods, and gifts that were ordered specifically by shogunal officials, which mainly fell into the category of curiosos. The former were gifts that were designed to show VOC appreciation for shogunal favor year after year, and were hence of set value that rarely changed much; the latter were given either to accompany a special request or to curry special favor with the Shogun and his officials, but always with an eye toward preserving the generally good relations that the Company had with officials in Edo and Nagasaki. We are further able to distinguish between the more formal gifts that were meant for the shogunal court in Edo and the Nagasaki bureaucracy, and the everyday gifts that were routinely given to those with whom the Dutch had daily contact. These latter items were most often lower level gifts of food and drink or one-off gifts of smaller materials objects.

We should mention here that there was a marked difference between gifts that were brought to Japan as general gifts, either because they were well received in the past or because they were exotic enough in nature to impress, and goods that were specifically ordered by Japanese officialdom, either for themselves or for the Shogun. If they were ordered for the Shogun, those items were relayed to the Dutch by a shogunal retainer who would record the order; if the items were ordered by daimyo for personal use, those demands (*eisen*) would be delivered either by a servant of the daimyo or a lesser official. From the mid-eighteenth century to 1862, these demands make up what came to be known as the *eisboek*, a ledger into which the Dutch recorded all such orders. These orders were often accompanied by quite startling illustrations, including detailed drawings of horses, dogs, and sophisticated manufactured goods such as clocks.[79]

These latter goods lead us to a final, and very important, distinction: between gifts that were given explicitly and purely as gifts, and those goods that were given to the Japanese officialdom but were "paid for." As Martha Chaiklin notes in her important study of Dutch material culture in Japan, there are a whole host of goods throughout the entire early modern period the Dutch brought to "sell" to the Japanese, but that really should be viewed as what I refer to as "quasi-gifts." That is to say, these goods either were brought at the explicit request of a Japanese official or were one-off sales to officials, mainly during the Dutch stay in Edo. The difference between "quasi-gifts" and the "official" gifts was that Japanese officials paid for the goods, although in many, if not most, cases, they paid a price which was low enough to be, in reality, a type of gift.[80] On more than one occasion the Dutch note in their diaries that many of these goods were sold for much less even than the intrinsic value of the good, and certainly much less than what the Company paid to have the item shipped from either Europe or Batavia. It is for this reason that these items, despite being sold, should really be seen as "quasi-gifts."[81] In 1654, for example, the chief merchant notes in his diary, again perhaps as advice for his future successors, that "accommodating high nobles... especially those who are related to the shogun, must almost pass off as a kind of gift."[82]

Most people who have travelled to Japan or read about Japan in any great depth know that gift-giving is an integral part of Japanese society, as indeed it is in many societies.[83] Gift-giving happens at every level of society, from state to state political relations, in the world of high finance, on special occasions such as weddings and births, and in everyday life between colleagues, friends, and family members. These latter types of gifts in particular create a web of reciprocity throughout society and serve to strengthen ties of both biological and fictive kinship. When the Dutch began to trade with Japan in earnest, they were incorporated into this pervasive system of gift-giving at every level. They were required to bring "institutionalized" gifts to the Shogun on the annual journey to court, just as were the other major daimyo of Japan. These gifts were presented in an ostentatious way so as to demonstrate symbolically and visually the power of the Shogun even over distant foreign countries.[84] The Dutch were also drawn into local systems of gift-giving wherever they happened to be, either in Nagasaki or in Edo. It was very common for VOC merchants to send gifts on holidays and other auspicious occasions, and on such occasions, the gift-giving would invariably require Japanese officials to send a reciprocal gift. One can see in the diaries kept by the chief merchants on Deshima that the Dutch became quite proficient in this gift culture. Their diaries are littered with the almost daily account of small gifts and reciprocal gifts passed between the Company merchants and the various Japanese with whom they were in contact. In short, the Dutch became enmeshed in this web of reciprocity that was and is still so prevalent in Japanese society.

In the following chapters, we will examine the routine of the annual *hofreis*, including the preparation of the gifts, their transport to Edo, their elaborate presentation, the return gifts given the Dutch, and the host of officials who received gifts. We will then delve deeper into the many varieties of gifts by category, including exotic animals and animal products, European manufactured goods, Asian luxury goods such as silk and spices, artwork, medicine, and finally the daily gifts of food and drink. And finally, I will demonstrate that far from being simply a curious feature of Dutch trade in Japan involving a few European trinkets and exotic animals, the practice of VOC gift-giving was an integral component of Dutch success, and it served, more than any other single institution, to ensure the continued prosperity of the Company as well as the incredible longevity of the Dutch presence in Japan. In other words, I will show that while the individual gifts themselves might engender a sense of frivolity and quirkiness, in reality, the institution of gift-giving was a central feature of Company success in Japan, as demonstrated by the repeated emphasis that the chief merchants continued to place on all levels of gifts in their diaries year in and year out.

1

Gift-Giving and the Early Modern Web of Diplomacy

Scholars have long recognized the power of gift-giving in social, economic, and political relationships. The French theoretician Marcel Mauss, writing in the 1920s, analyzed the role of gift-giving in building relationships among different social groups; in essence gift-giving builds bonds within in-groups and disparate groups by weaving an elaborate social fabric of giving, reciprocity, and social memory.[1] Through a society-wide system of exchange, including the social obligations embedded in gift-giving, Mauss argues that individuals are collectively bound together, and that, indeed, virtually every society at root, ancient and modern, has this in common, although certainly local differences prevail. In other words, the mechanism of binding society together through the giving and receiving of gifts is common to all human societies. Lewis Hyde brings Mauss' analysis of "archaic" societies into the modern world by writing about gifts and the gift economy in contradistinction to the rational, impersonal market-based economy of capitalism. Whereas the market economy is not necessarily concerned with personal relationships, gifts are used to strengthen interpersonal bonds by binding the giver and the receiver into an inextricable social relationship. Hyde notes that in contrast to material wealth, which makes a person rich the more that person hoards it, gifts are the opposite because "wealth" in the gift economy is accrued by giving gifts away, and thus accruing to oneself increased and closer relationships, the prestige and honor associated with largesse, and a network of obligatory reciprocity that one might call on in some indeterminate future.[2] Building on Hyde, Belk and Coon devise two frameworks within which to analyze gift-giving. The first is a model in which a gift is given with some sense of an expectation of reciprocity; in other words, and to be less than charitable, the gift is given with an ulterior motive in mind. The second is a model in which a gift is given as an expression of love,[3] although the theorist Jacques Derrida would counter that in the first model the gift is not, strictly speaking, a gift at all, in the sense that the giving is "tainted" by one's own motives in the expectation of some desired outcome.[4] Derrida goes so far as to posit (in what turns out to be a paradox) that the reality of a gift is not possible in human society because a gift is always given with some self-interested motive in mind. A true gift, according to Derrida, is something that is freely given with no thought whatsoever to anything in return; but in reality, such a mindset is more or less impossible, given the nature of humanity, although perhaps, the example of love above is the closest we can get to giving a true gift (perhaps Jesus recognized this when he spoke of self-sacrificial love as the ultimate expression of love). Even if a gift were to be somehow given with the total absence of any ulterior motive on the part of the giver, the receiver of the gift would still feel a variety of social obligations in receiving the gift, and thus the purity of the gift would also be compromised.[5]

Nathan Miczo posits that it is not the gift itself that is of primary importance, but the symbolism behind the gift, or in other words, the larger social action that the giving of the gift symbolizes.[6] The anthropologist Chris Gregory has referred to gift-giving as a mechanism through which we establish and maintain relationships through a system of reciprocity that creates a perpetual situation of indebtedness between the two parties. He identifies that gifts are given with the intention of creating a relationship, which at its core carries the social obligation to reciprocate. In other words, a gift is code for a social mechanism whereby complex webs of social indebtedness are created, and often the longer the period of time between receiving and reciprocating, the more firm is the indebtedness of the receiver, and hence the stronger the social obligation to pay the debt back.[7] Katherine Rupp, in a 2003 study of gift-giving and networks of reciprocity in Japan, found that by setting up a quid pro quo with one of her subjects, in this case letters of recommendation in exchange for English lessons, she unwittingly entered into a complex web of reciprocity from which she was unable to extricate herself without breaking, or at least damaging, a relationship, not to mention possible research data. From her personal experience, Rupp extrapolates anecdotal evidence that many people in modern Japan feel that gift-giving and the social obligations that result make the entire world of gifts more a burden than a pleasure.[8]

Moving to the early modern period, Cynthia Klekar uses English voyages to Japan and China in the seventeenth century to describe a world in which European-Asian state-to-state relations were not yet the norm (and would not be until the late nineteenth century), and relations between Western actors such as East India Companies and Asian potentates were mediated by "a cross-cultural language of gift exchange, reciprocity, and obligation that informed early modern conceptions of international trade and diplomacy."[9]

Gift-giving accompanied almost every initiative that the Dutch East India Company (and its English counterpart) undertook in Japan from their arrival in the islands in the early seventeenth century.[10] This was an effective strategy because gift-giving was not only a practice used in Western early modern diplomacy but also widespread in East Asian societies in which gift-giving was very much informed by practices such as tribute missions. If we were to extend our study even more broadly, we would find that gift-giving was a hallmark of early modern European interaction with many parts of the world: Christina Brauner, for example, analyzes European trading companies' use of gifts in their trade with West Africa, and João Melo writes about the gifts that the Portuguese "Estado da India" used to facilitate relationships with several Asian rulers.[11]

Klekar's magnificent study focuses largely on the initial voyage to Japan of Captain John Saris, the man charged by the East India Company with trying to get in on the silver trade, and as such, Saris' gifts were given very much with a specific intended outcome. In other words, the gifts that the English and early Dutch merchants presented to the Shogun were presented as part of a specific intention: to be able to establish trade in Japan. Thus, these gifts are examples of the first model explicated by Belk and Coon earlier, in which the gift is presented with a desired outcome in mind. Gifts may have been presented rhetorically as gifts of honor and respect, but in the end, everyone involved knew that the East India Companies expected a certain result and that these gifts were a down payment of sorts on that result. Company officials certainly conceived of their gifts in this way. They surely did not envision themselves actually becoming vassals of the Japanese Shogun, even though the Dutch occasionally wrote of themselves in exactly those terms, at least in letters to the shogunal court; and they surely did not think the gifts they presented were in any way an official demonstration of Dutch or English submission to the Shogun, even though the action of gift-giving might have implied such on the surface.[12] Rather, the gifts presented were transactional in nature. We know this is the case for the Dutch, given several remarks made in the VOC diaries in which the chief merchant specifically tells his successors to use the gifts as a way to curry favor with Japanese officialdom.[13] One such instance is in a diary entry for 1662 in which the chief merchant states,

> It would be better to keep their favor by a small presentation now than incur their displeasure, which would cost the company six times as much to gain their favor, apart from the damage which their ill will might bring about as happened

in Hirado, when the lodge had to be demolished, which was said to have been caused by someone who was unsatisfied because Mr. Caron had not presented him a gift.[14]

This is almost certainly a misreading of the removal of the VOC from Hirado to Deshima, but, be that as it may, it speaks volumes that the Dutch put so much weight on the importance of these gifts. For the VOC, the yearly gifts were simply the price of doing business, and in fact, when one looks at the accounting books that still survive, as well as in the letters sent from Deshima to Company officials in Batavia, it becomes clear that the gifts were just another expense, similar to the rent that the Company was obliged to pay the Japanese for the use of Deshima.

Gifts were also transactional in the sense that they were occasionally offered to bring about a desired outcome in a negotiation or to resolve a crisis between the VOC and the Shogun, an eventuality that occurred several times. Shogo Suzuki, for one, distinguishes between those gifts given to the Shogun on the yearly journey to court and those gifts given when the Dutch wished to discuss diplomatic or commercial affairs with the shogunal counselors.[15] It certainly was not unusual in early modern foreign relations for European representatives to travel to the court of a ruler to present gifts along with a petition, either for trade or for some other purpose. We've already seen that the Dutch, when they first arrived in Japan in 1609 seeking to establish a headquarters in Japan for their still nascent East India Company, made the journey to the shogun's court at Sunpu where they provided Tokugawa Ieyasu with admittedly paltry gifts along with a petition for trade.[16] The Dutch were warmly received despite a barrage of condemnation from their Portuguese rivals, and despite their anemic gifts, probably because of larger strategic geopolitical considerations on the part of Ieyasu.[17] The founding Shogun of the Tokugawa dynasty found it quite attractive to have another set of foreigners who could be played off against the Portuguese, the Catholicism of whom the Japanese consistently and increasingly found problematic. We also know that Ieyasu, in contradistinction to later Shogun, was eminently interested in overseas trade, as seen in his welcoming attitude not just to the Portuguese and Dutch but also to the English, Spanish, Chinese, Korean, and Ryūkayan Islanders, and in his willingness to tolerate a significant overseas Japanese population in places such as Manila and Ayutthaya. The *Ikoku Nikki*, a compilation of diplomatic correspondences by the Zen monk and close confident of Ieyasu, Konchi-in Sūden, contains a great many letters to overseas countries as diverse as Ming China and the Spanish Philippines.[18] In this spirit of openness, the Dutch were originally given essentially free rein to conduct trade in Japan, a boon that was, as Adam Clulow notes in his recent marvelous study of the VOC in Japan, out of all proportion to the paltry gift the Company initially presented.[19]

As we will have occasion to examine in a later chapter, lavish gifts always accompanied attempts to resolve various crises that arose between the Dutch and the shogunal court. The most famous example was the arrest and imprisonment of Pieter Nuyts, a Company servant who ran afoul of Japanese authorities because of his heavy-handed treatment of Japanese merchants on the island of Taiwan. After the Tokugawa suspended Dutch trade in retaliation, Nuyts was sent to Japan to answer for his actions, essentially sacrificed to the Japanese in order to restore trade, and was only released from his several-year captivity because of the tireless advocacy of the chief merchants, and also because the Shogun at the time was enormously pleased with a lavish gift of a metal candelabra.[20]

Another well-documented instance in which gifts were presented to the Shogun in an attempt to resolve a diplomatic crisis is from the farcical embassy in 1649 to the shogun's court in order to thank him for his treatment of several Dutch crewmen from the ship *Breskens* who had gone ashore in the domain of Nambu in search of provisions after their ship ran low.[21] The Dutchmen, because they did not arrive at Nagasaki, were arrested and forwarded to Edo for interrogation, the local populace convinced they were priests trying to enter Japan surreptitiously. While the men were eventually released after exhaustive interrogation to ensure the castaway Dutch were not in league with either the Portuguese or the Spanish, the *bakufu* insisted on a suitable display of gratitude, involving an official embassy from Holland. The Dutch chief merchant correctly assessed the situation when he writes that the Japanese were looking for a similar display of gratitude as that made upon the release of Nuyts.[22] After several years of back and forth, the Dutch finally cobbled together an "official" embassy led by a sickly man by the name of Petrus Blokhovius and his second-in-command, Andries Frisius.[23] As expected, Blokhovius died en route, Frisius went to the trouble to embalm his remains so as to prove to the Japanese that a high-ranking ambassador was indeed sent. The farce played out with the bestowal of lavish gifts on the Shogun in recompense for his graciousness in allowing the Dutch prisoners of 1643 to go free. The Dutch assured the Shogun that "the envoy had travelled four or five thousand miles from his country not for gold or silver or trade, but to pay reverence to the shogun."[24] This was a bald-faced, well, untruth, and the Shogun almost certainly saw it as such as well, but the shogun's honor had been served, and in return Frisius was presented with 500 *schuiten* of silver for his superiors in Batavia, 200 *schuiten* for himself, and ten "silk gowns" also for himself.[25] Frisius' gifts for the Shogun included the usual gifts of cloth and European goods, but also a "pyrotechnist" who fired off mortars and taught the shogunal guards how to fire them, and a finely crafted silver ship that was quite a hit at court. In the end, the Shogun was well pleased with the envoy, although his officials were apparently not pleased that the envoy had arrived aboard a ship packed with merchandise. It was good enough, though.

There were, of course, other nuances to the gift-giving that was a defining feature with European interactions with Japan. A long-established diplomatic model in East Asia known as the "tribute system" had its origins as early as the Tang Dynasty, although a more mature and coherent manifestation of the system arose during the Ming and Qing dynasties (Late Imperial China).[26] In this economic and political worldview, only rulers who were willing to make a formal recognition that the Chinese emperor (and by extension the Chinese empire) was the superior partner could partake in legitimate trade. Thus, potential trade partners were required to send embassies to the emperor's court to perform a ritual of submission, and in return, the emperor would "confirm" the rulers in their positions of authority in their own countries. Only then would merchants be allowed to engage in trade. Often the political embassy and the trade missions were combined into one trip for expediency, although in this Sino-centric worldview, legitimate trade was still conditional on a show of obeisance to the emperor.[27]

In this conception, VOC gifts could certainly be interpreted as a type of tribute paid to the shogun's court, especially since the outward trappings of the system were more or less all present, including an inherently unequal relationship that was the norm in East Asian international relations. Ronald Toby, in his seminal work *State and Diplomacy in Early Modern Japan*, has demonstrated that the Tokugawa were keen to systematically construct a Japanese-centered worldview in contradistinction to the Sino-centric order that had hitherto prevailed.[28] In other words, the Tokugawa were keen to portray Edo as the political, economic, and military center of East Asia rather than the capital of the Ming/Qing Empire. This supposed new world order required that foreigners perform their submission to the Tokugawa in order for relations to be officially sanctioned, in the same way that embassies to the Son of Heaven's court demonstrated submission. Yamawaki Teijirō states that for the Japanese, Dutch trips to Edo were framed as embassies from another ruler rather than from a commercial company, and the fact that the "embassy" came from "Europe" only increased the prestige of the Tokugawa.[29] This also explains the elaborate care the shogunal court took to maximize the visibility of several embassies from the Ryūkayan

Kingdom, the Choson dynasty, and the annual Dutch *hofreis*.[30] The Chinese Ming and Qing dynasties were unwilling to compromise their own carefully constructed Sino-centric world order, and so remained outside of the officially recognized Tokugawa foreign relations, which is why Chinese vessels, while perfectly welcome to trade in Nagasaki, were never allowed an official embassy to the shogun's court and, by extension, there existed no official relationship between the Chinese and the Tokugawa *bakufu*.[31]

The Dutch, however, were perfectly willing to perform their submission for the sake of Dutch East India Company trade, both in Nagasaki in their daily lives and also annually when Company representatives set off from Nagasaki on the journey to the shogun's court, where the central event was the shogun's reception of the Dutch and the ostentatious and closely choreographed giving of a variety of strange and valuable gifts. Timon Screech, in a lovely phrase, describes the Dutch performance at court as a "propaganda of Tokugawa moral worth."[32] Together these roles of submission and obedience played a role in reinforcing (and legitimating) the new Japanese-centered world order and, from the Dutch perspective, ensured continued Dutch trade with Japan for over 200 years.

Gifts were also given on special, celebratory occasions, such as the birth of a child to a Japanese official the Company had dealings with, when a new Shogun was installed, when an heir to the shogunal office was formally announced, or any one of a number of other auspicious occasions. The chief merchant writes in November of 1650 that the "crown prince" was about to be installed in Edo upon the retirement of the previous Shogun, and, because not all of the Dutch ships had arrived in Batavia on time that year, the factory didn't have the usual amount of "rarities" on hand to present extras. He continues in a note of veiled desperation by stating categorically that this was simply not acceptable because all of the daimyo would be present at court to observe the ceremony, and all would be expected to give gifts.[33]

Another celebratory occasion that demanded the giving of gifts was the Japanese holiday of *Hassaku*. This was celebrated on the first day of the eighth month of the Japanese calendar, and evolved over the years into an occasion for Japanese to present gifts to their immediate superiors.[34] In the case of the Dutch, this meant that they gave gifts to the *bugyō* of Nagasaki and other local officials they had occasion to come into contact with, usually smaller gifts of rarities.[35] The *Hassaku* gifts were, like other types of gifts, figured into the general cost of doing business in Japan.[36]

The continual practice of gift-giving over time was a means of maintaining the trust and patronage of influential members of the Tokugawa bureaucracy.

In other words, gifts were the social and economic lubricant that allowed the Dutch to thrive in Japan year after year, decade after decade.[37] The routine gifts given to the Nagasaki *bugyō*, the local daimyo from Kyushu, visiting daimyo, and what the Dutch referred to as "various secretaries according to annual custom" fell within this category.[38] As we will see in the following chapters, the Dutch continually plied Japanese officialdom with small gifts of food, drink, and trinkets, and these gifts served to engender a lasting spirit of amity that carried over from one chief merchant to the next, from one *bugyō* of Nagasaki to the next, and indeed from one shogunal administration to the next. This conception of gift-giving is illustrative of the conception of gifts with which we began this chapter: social mechanisms with which to bind people together in a complex web of obligation and reciprocity.

The daily lives of Company merchants on Deshima were framed by the concepts of obedience and submission. As we've seen earlier, as soon as a ship arrived at Deshima, the crew was mustered, the ship inspected, and the shogun's edicts read out to the Dutch. It was immediately clear right from the start that the Dutch were expected to conduct themselves completely in accordance with shogunal wishes. The entirety of Dutch official life on the island was regulated by shogunal decree, and for any official act, it was absolutely required that official permission be received at least from Nagasaki, and often from Edo itself. The fact that in over two centuries of life on Deshima there were no serious challenges to this authority demonstrates that the Dutch knew their place in this order and resigned themselves to a rhythm of life that was dictated from the political center of Japan. The court journey, arguably the climactic event of yearly life on Deshima for those who made the journey, was even more of an expression of submission and obedience, and was itself a large stage on which the Dutch could perform their submission to Tokugawa authority time and again. This was a world in which precedence was paramount, and even the slightest deviation from time-honored custom could be seen as a challenge to Tokugawa authority, a factor that led to an inherent conservatism in commercial relations with the Dutch, much to chief merchants' continual frustration. Claims such as that by Matthi Forer in his introduction to a translation of Jan Cock Blomhoff's court journey of 1818 that the overriding purpose of the journey was "to present the shogun with gifts, thus maintaining the cordial relationship that existed between the two countries" are too simplistic and misses the full complexity of gift-giving.[39] This may have been true, in a literal sense, for the weary Dutch who made the trip, but for both the Japanese and the VOC, the actual gifts were only part of the story. The Tokugawa used these embassies to illustrate the power and prestige of the ruling house, and to make sure that the daimyo were reminded, on a yearly basis, that the Shogun controlled, without a doubt, foreign relations and the flow of foreign goods into Japan.[40] As Adam Clulow notes, "The *Bakufu* was interested in foreign embassies precisely because they were grand spectacles that could be used to demonstrate domestic legitimacy."[41] The Dutch, on the other hand, treated these gifts as the cost of doing business, and later, as the necessary price to be paid in order to engage in the private enterprise that could lead to wealth for the chief merchants and his colleagues. This did not mean, however, that the Company was happy about the costs of the trip. The chief merchant on Deshima often complained in his diary of the expenses incurred on the trip, probably more for his superiors' eyes than anything. In 1770, for example, when the Shogun requested yet another Persian stallion, the chief merchant, in a palpable tone of exasperation wrote, "The Company does its utmost to fulfill the desires of the Shogun, notwithstanding our losses."[42] This episode has an even more frustrating epilogue in that the chief merchant recorded a few months later that the horse was ultimately rejected by the Shogun because it was half an inch too short, and so was unceremoniously given instead to another, presumably less discerning, official.[43]

While early journeys to the shogunal court were intended for specific purposes, either to obtain (or confirm) trading privileges or to put out a diplomatic fire that occasionally broke out, by the 1630s, the system of Dutch journeys to Edo became systematized into a highly regulated affair laden with symbolism and ritual. Year after year, the major aspects of the trip remained exactly the same, from the ritual of obtaining the myriad permissions to the audience itself to the gifts presented to the Shogun and his officials. The Dutch often complained about the expense of the trip, undertaken in the coldest part of the year, but to no avail. They tried persistently to minimize the amount of gifts they had to present; they tried to reduce the personnel that were required to make the trip; they tried a variety of ways to reduce expenses, especially as trade was reduced from a roar to a whimper throughout the seventeenth century and into the eighteenth century, but again, to no avail. One reason for this stubborn refusal to change the dynamic of the court journey was that the journey had quickly become a symbol of Tokugawa power and authority to regulate and control all aspects of foreign relations. The giving of gifts and the court journey itself was not at all the main point; rather the main point was that the gifts (and the journey itself) were physical manifestations of Tokugawa prestige. That even exotic Europeans came bearing gifts and literally bowing down to the Shogun simply added to the carefully constructed image of authority that the Tokugawa were eager to maintain, a phenomenon that Adam Clulow terms an "ongoing theater of submission."[44]

This latter point goes some way toward answering the question of why the court journey was so enduring, and, related to this, why it is that the diplomatic visits were of such importance to the *bakufu*. To answer these twin questions requires us to be flexible in how we view the court journey; in other words, I don't think that there is one simple explanation, but rather a multifaceted explanation. This is partly because of the fact that the *bakufu* attempted to reconcile two very different truths about the Dutch presence in Japan.

On the one hand, the Dutch were treated domestically as vassals of the Tokugawa, similar to other daimyo who were required to pay their respects to the Shogun on a regular basis, and indeed, to "attend" on the Shogun for half of their time as daimyo.[45] In this respect, the *hofreis* was rather like any number of daimyo processions to Edo that could be seen yearly up and down the length of Japan.[46] Similar to the daimyo, the Dutch were expected to travel in a certain style and with a certain predetermined number of "retainers," although unlike the daimyo, the Dutch would have preferred to minimize their retinue, as indeed they tried several times to do, generally to no avail. The VOC expenses included the rental of pack animals, palanquins, special barges for the shogunal gifts, and a relatively large retinue of people, from the Company surgeon to translators to porters. Any attempt to change this retinue was forbidden—a fact that often perplexed the Dutch but makes sense in the context of the *sankin kōtai*. Even when Company profits were severely curtailed toward the end of the seventeenth century and into the eighteenth, the Dutch were still expected to process to Edo in the same manner as before, even though such a procession cost the Company a not-inconsiderable sum of money.[47] And finally, the Dutch annual journey to court was codified at essentially the same time as the *sankin kōtai* system, in the mid-1630s. From this time all daimyo were required to attend on the Shogun on an annual basis, and the Dutch, it seems, were no different.[48] It is notable that neither the Ainu to the north nor the Ryūkayan Islanders to the south were forced to attend on the Shogun regularly, and yet the Dutch, arguably more foreign if not more exotic, were treated more as daimyo in this regard than as foreigners.

Constantine Vaporis and George Tsukahira, in their exhaustive works on the alternate attendance system, spell out in minute detail the daimyo processions to and from Edo, and the accounts are remarkably similar to the process undertaken by the Dutch. To be sure, there are marked differences. For example, once in Edo, the Dutch were not required to provide direct service to the Shogun as other daimyo were, particularly daimyo who were closely allied to the Tokugawa house. One could argue that the intelligence on world affairs that the Dutch provided was a type of military service, but this differed fundamentally from the daimyo who were required to perform specific military duties for the Shogun such as guard duty around the shogun's castle. Another difference is that the Dutch were not required to leave hostages in Edo, namely, their families and, more specifically, daimyo heirs. One could argue that the Dutch were themselves already hostages on the "prison" island of Deshima, and so there was no need to take greater pains to ensure Dutch subservience, but I think this is an instance in which we're comparing apples to oranges. The reason why daimyo hostages were required was to prevent the threat of provincial rebellions and military alliances; clearly, the Dutch in their very limited numbers and limited military resources were not on a par with the great military houses in western Japan such as the Shimazu of Satsuma, at least early in the seventeenth century when these decrees were formalized.

It is increasingly clear, through the work of military historians of Asia over the past several years, and most recently in the work of Tonio Andrade, that Europeans in the seventeenth century held no great advantage over Asian militaries, certainly not on land.[49] There was never any real question, for example, of a serious European invasion of China or Japan, mostly because the militaries of the Tokugawa confederation and the Qing dynasty were quite formidable, but also because European numbers and technology were simply too limited. At any given time in the seventeenth century, European military forces available for a serious military conflict would number perhaps a few tens of ships at most, and perhaps a few thousands of troops. Certainly, European military technology was advanced in the seventeenth-century context, but Asian rulers were very adept at adapting that technology for their own militaries so that if there was a gap at all in military capabilities, it was very small and of short duration. And of course, such a gap could be more than compensated for by the fact that Chinese and Japanese armies were far larger than anything Europeans could assemble in Asia, and just as well organized as European forces. The one area that Andrade identifies in which Europeans had a clear military advantage was the so-called "renaissance fort" that allowed Europeans to withstand concerted attacks by besieging armies, but of course this situation did not hold in the case of the Dutch because they had no such strongholds in Japan.[50] While the Japanese were right to be concerned that Dutch ships could easily prey on Japanese shipping, not to mention Chinese ships coming to Japan, there seems to have been little real concern over Dutch military strength within Japan itself.

To return to the Dutch journeys to court, however, the *hofreis* quite closely resembled daimyo processions to Edo as they fulfilled their mandated obligation to attend on the Shogun, a point that Marius Jansen makes explicit in his magisterial *The Making of Modern Japan*.[51] They were required to come to Edo every year, spending sizable sums on an extensive retinue and other expenses such as lodging.[52] They were required to attend on the Shogun by providing intelligence and by performing an act of submission in an audience that made it perfectly clear the Tokugawa commanded the allegiance of even foreigners from the farthest reaches of the globe. And finally, the Dutch went to great lengths on these journeys to demonstrate both verbally as well as in their actions that they were "vassals" of the Tokugawa, ready to serve when needed and complying, however grudgingly, with all Tokugawa edicts, no matter how tiresome.[53] Jansen states that, unlike the Chinese, who were only ever viewed as merchants and thus were never permitted to come to Edo, the Dutch were viewed as representatives of a great nation, and so the chief merchant's status changed from that of merchant to one of daimyo for the purposes of the journey to court.[54] Timon Screech notes as much when he refers to the journey to the shogun's court as a "semi-ambassadorial" journey.[55]

On the other hand, the Dutch were clearly not simply another daimyo retainer. The Dutch were quite obviously foreign, and in fact, the very fact of their foreignness is probably what continued to interest the Tokugawa. In this regard, the Dutch were representatives of a foreign power traveling to Edo to pay their respects to the Shogun, even though the *bakufu* was quite aware that the Dutch were not traveling straight to Japan from Europe but rather came from the VOC headquarters at Batavia.[56] The Dutch allowed the shogunal court to legitimately claim to be receiving embassies not only from nearby foreign lands (Korea and the Ryūkayan Kingdom) but also from afar. The key element of the pageantry at court when the Dutch visited was the various ostentatious rituals of submission. Not only did the barbarian Dutch come to submit in some theoretical way to the shogun's will but they also performed their submission with the presentation of formal gifts, the "curiosos" they brought from Europe, and with the displays of humility involved in the audience. The symbolic submission on the part of the Dutch served as a concrete reminder to all and sundry at court that the Tokugawa commanded respect even from as far afield as Europe.

The foreignness of the Dutch was most forcefully brought home during what could be, in Dutch eyes, an often-humiliating audience with the Shogun. The Dutch chief merchants were made to approach the Shogun on all fours, eyes averted from the shogunal presence, and to prostrate themselves facedown before a usually obscured Shogun before backing out of the room, again on all fours, as if embodying the act of groveling.[57] On top of this, however, the Dutch were often, especially in the first century or so of the court journeys, made to "act foreign." That is to say, the Dutch were made to dance in a Dutch fashion, to sing Dutch songs, speak Dutch to each other, greet each other in the Dutch manner, and were even asked to demonstrate kissing![58] On one occasion, the young son of one of the Dutch merchants accompanied his father on the court journey, and, during his stay in Edo, the child was asked to sing foreign songs for the Japanese officials.[59] When such gratuitous displays were no longer required to be performed in this way, the diaries make it perfectly clear that the Company servants were quite relieved.[60] A similar phenomenon occurred when Ainu appeared before *bakufu* officials: they were forced to appear in native dress, not only to satisfy the Japanese craving for the exotic but also to demonstrate their foreignness vis-à-vis the Japanese.[61] I think that something similar happened in the Dutch case. The more foreign the Company servants appeared, the more it was brought home to the Japanese political and military elite that the Tokugawa were the center of an East Asian world order in which even far-off foreigners came to pay homage to the Shogun.

The VOC merchants' readiness to "kowtow" to the Shogun elicited some criticism in Europe, and later in America. This is seen most obviously in the case of European embassies to the Chinese emperor in which the Dutch had no problem performing their submission to the emperor in exchange for trade, whereas the English steadfastly refused to perform the ceremonial gestures of submission.[62] But the same criticism was leveled at the Dutch for their action in Japan as well; the essayist Oliver Goldsmith roundly criticized the Dutch for being willing to prostate themselves to the Shogun in order to advance their commercial interest, although certainly the fact that the English and Dutch were rivals in East Asia must surely have had something to do with his criticism.[63] Later, American writers in the mid-eighteenth century also criticized the Dutch demeanor in Japan, arguing that the Americans should take a more martial approach to interactions with the Japanese. The Dutch themselves made it clear to the Shogun and his officials that they were willing to speak the language and rhetoric of vassalage in order to maintain Dutch access to Japanese markets, although, as Adam Clulow points out, this was a phenomenon that was not that unusual in Asia when Europeans often used this rhetorical language to obtain their real commercial objectives.[64]

Another way in which the Dutch were treated as foreign was in the yearly interrogation to which they were subjected.[65] This was on top of the annual written report on the goings-on in Europe and among the Europeans in Asia that the Company was required to submit upon a ship's arrival in late autumn. These reports, called the *fūsetsugaki*, painted a rough picture of Europe in the early modern period (at least the picture the Dutch wanted the Shogun to see), and they were immediately translated from Dutch into Japanese and forwarded to Edo for inspection.[66] Aside from these yearly reports, the Dutch were often interrogated for hours upon their visits to Edo, sometimes about particular happenings and sometimes about general global knowledge. The Dutch chief merchant often portrayed these sessions as exhausting and tedious, especially when several different officials asked the Dutch the same questions over and over again, sometimes day after day in the event of a particularly pressing incident or concern.[67] Through the Dutch reports, along with similar Chinese reports, the Japanese were able to keep relatively well informed about what was happening in the wider world, even though all Japanese foreign travel was officially banned in the 1630s as part of the comprehensive *sakoku* decrees that formalized, and to a certain extent crystalized, Japanese foreign policy for the next two and a half centuries.[68] This particular aspect of the Dutch court journey reinforces the Dutch role as vassals to the Tokugawa in the sense that just as daimyo retainers were expected to provide military service at court, so the Dutch reports provided a kind of military intelligence for the *bakufu*. Especially in the decades immediately after the Portuguese were expelled in 1639, the Dutch were routinely interrogated as to Portuguese and Spanish activities in Asia and were warned in no uncertain terms that the Dutch were to report immediately to Edo any intelligence that they learned about a Portuguese or other Catholic plot to come to Japan.[69]

At least on a symbolic and rhetorical level, the culmination of the *hofreis* was the presentation of the official gifts to the Shogun. Relatively early on in the Dutch court journeys, the value and the type of official gifts were more or less set and consisted of a variety of silk goods and other standard luxury goods from Asia. Other gifts were also presented that might be considered far more exotic, such as large fauna and fine works of European craftsmanship, but these gifts were much more irregular, and many of them fell into a category that, as we noted earlier, can be thought of as "quasi-gifts."

The official gifts that the Dutch brought year in and year out were so routine in nature, and the value of the gifts were so set, that it is possible to view the presents not as gifts in the classic sense of gift-giving as laid out in the beginning of this chapter, but rather as a type of "import" tax. In other words, apart from the rent that the Dutch paid to the landlords in Nagasaki for the privilege of being imprisoned on Deshima, the VOC was not required to pay anything resembling a yearly levy on trade. The goods that the Company forwarded to Edo could thus be thought to represent, in effect, a certain percentage of Dutch profits in Japan, especially after the Japanese placed an official annual limit on the value of Company trade. Even after the Company was given permission to journey to the capital once every four years instead of once every year, they were still required to forward the same amount of gifts to the court in Edo, reinforcing the view that these good could be conceived of as a sort of tax, and the fact that the luxury goods fit in well with the ostentatious display of wealth that a rapid urbanization engendered in Edo-period Japan made the gifts all the more valuable.[70] Frits Vos states as much when he notes that "once a year, and later once in every four or five years, the tedium of their existence was relieved by a court journey to Edo ... [and presented] gifts which had often been ordered beforehand and were in fact a kind of tax levied for the privilege of being allowed to trade in the empire."[71]

By the mid-seventeenth century, the formal audience with the Shogun was completely prescribed and rarely changed, and this extended to the official gifts given to the Shogun (and often the heir to the shogunate). Occasionally, the Dutch would be able to catch a glimpse of the Shogun behind a screen, but they were never able to physically interact with him, and this lack of physical interaction extended to the gifts.[72] The gifts were displayed in the audience hall, the Dutch went through the motions of being received in audience by the Shogun, and then the audience was over. The Dutch only learned about the Shogun's pleasure at the gifts (or displeasure as was sometimes the case) secondhand through a shogunal official who would congratulate the Dutch on their audience. The real interaction was with the shogun's councilors, the Nagasaki *bugyō*, and other influential daimyo who happened to be in Edo (and of course high-ranking officials who visited Nagasaki). These officials were also all given formulaic gifts of varying quantity after the audience was concluded, but it is often with these officials that we truly get a sense of the astonishing array of "quasi-gifts" that mediated these relationships.

Another aspect of gift-giving that was quite prescribed was the "return gifts" given to the Dutch by the Shogun, and then by other shogunal officials in turn. Early gifts often consisted of gifts of silver in addition to Japanese kimono. This tradition became standard across the years, especially the gift of kimono.[73] In later years, especially, these kimono became quite fashionable in Europe and so became a valuable export item for the VOC.[74] Many of the diaries in the eighteenth century state that these robes were handed over to a tailor in order to be "remodeled in the Dutch fashion."[75] Once the Shogun presented the Dutch with this symbolic gift, all of the shogun's officials who received gifts would then also provide the Dutch with return gifts of their own. These were usually utile items, often times gifts of food and drink, although some higher-ranking officials provided the Dutch with a lesser number of "gowns," such as the designated heir of the Shogun.[76] In the eighteenth century, the Dutch routinely received gifts of eggs and stone bass for their consumption, and occasionally gifts of *sake*.

By their very nature, these gifts, including a whole range of large and small animals from birds of paradise to water buffalo, European manufactured goods, some of them distributed, as noted by Martha Chaiklin's study of Dutch material culture in eighteenth-century Japan, surprisingly liberally around Edo and other "shogunal cities," represented in discrete packages the exotic nature of the Dutch and the fact that they were traveling thousands of miles explicitly to attend on the Shogun and to submit to shogunal authority.[77] It's easy to think of the telescopes, spectacles, medicines, and artwork of various stripes as curiosities, and indeed the Dutch often refer to these items as *curiosos* in their diaries, but to the Japanese, these quasi-gifts were loaded with symbolic meaning and carried the connotation of Dutch submission and shogunal authority. In this regard, the VOC became not only a mechanism for distributing European goods and Southeast Asian luxury goods liberally among the upper crust of society but also a vehicle through which the Tokugawa polity could affirm, especially vis-à-vis the other potentially rival daimyo, the far-reaching authority of the *bakufu* in foreign affairs, and by extension in domestic affairs. The fact that the various daimyo, friend and foe alike, shared in the lavish bestowal of European and Asian consumer goods only served as totemic reminders of Tokugawa power and prestige.

While it is certainly true that the Dutch seem to have been a form of diversion for many daimyo, especially powerful daimyo who passed through the region on their way to Edo, it is also true that these powerful daimyo, exactly those whom the Tokugawa needed to impress their power upon, would have made the connection that the Dutch presence in the *bakufu*-controlled enclave of Nagasaki represented the projection of Tokugawa power far from the political center. Although Company servants often complained of the burden of being a spectacle, rather like an animal in a cage, such complaints are invariably followed by a stoic resignation and the sense that these minor inconveniences were part of the cost of doing business in Japan. For the Tokugawa, as well, it was to their advantage to be able to display the Dutch both in Edo and at Nagasaki, however corralled they may have been, as a reminder to all and sundry of their absolute authority.

Whether in daily life on the island of Deshima or at the Shogun's court in Edo, the Dutch found themselves in the position of having to "perform their submission." This was most obvious when the "Holland Captain," as he was known officially at court, prostrated himself facedown in front of the Shogun, therefore literally and metaphorically performing an act of submission. However, I would argue that the Company's whole choreographed existence in Japan, or at least the high points of the year, such as the arrival of ships, the unloading of cargoes, the sale of merchandise, the trip to Edo, and the departure, were all framed by this performance of submission.

When the Dutch ships arrived at Deshima, there was an elaborate and essentially unchanging procedure that accompanied the arrival. Over the course of years, such procedures took on more of an air of ritual than of practical or precautionary procedure, and to change even the tiniest aspect of the arrival seemed nearly impossible. The same was true for most other aspects of life and business on the island. The chief merchant often sent requests to the Nagasaki *bugyō* seeking to change certain onerous aspects of life on the island, but almost always to little avail. A simple request such as sending one fewer member on the *hofreis* in order to save money in a straitened economic environment was treated as an enormous and consequential change to established routine, and so was consistently denied until the *hofreis* was changed to every other year, and then once every four years much later in the Tokugawa period.

I would argue that one reason why changes to the established routine were difficult was because the entire VOC presence in Japan was an elaborate pageant meant to demonstrate Dutch submission to the authorities in Edo, and, by extension, shogunal authority in Nagasaki. In this conception, every gift bestowed on Japanese officialdom, every petition made to the Nagasaki *bugyō*, no matter how many times it was denied, every instance of Dutch compliance with the arcane rules of trade and behavior, and certainly every journey to the shogunal court was an opportunity for the Dutch to perform their submission in myriad ways and in myriad settings. The fact that many of these daily or yearly routines took on the air of a liturgy and ritual simply highlights the nature of Dutch symbolic submission while, at the same time, demonstrating concretely that the Shogun was the legitimate arbiter of power in Japan with absolute control over the barbarians who came humbly and meekly to Japan.

2

Horses and Camels and Birds of Paradise, Oh My: Exotic Animals as Gifts

On January 6, 1647, the chief merchant of the Dutch factory on Deshima, Willem Vertseeghen, mounted his horse and prepared for the official audience with the Shogun during that year's court journey. It was a rather stranger than usual retinue that paraded through the streets of Edo that day, as related in Versteeghen's diary:

> At Eight o'clock we set off for the castle in this order: at the head the two camels covered with black velvet, muzzles, and straps, led by two men, then the two cassowary sitting in a wooden cage, carried by six men, two beautiful, white cockatoos in a large birdcage with copper wire netting on top and at the sides, carried by two men. Then, following behind, fourteen cases with gifts, one after the other and, depending on the weight, carried by a number of men, and the presentation trays, then I followed in a palanquin, four Dutchmen on horseback, and a black, who walked beside the palanquin with several servants. We were accompanied by two noblemen, the interpreter and his son, three sons of the landlord and other retinue. We attracted a great deal of attention.[1]

We are able to partially reconstruct the history of these camels in Japan through the diaries of the chief merchant. The animals seem to have arrived on the island when the ships arrived between September and October of 1646, and were subsequently presented to the Nagasaki *bugyō* for inspection on November 3 of that year. The diaries report that he was well pleased and would need several days to inspect the gifts. On November 29, the gifts were packed up on the specially designated barges to be sent ahead to Edo (we are told that the camels commanded their own barge, as well we might imagine, given the size of camels and the fact that there were two of them). On December 22, the Dutch became somewhat distressed about the camels and felt the need to send for the surgeon to attend to them because they were "a bit off color." In order to ensure the health of the animals, it was decided that the animals should rest in Osaka, "because the camels are not accustomed to this type of traveling and are rather tired and sickly, they should stay here for a day with two servants and a groom and they can follow at their ease as soon as possible." Clearly, the camels were the highlight of that year's gifts to the Shogun, and every care was taken to ensure that the beasts arrived safely, or at least alive.[2]

Three days later, on December 26, the Dutch received a messenger who related the welcome news that the camels were apparently on the mend, were back on the road toward Edo, and would follow at their leisure. The Dutch arrived in Edo ahead of the camels (December 30), but because it was the custom for the Dutch to send the gifts to a shogunal official to be inspected, they came up with the acceptable compromise of writing a memorandum about the camels in lieu of the actual beasts themselves. The animals subsequently strode into Edo on January 3, undoubtedly attracting a fair amount of attention, and immediately the chief merchant ordered an interpreter to send an official notice to the Nagasaki *bugyō* in Edo at the time, who responded that he was pleased the animals arrived safely. Three days later, on January 6, the Dutch lined up in the procession described earlier and set off for the shogun's castle, the camels clearly the main attraction for that year.

The camels were placed in the courtyard of the Shogun where not only the Shogun and his close confidants but all of the "nobles" could also view them.[3] In fact, the Dutch describe how "the whole castle seemed to be running wild" and that "every nobleman had come to the castle, and all had gathered to view the rarities we had brought." A few days later, the Company's patron, Inoue Masashige, told the chief merchant that "your gifts, with the inclusion of many rarities, have pleased His Majesty, which is good for the Dutch, and a great honor for you." One could argue that episodes such as these provided a momentary, pleasant diversion for the elite of Edo, and this was undoubtedly true. However, it is also undoubtedly true that displays such as these served to reinforce the power of the Tokugawa in that rarities and exotic animals from the very ends of the earth were brought to Edo by Western barbarians simply for the pleasure of the Shogun; these spectacles additionally served to elevate the status of the Dutch as they quite clearly had the means to bring such monstrous camels and technological marvels all the way to Japan. And finally, by continuously satisfying the desires of the shogunal elite in Japan, the Dutch ensured their own continued commercial success in Japan.

On that same trip, another member of the shogun's government in Edo approached the Dutch and asked if he could have a male buffalo, because the buffalo the Company had given him earlier recently died, leaving the official with only a female buffalo, who was apparently lonely without her partner.[4] The buffalo in question originated from Southeast Asia, and it speaks to the willingness of the Dutch to satisfy what must have been expensive and logistically difficult demands that they not only seriously considered such requests but often were also able to fulfill them in, what in the early modern era was, relatively short order. This was facilitated by the fact that the Dutch had several factories strewn across Asia, from Japan in the east to Persia in the west, with Batavia serving as the Company headquarters. Letters flowed across Asia, including letters requesting various rarities for potentates such as the Japanese Shogun. Sure enough, a year later, on November 20, 1648, we read in the diaries that the official in question took ownership of not just one buffalo, but two (and it would have been three except that the third [and the smallest, for what it's worth], died shortly after arrival in Japan).[5] Thus for two years in a row, the Dutch brought large, exotic fauna with them: two camels in 1647 and three water buffaloes in 1648. But, that's not all. In 1647, the Dutch also managed to bring to Edo a cassowary, two cockatoos, and a civet cat that died en route to Edo that they nevertheless had to pickle and carry with them because the authorities were expecting it. In 1648, the Company brought a white deer, a parrot, and of the course the aforementioned three buffaloes.

Another notice of buffaloes arriving on Deshima is of interest because of the extended negotiation over delivery of the beasts. Four of the animals arrived on August 26, 1659, intended for the shogunal intendent of Osaka, who had an interest in exotic animals. The Dutch argued that rather than deliver them personally to Osaka while on the court trip to Edo, the official should make his own arrangement to come and get them. The Dutch must have prevailed on this point because we are told on February 3, 1660, that the buffaloes remained behind on Deshima, although the expense of delivering the beasts must have been only slightly more than actually stabling them on the island. The next we hear of the beasts, the Dutch again requested about the status of the buffaloes, but rather than come to a conclusion, we are told that there was a request for yet more buffaloes, to which the chief merchant wrote that even as it was, the four buffaloes already on the island could not get enough to eat! Finally, on June 3, we are told the beasts were loaded on a barge and shipped to Osaka, where they arrived after a journey of twelve days. The animals are mentioned frequently during their long stay on Deshima as objects of wonder for visiting officials who enjoyed looking at the beasts, along with the other attractions such as the billiards table and, naturally, the food and drink.[6] While it is true that these couple of years were extraordinary in that the Company did not bring large fauna to Edo as a matter of course, but rather more infrequently, the Company did regularly import smaller animals and animal products to Japan for gifts and quasi-gifts for the officials in Nagasaki and Edo. This chapter will be devoted to examining some of those exotic animals as well as the more routine animals and animal products.

Megafauna

Of all the animals given as gifts or quasi-gifts through the centuries of VOC trade with Japan, the large fauna such as the aforementioned camels, or elephants, horses, and indeed buffaloes have the ability to most inspire the imagination. One of the reasons this is, I think, is that the logistics of moving these large animals across oceans must have been quite enormous. Take the camels as one example; moving them from western Asia to the farthest reaches of East Asia must have been quite a feat of planning, even given the fact that many of these animals were accompanied by what the Dutch call "grooms," people, often natives of the regions whence the animals came, who knew how to care for the animals. The same could be said for the Persian horses that we'll see later, or especially the elephants that came from Southeast Asia. Moving these animals across the ocean, on journeys that were marked by violent storms and by their duration, must have made many a ship captain feel like Noah, if not in piety, then certainly by the animals on board. Even the letters requesting such beasts sent from Japan to Batavia and then forwarded on to the various factories in Asia, and the return "merchandise" sent from these factories back to Batavia and then finally to Japan is a feat of early modern bureaucracy startling in scope.

Another reason these animals capture the imagination is that, as we noted with the earlier diary entries, they were paraded, sometimes literally, through Japan to the shogun's capital precisely because they were so exotic. By the 1640s, all Japanese travel to other lands was strictly forbidden and so most Japanese would never have had occasion to see a camel, much less an elephant. The sheer exotic nature of these beasts was what made them particularly valuable as presents: foreigners from the very ends of the earth took great pains to deliver these almost fantastically strange creatures to the Shogun. Is it possible to have a more potent symbol of the power of the Shogun than this? This was certainly true in the first several decades of shogunal rule as the Tokugawa house took great pains to impress upon their fellow daimyo, the court nobility in Kyoto, and the warrior bands that accompanied the daimyo to Edo that they were indisputably the military rulers of Japan.

The truly exotic megafauna sent to the Shogun were camels, elephants, oxen, and especially Persian stallions. Camels were brought to Japan on two occasions, in 1647 and in 1821, when another pair of camels arrived in Japan, but never made the trip to Edo since they were rejected as gifts by the Shogun. The latter two camels are immortalized in a series of images made in 1824 by Utagawa Kuniyasu. Utugawa's representation shows the two camels with one rider each and a couple of strangely dressed attendants, and is accompanied by an elaborate description of the animals' diet, size, and place of origin.[7] Martha Chaiklin notes that because the camels were rejected as gifts, they were given to one of the mistresses of a Dutch merchant who charged admission to see the animals and thus made a pretty penny.[8] It's hard to miss the disparity between the reception given these two sets of camels. The first set in 1646 were draped in black velvet, their health meticulously attended to by a physician; they were received with great ceremony in Edo and were viewed with wonder by many warrior elites in the courtyard of the shogun's palace. The camels brought in 1821, however, were unceremoniously rejected as gifts and given to a prostitute to make whatever money she could off of them. There are several reasons for the different receptions, but one is surely that in the 1640s, the Shogun was still solidifying his power over the daimyo, whereas in the 1820s, such exotic gifts simply represented a cost that the shogunate was unwilling or perhaps unable to bear.

On February 1, 1659, as the chief merchant was preparing to leave for Edo on the yearly court journey, he showed the Nagasaki *bugyō* two white oxen from Bengal that were intended for the Shogun as gifts. According to Chief Merchant Wagenaer, "When [the *bugyō*] saw that the old copper horns of the animal had been gilded and that they were bedecked and betasselled with quite a few bells and silk trimmings, he burst out laughing and said that His Majesty would be extremely pleased with them if only they arrived in Edo as smooth and fat as they were now."[9] The pair of oxen had arrived on Deshima aboard the *Venenberg* on September 6, 1659, and were presented to the *bugyō* for inspection, along with a specially made carriage, on September 10. He was very much impressed with the animals saying that they were quite rare and were sure to be well received in Edo. A minor crisis erupted when it became apparent that one of the oxen began to lose a considerable amount of weight and thus a "cow-master" was called in on December 21. The diagnosis was that the oxen were not used to the cold weather and that they should be given blankets and a diet of boiled barley and beans. This remedy must have worked, because the merchants arrived with the beasts in Edo on April 4, and we are told that on several occasions high-ranking personages came round to the Company's lodgings to have a look at the oxen. The audience with the Shogun occurred on April 19, and the oxen were "beautifully caparisoned and harnessed to the carriage" and sent ahead to the shogun's palace. After the audience, two Dutch merchants instructed the Japanese attendants how to harness the oxen and manage them, and with that the two rare white oxen pass from the pages of history into what one can only hope were pastures of plenty.

Horses were imported with much greater frequency than other large animals throughout the seventeenth and most of the eighteenth centuries. Unlike camels and oxen, horses were prized by the Japanese as a utilitarian instrument of war, and for a country that was ruled by a class that identified first and foremost as warriors, horses made an especially apt gift, especially the magnificent steeds from Persia and the Arabian Peninsula. In 1668, for example, two Persian steeds were presented to the Shogun and were sent to the shogunal stables where, eight years later, they make another appearance when the chief merchant was told that the horses had sired many offspring that were of even finer quality than the original gifts.[10]

When these two horses were originally brought to Japan in 1667 and designated as gifts for the Shogun, the Nagasaki *bugyō*, as was usual, requested to inspect them. Accordingly, on February 3, about a month before the court journey, the chief merchant presented the two horses, only to be told that the horse caparisons were not at all appropriate and should be replaced. Chief Merchant Ranst argued that the horses were sent from Batavia bare and that the Dutch could not be expected to know how the Japanese caparison their horses. After some back and forth, the *bugyō* summoned the Dutch and told them that "because this gift of horses would please the Shogun very much and he would therefore view them personally, it would be proper if we prepared a couple of proper caparisons made up nicely."[11] This done, the horses made the court journey, and on April 7, a Japanese attendant told the Dutch to ready the horses for an audience with the Shogun two days later. One snag was that the *bugyō* neglected to inform the shogunal court that the two horses had "dapple grey" coats and so when they were presented to the Shogun initially, they were rejected and the Dutch told to present them instead to a couple shogunal officials. After much reconsidering, however, the two senior officials at the court informed the Dutch that

> his majesty has taken into consideration that the horses had been brought to Japan across the sea at considerable trouble and expense. If [the Shogun] did not accept them now, it would entail even more difficulties and expense. Their

coats had been the only reason they had not been accepted with the other gifts. His majesty has overlooked this fault and will now accept the horses. He is very pleased with them as, apart from the fault they are perfect horses, which is the [chief merchant]'s good fortune.[12]

In 1725, five more Persian horses were brought to Japan at the request of Tokugawa Yoshimune in an attempt to try to improve the Japanese horse through cross-breeding.[13] The Shogun also extended an invitation to the noted equestrian H. J. Keijser, who arrived with the five horses, made the journey to Edo, and instructed shogunal attendants, and apparently Yoshimune himself, in the methods of Western horsemanship.[14] After leaving Japan, he returned again in 1734 with six more horses, made another trip to Edo, and spent six months instructing the Japanese. Keijser's exploits in Edo are recorded in an official diary, which was handed over to the chief merchant on his return to Deshima and forms part of the Company's official diaries for the years 1734–35[15]. The Shogun, apparently quite satisfied at Keijser's performance, asked for another equestrian, and so a Dutchman by the name of Jan Jephart Werner later made the journey to court and also instructed the Japanese in Western equestrian techniques.[16]

The import of horses continued, including some rather detailed back and forth between shogunal retainers and the Company as the Company tried to present horses the Shogun would find acceptable. One horse was rejected, for example, because it was white, an inauspicious color, and others had died on the way to Japan. In both 1769 and 1771, stallions were rejected—on one occasion because the horse was a half-inch too short. Two years later, a shogunal official asked the chief merchants why the Dutch had not imported a Persian stallion even though the Shogun continually asked for one, to which the chief merchant replied, with an obvious hint of exasperation, that it was extremely difficult to find a horse that fit the shogun's exacting expectations![17] Finally, in 1778, two horses were presented to the Shogun Ieharu, who accepted them and put them into his stables. The Dutch were later to learn that a year after the horses were accepted, the shogun's son, Iemoto, was killed when one of the horses bucked him from the saddle.[18] This tragedy prompted the Japanese to break off requesting horses, and thereafter we read of no other horses arriving at Edo.

An interesting side note tangentially related to horses involved a finely crafted carriage the Dutch imported to Japan specifically as a gift for the Shogun. In a diary entry for the year 1734, we read that the carriage arrived on the island along with several horses and the aforementioned Keijser. While horses were generally accepted by the Shogun as gifts, the carriage was specifically rejected as a gift, not once, but repeatedly. In October of 1734, we are told in a diary entry that the carriage and the horses were a blatant attempt to extract more copper exports from the Japanese, and in the case of the horses, this strategy often worked, for in recompense for horses, the Dutch might be allowed to export slightly more copper for that year. And yet the carriage itself was rejected as a gift.

The carriage was first rejected in 1734, the year it arrived on the island. Incidentally, other presents for that year included a gold pocket watch, a clock, three violins, a chandelier, two pieces of field artillery, two paintings, a leopard, and seven turkeys. This would have been in addition to the usual gifts of cloth that made up the bulk of the usual presents, so most likely the VOC was trying to attain their desire for more trade with an overwhelming array of gifts. And indeed, the Dutch attained that year two hundred extra chests of copper for their efforts. And yet the carriage was still rejected as a gift. Another rejection of the carriage, along with some of the other gifts from 1734, including the gold pocket watch, came in September of 1737 when the Dutch were told that these gifts were "not to the shogun's liking." This did not stop the Dutch from again presenting the carriage as a gift in 1738, although again the carriage was rejected. For that year also, however, we are told that the Dutch received an extra two hundred chests of copper because of additional horses presented to the Shogun. In September of 1738, the Dutch were told definitively that the unloved and rejected carriage should be returned to Batavia on the next ship because the Shogun would not accept it as a gift.

Why were the horses accepted as a gift and the carriage not? One explanation is practical and is offered up by Leonard Blussé when he notes that the only figure to ride around in something similar to a carriage was the emperor in Miyako. For propriety's sake, then, the Shogun simply could not accept the gift without the potential for political scandal.[19] However, there could also have been another reason why the Shogun repeatedly rejected the carriage. Perhaps the *bakufu* was worried about creating a precedent by accepting extraordinary gifts such as this carriage and thus being forced to continually offer more copper in return for such lavish gifts.

It was one thing for the shogunate to accept horses and to allow the Dutch to take away a few hundred extra chests of copper in return: the Shogun was personally very interested in horses and ultimately horses were military items essential to any warrior. The carriage, on the other hand, was an item that had never been requested by the Shogun or any of his officials; was not in any real way useful militarily, even tangentially; and was probably a blatant attempt by the Dutch to import exotic things to Japan to increase their copper quota for the year. If this carriage was accepted and the copper increased in one year, then who knows what exotica would have shown up in Japan the next year, and because precedent was such an important part of official life in the Edo period, the *bakufu* might have had to respond to these "curiosos" by increasing the copper quota again and again. This the *bakufu* simply couldn't do since Japan's supply of copper was becoming more and more strained, given the existing mining techniques. Ultimately, therefore, the Shogun rejected this carriage, but accepted the gift of horses as well as the "gift" of the equestrian specialist.

Two elephants were imported into Japan, one in 1727, and one in 1813 when Dutch trade was taken over by the English during the Napoleonic Wars and when Batavia was occupied by English forces. In that year, Thomas Raffles sent a ship to Deshima in an attempt to open up Japanese trade to English shipping and he thought that the gift of an elephant might sufficiently impress the authorities in Edo. In a list of expenses for the voyage to Japan, Raffles listed a sum of 268.80 Spanish Dollars for "Food for the Elephant and Other Animals."[20] The Russian captain Vasili Mikhailovich Golovnin provides a description of the elephant in his account of his captivity in Japan:

> An elephant, which the Dutch had brought from the island of Sumatra, as a present for the Japanese emperor, was described with the greatest minuteness imaginable. No circumstance was omitted, the place of his nativity, his age, length, height, thickness, the food he was accustomed to consume, and how many times in the course of the day, and in what portions he was supplied with the various articles, were all carefully noted. A native of Sumatra, who was the keeper of the elephant, was described with corresponding precision.[21]

Golovnin also claims that the elephant was imported by the Dutch when, in fact, it was brought by the English who were occupying Batavia at the time. Golovnin gives over a considerable portion of the narrative in this section of his book to the embarrassment that the Dutch felt at having had their headquarters taken over by another country; the Dutch were probably quite right to be concerned and took special pains to hide this fact from the Japanese in their yearly reports. The other elephant arrived in 1727 and was the subject of much wonderment. The elephant was given a pass to journey through the country, and it made its way to Miyako where it was granted an audience with the emperor before being paraded to Edo to meet the Shogun. The poor beast ultimately came to an unfortunate end as it eventually starved to death in 1742, but its bones were buried at Hōen-ji just outside of Edo, whatever small consolation that may be to the unfortunate elephant.[22]

The final example of large animals brought to Japan as gifts is a pair of asses from what is today the east African country of Ethiopia. The two animals were sent to Batavia as a present from the ruler of that kingdom, and the governor-general of the VOC hit upon the idea of sending them to Japan as a special present for the Shogun. Accordingly, they were loaded onto a ship and arrived in Nagasaki in 1675 where they caused a sensation with the Nagasaki *bugyō* and other officials. Cynthia Viallé relates an amusing story about the asses and the usual inspection of gifts by the *bugyō*. The Nagasaki *bugyō* was quite pleased with the animals, but apparently thought that the tails needed to be longer, and so ordered that tail hairs from horses be woven together to make the tails of these asses more comely for the Shogun.[23] This done, the asses made their way to the shogun's court in Edo in 1676 where they were received with great pleasure and placed in the shogunal stables.

Birds

Perhaps the greatest and most varied type of animal gift to the Shogun and his officials was the gift of birds. It is well known that the Tokugawa were quite serious about hunting with hawks, and so vassals often presented the Shogun with hawks to satisfy this pastime. Brett Walker, in his study of the Ainu, examined the gifts sent to the Tokugawa by the Matsumae family charged with the administration of Ezo and with maintaining relations with the indigenous Ainu. Among the most prized gifts were hawks from the northern island, and Walker details how the Matsumae brought hawks to Edo as gifts for the first several Shogun.[24] The Shogun knew of the hawks that were native to Europe and asked specifically for some specimens to be sent to Japan, but the Dutch had to reply truthfully that because the journey to Asia was so long, the birds were not able to survive the trip and the Company could therefore only bring to Japan species from areas such as Southeast Asia.[25]

Probably the most exotic birds to arrive in Japan were ostriches and cassowaries, both quite large and flightless birds. As we have already seen, a cassowary was part of the retinue in the court journey along with the pair of camels in 1647. The cassowary was described as being in a large cage that was carried to the shogun's palace by six men. In June of 1654, the Dutch received the servant of the Nagasaki *bugyō* who, "came to inquire what kinds of rare birds are found in Batavia and in Java. Lord Tōdō Daigaku-Sama, who is a great lover of strange birds, would like to know. Last year some cassowaries and turkeys were ordered for him."[26]

Cassowaries are flightless birds that are native to Australia and New Guinea and could grow to be almost human size. Notable features of the cassowary are its domed head with horns, its black plumage with brilliant red spot on its neck, and its large spike on its inside toe. Needless to say, for Europeans, as for Japanese, the cassowary was undoubtedly an odd specimen of bird and elicited wonder from those who saw one for the first time. Maria Belozerskaya relates the first such bird brought back to Amsterdam by the Dutch: a gift from a Javanese ruler to a Dutch ship captain in 1596. The bird arrived in Holland the next year, was a sensation, and ultimately ended up in the animal park of a nobleman.[27]

In 1657, the Dutch were preparing to transport a cassowary to the Shogun on the court journey for that year when the servants responsible for packing the gifts on the specially designated barges informed the chief merchant that there was no room and so proposed a separate barge for the bird. The diary for January 14 tells us, "the skipper was very willing to transport it, yea, he was honored that his barge was chosen to transport a shogunal gift."[28] The next we hear of the bird is on February 20 when the Dutch were newly arrived in Edo. The chief merchant writes that some elites had come round to the lodging and were keen to rifle through Dutch curiosities, and that they also enjoyed ogling the cassowary in the garden of the house in which they were staying, although later the chief merchant writes that "the whole afternoon many important persons have been coming and going. Most of them use the pretense of coming to see the cassowary to come up to my room for some refreshments." Again, writing the next day, the chief merchant states with understandable exasperation, "The usual pretext for most of the visits and annoyances: to view me or the cassowary like two strange monsters."[29] On February 26, on the eve of the audience with the Shogun, the chief merchant relates that

> the cassowary, which is still in good health, has been cleaned, and his cage as well. I had it decked out with finery. A new collar with large bells was hung around its neck and a pair of silk garters were tied above its [a small section of the manuscript damaged and illegible] . . . so that tomorrow it will also appear well groomed.

Thereafter, a comical scene occurred in which the chief merchant states dryly that "at the urgent request of our landlord and interpreters, who insist that this is obligatory, we went to the *furo* or bath. We washed and cleansed ourselves thoroughly." One can imagine that given what we know of European hygiene of the day, the cassowary was not the only odor that needed to be expunged before the audience with the Shogun.

Cassowaries were notorious for being omnivorous as they would eat more or less whatever happened to be at hand. Perhaps this is the reason why Tokugawa

Ietsuna rejected another bird as a gift in 1663; given the potential lifespan of several decades, it would have been costly to maintain, especially once the novelty of the bird wore off, which seemed to happen quite quickly in early modern Japan.[30] In any case, the bird most likely was carried back to Nagasaki with the Dutch that year. The next we hear of the bird was on an apparently uneventful January 11 when we read that "the cassowary has died. Nothing else happened." This was probably the cassowary that was rejected in 1663. Thereafter, it would be over a century and a half before the Dutch would again present a cassowary as a gift, and when they did, in 1825, that bird was also rejected, as was the poor elephant that we met earlier.[31]

On January 29, 1658, the chief merchant related in his diary that an ostrich was put in a specially constructed cage and sent to a barge that was rented for the express purpose of delivering the bird to Edo as a gift for the Shogun.[32] When the Company arrived in Osaka, a special pass was requested of the shogunal officials there so that servants could carry the ostrich overland to Edo, and the intendant replied that because this was a gift for the Shogun, as many men as were needed should be employed. The party subsequently arrived in Edo on February 5, and by February 6, already several people had come to the Dutch lodgings to see the ostrich, whose feathers had apparently grown quite beautiful. On February 8, the chief merchant requested that some Japanese carpenters construct a new cage for the ostrich in preparation for the audience with the Shogun as the old one was found to be in ill repair. The next day, the Shogun was informed of the bird and that it was the talk of Edo. The audience came on February 17, and as the Dutch were preparing for it, two high-ranking officials "asked after the nature and qualities of the ostrich—everyone was gazing at it with great wonderment—and where we had procured it, its age, how much taller it would grow, and suchlike. I replied truthfully and to the best of my knowledge." The chief merchant noticed that as he went in to the audience chamber, the ostrich had been arranged in such a way as to afford the Shogun a view of the bird while the Dutch were paying their respects. In other words, the ostrich, like other exotic animals before and after it, was part of an elaborate pageantry designed to call attention to the power and prestige of the Tokugawa family. In this case one wonders which was the stranger sight—the ostrich or the *Oranda Kapitan*.

Two days after the audience, the Nagasaki *bugyō* requested a fuller description of the ostrich and where exactly it came from:

> It is said the shogun has a look at it twice a day and it is much appreciated. He wants to know where it comes from, the distance in miles to the Cape of Good Hope to Holland and also to Nagasaki; the size of the African domain;

also the produce of the land; was this ostrich male or female; how were they caught; did they live on land or in water; were they shy of humans; did they attack them; what was its age; and how much taller would it grow; and more suchlike questions.

We are told that about a week later, the Shogun apparently appointed six people to care for the ostrich, to which the chief merchant adds, "if this is true, then all the trouble which we experienced on the way with this bird has been well worth it and all our expense richly recompensed." The story, however, had a rather unfortunate coda, as related in a diary entry for July 14, 1658, just five months after presenting the bird to the Shogun:

> I was told that the ostrich which we had presented to the shogun this year had died. The shogun had taken much pleasure every day in seeing it run. One rainy day, while running, it had hit its chest against some wood lying about there and it had fallen to the ground and within view of the shogun it died. Apparently they have chased the bird too much and tired it out, and thereby killed it.[33]

Thus, ended ignominiously the great ostrich spectacle of 1658.

As Martha Chaiklin tells us, many high-ranking daimyo had a great passion for exotic bird collecting, and the Dutch catered to this in selecting their gifts and quasi-gifts. To be sure, many of the birds brought to Japan were ordered specially by the daimyo, especially when the Dutch began to keep what is known as the *eisboek*, or the "registry of requests."[34] Because birds were more or less in constant demand, the Dutch routinely brought a great many species with them to Deshima.[35] On January 28, 1652, we are told that among the gifts that the Nagasaki *bugyō* inspected that year were nine birds of paradise, of which it was determined that five would go to the Shogun.[36] Two days later, the VOC's main patron in Japan, Inoue Masashige, sent for some of the birds of paradise so that he could have their likenesses painted on a Japanese folding screen. On February 5, the Company sent the remaining birds of paradise to Inoue, and then we hear no more of them, so it is logical to assume that he either kept them for himself or, as he was wont to do, used them for his own purposes as gift items in the capital.

Birds of paradise are native to eastern Australia and New Guinea, and were especially prized for the spectacular plumage found on the males of the species. This species probably came to be best known in Europe when Alfred Russell Wallace published the results of his eight-year expedition to the Dutch East Indies in a book entitled *The Malay Archipelago* in 1869, a book whose subtitle was *The Land of the Orang-Utan and the Bird of Paradise*.[37] Because these birds were so beautiful and strange, they were used primarily as gifts for shogunal officials and the more illustrious daimyo.

On the same court journey, an interesting incident occurred in which a shogunal official came to the Dutch residence with a box of what he presumed were rare bird feathers.[38] This official claimed that he ordered more and that he was told by the previous year's chief merchant that they came from around Batavia in what is today Indonesia. Chief Merchant Van der Burgh replied that he was sure the requested feathers would arrive on the ships for that year as he personally saw to it that the order was placed. Indeed, on November 28, 1653, we are told that the Dutch had received two barrels of "Dutch bed feathers."[39] The exotic nature of these feathers is demonstrated by the fact that the Dutch thought no more of them than to use them in pillows, while for at least this particular Japanese official, they were a treasure to be, well, treasured.

Many other birds were sent to Japan, the most common being exotic "collector" birds such as cockatoos, canaries, parrots, and the like.[40] An indication of how seriously the Japanese took their birds is found in an incident in 1776. That year, the chief merchant writes that as the servants were unloading the dogs and birds from the newly arrived Dutch ship, a careless bird keeper left the door of a cage open and all of the birds escaped. The Japanese were not happy with this avian declaration of independence, and so the Dutch were forced to write a letter in which the incident was explained, presumably to demonstrate the Nagasaki officialdom's innocence in the great bird escape.[41]

In 1647, we read of a dodo that arrived in Japan, and that a daimyo who came around to look at it, along with some deer, was pleased with the animals.[42] Along with larger animals such as the aforementioned examples, these animals were perhaps the most ostentatious examples of Dutch subservience to the Shogun. In several instances, animals played the leading role in the audience with the Shogun, a spectacle that was by no means a closeted affair. The Dutch diaries make it abundantly clear that the audience, formulaic and scripted as it may be, was entirely designed to be a spectacle for daimyo consumption. The Tokugawa specifically designed these audiences to highlight the exotic nature certainly of the Dutch themselves, but also of the gifts that the Dutch brought, and the most exotic of these gifts were the live animals. Camels, horses, asses, tiger cubs, oxen, water buffalo, and the like, to be fair, were quite rare gifts, but exotic birds, including cassowaries, ostriches, and "collector" birds, were more common, and these combined with the other exotic gifts that we will discuss in the next chapter served to demonstrate in a strikingly colorful and forceful nature the grandeur and the power of the Tokugawa, for in the end, the animals and the other exotic gifts were brought from the ends of the earth to pay homage to the Shogun and to the long line of Tokugawa who held that position.

Animal Products

Aside from the menagerie of live animals brought to Japan aboard VOC ships, the Company took special pains to also bring various animal products especially popular in Edo and beyond. One of the most popular of these animal products was animal horn, including narwhale tusks, rhinoceros horns, and of course elephant tusks, which is not at all surprising given that even today the illegal trade in ivory seems to be thriving, despite decades of activism and millions of dollars spent in an attempt to enforce a general ban. The Dutch were able to obtain a ready supply of tusks and horns in their factories in Siam (Ayutthaya) and Burma from whence they shipped them to Japan for a hefty profit, to be used as valuable gifts for shogunal officials. And as for narwhales, the Dutch were able to procure a supply from trade with the Inuit in Greenland, from where the prized horns would be shipped to Batavia and then on to factories such as Deshima.[43] An examination of the cargo arriving in Japan as seen in the Dutch diaries, and until the early 1660s in the diaries of the VOC headquarters on Taiwan, show a steady flow of ivory from Southeast to East Asia. The trade in elephant tusks is beautifully illustrated in a print from around 1845 in which a Dutchman is shown weighing several tusks on a wooden scale.[44] These tusks were obviously for sale, but it was certainly not unusual for the Dutch to select gifts for the Shogun from among the animal products that arrived on the yearly ships, in consultation with Nagasaki officials. In fact, most of the animal products seem to be included in the gifts precisely in this way, that is to say that the tusks, rhinoceros horns, ray skins, or whatever item it happened to be were examined, and a few choice specimens selected and included in the gifts to "His Majesty." On November 7, 1648, for example, we are told that "the goods which will be sold at the first sale have been displayed. Two secretaries of the Nagasaki *bugyō* inspected the ray skins, of which they took fifteen to show to the *bugyō*, who would select the ones to be presented to the shogun."[45]

On November 18, 1667, the following entry appears in the diary of the chief merchant of the VOC on Deshima:

> The interpreters brought me the horn of a unicorn. It measured 2 ½ ells and weighed 69 taels. A private person had imported it and had sold it to the Japanese

merchants for 500 taels of *schuitzsilver*. The officials had seized it in order to use it as a gift for the shogun this year. They ordered that the money should be returned. Although I could stop this for one day by arguing that several pieces had already been sawed off and sold to private Japanese individuals, and therefore it would be inappropriate to present this horn to the Shogun, especially because we could send for a horn from Europe which would show how it had been attached to the animal and which would therefore be much more suitable for and more agreeable to the Shogun. The interpreters let me know that they understood my arguments, but nevertheless they stood by my previous order to present the horn to the shogun. Textiles of equal value could be deducted from the shogun's gift. Quite frankly, for the company it does not matter either way and it is best to present whatever these gentlemen think pleases him most."[46]

Probably the best account of unicorn's horns in Japan comes from the Swedish physician, Carl Peter Thunberg, who spent a year on Deshima in the service of the VOC in 1775–76 and later wrote an account of his stay on the island. Of the unicorn horn he writes:

Unicorn's horn (unicornu of the *monodon monoceros*) sold this year . . . very dear. It was often smuggled formerly and sold at an enormous rate. The Japanese have an extravagant opinion of its medical virtues and powers to prolong life, fortify the animal spirits, assist the memory and cure all complaints. This branch of commerce has not been known to the Dutch until of late, when it was discovered by an accident. One of the chiefs for commerce here, on his return home, had sent from Europe amongst other rarities to a friend of his who was an interpreter, a large, handsome, twisted, Greenland unicorn's horn by the sale of which this interpreter became extremely rich and a man of consequence. From that time the Dutch have written to Europe for as many horns as they could get, and made great profit from them in Japan.[47]

Thunberg then goes on to relate what prices one could fetch for the unicorn horn, and makes special mention that if one was able to smuggle the horns to Japan and sell them privately, the profits were much greater than if one had to sell them officially. These horns were obviously the horns of the narwhale, but because the trade was so lucrative, "and because no one could deny the corporeal existence of these splendid ivory shafts, the unicorn myth was kept alive by unscrupulous merchants."[48] It is interesting to note that even as the Dutch were bringing "unicorn horns" for gifts, there was a fair amount of skepticism on the part of Japanese officials. Inoue, for example, took a goodly amount of convincing before he was willing to accept Dutch claims that what he was being presented with was actually a unicorn horn.[49] In the end, he accepted it, but I get the impression that he did so more as a way to keep the Dutch from losing face than from any sense of true conviction. Here again we are reminded of the nature of "quasi-gifts": on January 26, Inoue Masashige came to get the goods he ordered and inquired about the price. The chief merchant notes that they quoted the same low prices as usual to maintain the fiction that he is actually paying for these goods.[50]

Another category of animal product that was quite popular and often used as gifts was animal skins. In particular, deerskins and ray skins were often included in the list of gifts for the Shogun, at least in the seventeenth century, although occasionally we hear of more exotic skins, such as a request for two lion skins in 1778.[51] Deer skins came primarily from VOC factories in Siam, Cambodia, and Taiwan, although in 1662, the Company was kicked off of Taiwan by the forces of the pirate/merchant/patriot/rogue Zheng Chenggong, better known in the West as Coxinga, and Company trade in Siam began to dwindle in the same year when the king of Siam imposed a monopoly on all foreign trade, preferring to send his own ships, manned mainly by Chinese crews, to Japan.[52] Before these setbacks, however, the Dutch would routinely ship tens of thousands of skins to Japan every year. In 1637, for example, the chief merchant complained of the scarcity of skins for the Japan market that year, saying that there were only 61,000 available.[53] The skins were used by the samurai class in particular to fashion garments to be worn underneath armor, particularly useful because of the ability of the skins to repel moisture. The skins could also be smoked and lacquered and then used to make high-quality bags for the urban elite in cities such as Edo, Osaka, and Miyako.

Ray skins were imported from places as far afield as Siam and San Thomé, on the east coast of the Indian subcontinent, where in 1635, the Dutch discovered that there were large profits to be made from this product and began to buy up as many ray skins as possible.[54] These skins were particularly valuable in Japan as they were used to cover the hilts of the ubiquitous swords that every samurai was entitled by law and heredity to carry.[55] In May of 1668, we read that a major official in the shogunal government requested thirty ray skins among the next year's gifts.[56] Ray skins were rather ubiquitous in VOC ships coming to Japan in the seventeenth century, and we know that they were prized as gifts to the Edo elite because Dutch diaries repeatedly note that the Nagasaki *bugyō* inspected the skins and chose the best for the *hofreis* to Edo.

Finally, there are a whole host of animal products that were given in very small quantities, and sometimes as one-off gifts. These are at times quite bizarre, such as the gift in 1644 of a jar of elephant fat, a case containing an elephant's liver, and a box with a rhino's liver. Two days later, in thanksgiving for these wonderful gifts, the daimyo sent the Dutch two barrels of *sake*.[57] I leave it to the reader to judge who got the better deal. The elephant fat was medicinal, and it must have been efficacious, for occasionally we see other requests for it. In 1652, for example, we read that among the requested items for that year was another jar of elephant fat along with an elephant's spleen for good measure.[58] And in 1654, the Nagasaki *bugyō* was quite taken with the gift of shark brains given him that year.[59]

As with other gifts brought to Japan on board VOC vessels, the exotic animals and animal products discussed in this chapter are much more than simply tokens of gratitude to the Shogun, or even a "quid pro quo" in order to ensure continued access to the Japanese market; rather these gifts were physical manifestations of a political reality that the Japanese ruling elite in Edo were trying assiduously to construct. The Tokugawa and their vassals were trying to demonstrate that Edo was not just the political and military metropole of Japan but also the center of a Tokugawa-centered political order that encompassed all of East and Southeast Asia. As we've noted before, gifts were a way to demonstrate Dutch reinforcement of this world order, and exotic animals in particular were among the most effective ways to hammer this point home. The expense of shipping these beasts; the sheer logistics of transporting them hundreds, if not thousands, of miles to Edo; and the care that the Dutch took to ensure these animals arrived safely were all signs that the Dutch were submitting to Tokugawa authority in the region. Exotic animals not only caused a sense of wonderment and spectacle among the assembled daimyo in Edo but also served as biological signs of Tokugawa authority, a consideration that was eminently important in Tokugawa Japan precisely because the Shogun were not absolute despots, but had to continually contend with other military houses that could be quite powerful in their own right. What better way to reinforce power and authority than to have Europeans, themselves exotic and foreign, bring strange and wonderful creatures to the Shogun from the ends of the earth?

3

Most Exquisite Curiosities of Nature and Art

While animals were biological examples of the nature of exotic gift-giving in Japan, works of art, including paintings, engravings, carpets and tapestries, maps and globes, and finally works of fine craftsmanship such as metalwork and glassware, were man-made manifestations of the "exotic" that the Dutch brought to Edo to be spread around the upper crust of society more or less liberally. And just as animals were desirable because of the symbolism of having been transported at great expense from the ends of the earth, so too were works of art symbols that the distilled creative genius of Western civilization was being transported many thousands of miles expressly to gratify the Shogun. Domestically, of course, this was powerful symbolism, the more so because these objects were prominently displayed as the Dutch processed into the shogun's audience chamber for the gathered political and military elite of Edo-period Japan to see.

As Martha Chaiklin and others have noted elsewhere, the demand for European manufactured goods, and in this case artistic works, was so great because they were ostentatious items meant to convey status, connections, and influence.[1] As L. M. Cullen notes, "These items were widely diffused among a restricted group in Nagasaki but more especially within a well-placed Edo circle, either collectors of the exotic or alive to their artistic or scientific import."[2] The Dutch responded to the demand for these items by using them as gifts and quasi-gifts for the myriad officials with whom they came into contact on a regular basis. Often Japanese officials would request various luxury goods, and the Dutch would do their best to fulfill the orders, but on several occasions, we read in the diaries about instances in which an official, visiting either Deshima or the Dutch residence in Edo, comments favorably on an item, whereupon the Dutch hand it over as a token of their "esteem."

I am aware that it's certainly possible to stretch the argument a bit—sometimes a beautifully crafted piece of Dutch manufacturing is just that, an object to have around the house and show off to visitors—but I don't think it's too much to argue that on some level *objets d'art* carry within them at least the faint imprint of Tokugawa power and prestige, at least at the upper crust of society, and in the premodern era, that is really what we're talking about when we examine luxury goods and their consumption. To take just a single example that we'll discuss more at length further, the Dutch imported an "oval case with twenty-three different female faces" as a gift for an official in 1643. The gift in and of itself was certainly exotic and must have been at least moderately intrinsically valuable, but the real power of the case lay with what the case represents. First of all, these types of foreign luxury goods were brought to Japan in Dutch ships, a process that was made possible by the power and prestige of the shogunal authority. Therefore, the very people in Japan to whom the Shogun was most keen to demonstrate his legitimacy were also often the very people who were receiving these luxury goods as gifts. In that sense, the aforementioned case was much more than a "rarity" or a "*curioso*" to use the Dutch phrase, but was also a totemic reminder of Tokugawa power and prestige. Furthermore, when the leading daimyo of the realm displayed these luxury goods, as they surely must have, or used them to give as gifts to others in Edo, they were literally displaying a symbolic representation of the shogun's control over all things foreign.

This chapter will examine what I will refer to as *objets d'art* broadly defined. This category is a somewhat nebulous one, and at times the categories in this book will overlap, such as when the Dutch brought elaborately decorated telescopes to Japan. I have chosen to include such objects into a separate category of scientific paraphernalia, including telescopes, spectacles, medicines, treatises, and the like. For this chapter, we will mainly examine paintings, tapestries and carpets, fine metalwork, glasswork, maps and globes, and decorative weaponry. These were all objects that were inherently meant for display because of their beauty and novelty, but in being so displayed, the owners were also displaying, wittingly or not, the power and prestige of the Tokugawa, the undisputed arbiter of foreign relations in Japan, and, as demonstrated physically through these and other gifts, the political center of Japan.

Carpets

An article often listed among the presents for the Shogun is what the Dutch referred to as an *alcatief,* or in plural, *alcatieven*. These were carpets, often Persian in origin, usually made of silk, but possibly also wool, and that seem to have been much in demand in Japan. In October 1668, for example, shogunal officials specifically requested that the next year's gifts include a number of these carpets.[3] A reference to one of these carpets is found in the *Tokugawa Jikki*, in which it is stated that the Dutch embassy for that year brought a number of gifts for the Shogun, including a "flower patterned carpet."[4] References to *alcatieven* run fairly consistently throughout the chief merchants' diaries, including several requests by shogunal officials. As we have had occasion to note earlier, Saris brought a present of a "Turkish" carpet to Ieyasu in 1613, and as this was the very first visit of the English to the Shogun, one can imagine that the gifts on this occasion would have been selected judiciously and specifically to impress. It is perhaps not surprising that Persian carpets should have been viewed as luxury goods and exemplars of superior artistry as even today fine Persian carpets are considered a mark of cultural refinement, especially if the Persian carpet in question were made of silk.

One instance involving carpets illustrates nicely how items meant for sale at a profit could sometimes turn into what effectively amounted to a gift. In October 1740, we read that the Company imported several "Bengali carpets" to sell. However, after a great deal of negotiations, it emerged that the prices offered were too low for the Company, the ostensible reason being that several pieces of "Bengali ware" had been imported that year on Chinese ships, driving the prices down. Rather than sell the pieces at a loss, the Company decided to send the carpets back to Batavia. The next year, however, a shogunal official inquired about the carpets from the year before, only to be told that they were slated to be returned on the next ship. The official continued to inquire about the carpets, saying that he really needed them to give to high-ranking officials in Edo. The chief merchant convened a special meeting of the factory and it was resolved that because the official who requested the carpets had been a "true friend of the company," and, probably more to the point, because to refuse this request could spell trouble for the VOC, they would sell the carpets at a heavily discounted price. This is a perfect example of a "quasi-gift." It is true that the goods were sold, but the Company sustained a loss on the goods for reasons of expediency for the Company.[5]

On one occasion we read of an interesting negotiation concerning a "rug" that the Dutch intended to give as a gift to the Shogun, a negotiation that reveals the rhetoric of gift-giving that the Dutch routinely used with shogunal officials. On October 6, 1649, a few Japanese officials came to the Dutch and suggested for whatever reason that the rug (which the Shogun specifically ordered a few years before) be taken off the lists of gifts and sent to Edo as an item for which the Shogun would pay. The Dutch replied, according to the account in the diary for that day, in quite hyperbolic language: the Dutch company would, under no circumstances, accept payment from the Shogun because the Dutch held the Shogun in such high regard, and, in fact, even if the rug were "ten times more valuable," they would gladly give it as a gift because their sole concern was to see to it that the Shogun has everything he desires. The Dutch concluded this reply by reminding the officials that the Dutch are very happy to know what the Shogun wants every year so that they can be sure to supply him accordingly.[6]

Maps and Globes

Although not often thought of as "art" as such, globes and maps were imported into Japan largely because of their value as fine examples of European craftsmanship. While it is true that the Japanese were curious about Dutch knowledge of the world, and routinely questioned the Dutch closely about various aspects of global geopolitics, the Dutch took special pains in their diaries to highlight the artistic aspects of the globes that were intended as gifts. In November 1647, for example, the president of the Dutch factory noted that a large globe was intended for the Shogun that year, but not any old globe, for this one stood on a fine ebony stand with marbled pillars.[7] Ten years later, in 1657, Zacarias Wagenaer, chief merchant, was told that the Shogun had requested two globes be included in the presents for next year: a terrestrial globe and a celestial one.[8] Indeed, we read in a diary entry for January 1659 that two globes arrived in Japan with detailed instructions on how to use them.[9] Given that gifts generally took about two years to arrive in Japan from the time of request, it is logical to assume that these two globes were the ones requested in 1657, although the diary entry for 1659 does not contain a specific reference to this fact, nor does the entry describe the nature of the two globes.

An interesting scene involving the gift of a globe reveals the extent to which the Japanese were serious about not allowing any trace of Christianity into the country.[10] In November of 1648 the Dutch received a visit from a man named Sawano Chūan, whose real name was Cristovão Ferreira, a Portuguese Jesuit priest who was captured in Japan in 1633 after the Tokugawa had forbidden of pain of death the propagation of the Catholic faith, and banished all priests from the country. Ferreira was tortured using the infamous "pit torture," and after several hours recanted his faith. Becoming a Buddhist, he changed his name to Sawano Chūan, married a Japanese woman, and worked for the *bakufu* in various capacities.[11] On this occasion, we see him on Deshima advising the Dutch that the globe they intended as a gift would be quite unacceptable because it contained a section in which various saints' names were inscribed. The Japanese censors would surely discover this, and no doubt a robust investigation would ensue. In short, the apostate priest advised the Dutch that they should either remove the names from the globe or send it back to Batavia so as to spare setting in motion the elaborate state-sanctioned mechanisms to ensure that no trace of the faith entered Japan. Ferreira's warning must have been heeded, for there is no record of a globe being offered as a present for the next several years.

A particularly interesting case in which a map was designated as a gift for the Shogun appears in the chief merchant's diary for September 18, 1647. In that year, the Company's patron came to inspect the gifts for that year, which was the usual custom. Inoue Masashige spotted, among other rarities, a world map. It seems that the Dutch were advised to leave the map out of the gifts because "according to the interpreter, Japan would look too small compared to the rest of the world in the eyes of the Shogun."[12]

In 1663, chief merchant Indijck writes in his diary in April that he was asked to explain the contents of "eight small and ten large maps" that were included in that year's gifts for the Shogun.[13] A few days later we are told that permission to depart back to Nagasaki had been delayed, perhaps because the Shogun was ill, but there may have been another issue, as Indijck writes, "we believe that the explanation of the aforesaid maps are the principal cause of the delay." Six days later the chief merchant was called to the house of one of the leading shogunal councilors and, "after some small talk, he placed before us the world map which we had presented to the Shogun the other day. We pointed out what he asked us. It was all noted on small pieces of paper, which were pasted on the map." The first point to notice is that the Dutch had given the Shogun eighteen maps as a gift that year, which by any account is rather a lot of maps. The second is that the Japanese officials seem to have taken these maps quite seriously and to have studied them, even making notes on them after having asked the Dutch to interpret the maps. This instance highlights nicely the different roles that the Dutch played in Japan: the VOC as a global company trying to make a profit, the Dutch as a living symbol in Japan of the shogun's total usurpation of all foreign affairs, and finally the Dutch as the shogun's faithful vassals, not only bringing gifts on a yearly basis and prostrating themselves in audience but also supplying valuable intelligence to the regime.[14]

Decorative Containers

Another common type of artistic object imported into Japan specifically for gift-giving is what we might call ornamental cases, sometimes specified in the diaries as jewelry cases, but not always. The most unusual of these was mentioned in June 1643 and, as we've had occasion to see already, described as an "oval case with twenty-three different female faces." The object was given as a gift to a high-ranking official who then requested that the Dutch add the nationality of each costumed figure, which would imply that the designer of the case was attempting to illustrate various ethnicities with whom the Dutch came into contact, although that must necessarily remain in the realm of speculation.[15]

In February of 1656, the Dutch were in possession of a small, embroidered jewelry "coffer," and because it was rare, they thought that it would make a particularly suitable present for the Shogun that year. This year offers us a glimpse into the entire process of gift-giving in Edo as the diary for 1656 contains detailed entries about the elaborate rituals surrounding the audience, the subsequent process of giving gifts to other high-ranking officials, and then receiving the "return gifts."[16] First of all, as soon as the Dutch arrived at court in early February, they immediately had a list of all the presents for the Shogun translated into Japanese and given to the official responsible for overseeing the Dutch, Inoue Masashige.[17] Next, the "rarities," as they were generally called, were themselves sent to Inoue for his inspection. This was not simply so that his curiosity might be sated, but we know from several entries in the Dutch diaries that he advised the Dutch which presents to set aside for the Shogun and whether the gifts should be increased or decreased for that year. In the meantime, a steady stream of shogunal officials and their retinues came to the Dutch lodgings to have a look at the rarities and to be entertained liberally with wine and treats: the diary notes, for example, that on February 6, the officials left "full of gratitude," which might have been a kind way of saying that they left "full of wine."

Artistically rendered cases were also used to wrap other items that were themselves intended as gifts. In particular we read in the diaries that bottles of wine, along with glasses, could be wrapped in specially designed cases that would then be wrapped in decorative ribbons. Similarly, on a couple instances, we read of "spyglasses" that were packed in decorative ivory cases and then used as gifts. On one occasion, we read of six spyglasses that were intended as gifts for the Shogun. When the *bugyō* inspected them he told the Dutch not only to clean the lenses but also to wrap three of them in fine golden leather.[18] The new wrappings must have been to his liking, because a few days later he praised them for their beauty. Similarly, we are told that a large compass intended as a gift to a powerful daimyo was set in a case of marbled wood. One can imagine that the case itself would have lent the compass more prestige than it ordinarily would have alone, and that the artistically rendered box was part of the overall desirability of the object as an item of conspicuous consumption.[19]

Paintings and Engravings

While most of the objects of art discussed hitherto have been works of fine craftsmanship, there were numerous instances of paintings, engravings, and tapestries given as gifts. In January of 1664, for example, the Dutch brought to Japan two large paintings, one depicting the Battle of Flanders and the other a picture of a naval battle between the English and the Dutch.[20] These two paintings in particular make an extended appearance in the diaries; the first was on January 6 in an entry in which the chief merchant states that the previous holder of that office left instructions for the two paintings to be sent to Edo as gifts for the Shogun, but "considering that such large pieces with their heavy frames and cases cannot be transported overland without enormous effort and incurring excessive costs, we decided to communicate this matter to [the Nagasaki *bugyō*] and ask his advice about whether these paintings would find favor with the shogun or not."

The next day, two interpreters took the two paintings to show the Nagasaki *bugyō*, and, on their return, the chief merchant reports that "after he had seen them . . . he liked them very much and said that the Shogun would undoubtedly be very pleased with them. He gave orders to store them carefully and to convey them to Edo with great care to prevent them from being damaged." However, after affirming that the Shogun would be pleased with the gifts, the *bugyō*, clearly enamored of the paintings, suddenly declared that they would be inappropriate for the Shogun. The chief merchant, although not explicit in the diary, certainly seems to suggest that the *bugyō* had an ulterior motive in the verdict, namely, his own interest in the gifts. When he first viewed the paintings on January 7, for example, the diary relates that

> his honor declared that he would have liked to keep them at his home for two or three days for his own pleasure, but he had not dared to for fear that some disaster might occur. Therefore, he sent them back to us, but with the express orders not to pack them again until he had had another careful look at them.

The Nagasaki *bugyō* remarked, perhaps a bit wistfully, that "the Dutchmen had many things in their country which were very rare here. If they knew those things and brought them here, the Shogun would be pleased."

The chief merchant later wrote that the *bugyō*'s excuses were "feeble" and noted that these very paintings had been ordered six years ago for the Shogun.[21] The *bugyō* apparently felt that the paintings, "depicted very sad scenes, such as dead people, and sinking and burning ships. These were, he said, scenes which one could not present to someone with such a tranquil mind as the Shogun without upsetting him badly." He continues on to say that the Company "owed the shogun a great debt of gratitude for his favors, which can only be paid back with an open and generous hand, for which purpose we thought the paintings would have come in very handy." In the end, the chief merchant accused the Nagasaki *bugyō* of wishing to take the paintings for himself and then later present them to the Shogun as a gift, which is probably what many of the gifts the Dutch bestowed on Japanese officials were destined for.

On a similar martial theme, Charles Boxer relates that in 1635, two copper engravings were presented to the Hosokawa family, a powerful family with whom the Dutch had frequent contact. One of the engravings was the Siege of Hertzogenbosch and the other depicted the Defeat of the English off Isle de Ré.[22] Christopher Duffy states that in the seventeenth century, "there was a passing fashion for English and Dutch engravings and maps."[23] On that note, an entry in the Dutch diary for February 27, 1658, notes that Inoue requested a beautiful map of the world along with pictures of battles on land and at sea, noting that the shogun's other maps and pictures had been destroyed in a fire.[24]

Nicholas Couckebacker, chief merchant at Hirado in the 1630s, noted in 1633 that paintings were given not only to the Shogun but also to several of his officials. The paintings designated for the Shogun were specifically described as paintings of ships. Two years later, he also noted that paintings of ships were given to the daimyo of Hirado, the official in whose domain the original Dutch factory was established in 1609.[25] Earlier, we learn from Richard Cocks, the head of the English factory in Japan from 1613 to 1623, that the Company presented the (Japanese) wife of the celebrated Englishman William Adams a picture of King Solomon. We know nothing else about this particular picture, whether, for example, it was a painting, a drawing, or an engraving, but we do know that the English happened to have a picture of Solomon to hand, and that for whatever reason, Cocks thought that Adams' family would enjoy it!

Five paintings by Willem van Royen were presented to the Shogun Yoshimune in 1724 as gifts, two of which were subsequently hung: *View of the Rhine* and *Still Life with Peacock*. Timon Screech tells us that these paintings were still being admired a hundred years later and that they were copied by Japanese artists who had begun attempting to paint in the Western style.[26]

Another item that was imported into Japan as gifts, at least in limited numbers, was tapestries. In November of 1633, the Dutch diaries at Hirado list a number of goods that were reserved as presents for the Shogun. Among the list was an item referred to as a "Dutch tapestry showing the History of Rebecca."[27] This is interesting in that this was at a time in which Christianity was being zealously persecuted in Japan, to the point that the English were forced to not display the English flag because of the Cross of St. George. One can only imagine, therefore, that this particular tapestry was not presented to the Shogun as a religious item of Judeo-Christian provenance, but purely as a work of art.

While we do not have many examples of musical instruments given as gifts to Japanese officialdom, we do have a few. One example is a harmonica that the Nagasaki *bugyō* became enchanted with after hearing it played and suggested that it be given as a gift to the shogunal heir. The chief merchants agreed, wrapped it up, and sent it off for its new purpose. In 1648, the Dutch sent a trumpet to Inoue Masashige so that he could have the design copied, although to what end we don't know.[28] We also read of a trumpet given to a daimyo, along with a quadrant and a bottle of tent wine. The Dutch record that the daimyo sent the quadrant back because he didn't like it, along with a torrent of abuse for the Dutch, saying that the Dutch didn't come to the capital out of love for the Shogun, but merely for their own ends. He presumably enjoyed the trumpet well enough, and given the invective, the chief merchant records, perhaps too much of the wine as well.[29] We also read of a standing street organ that was given as a gift to the powerful daimyo Shimazu Shigehide in 1788. Timon Screech tells us that by this time Western music was out of fashion, and so the organ was unceremoniously taken away.[30]

A Tale of Two Lanterns

The final category of artistry that was used as gifts in Japan is fine metalworking, a broad category that includes many objects, but that also includes one of the most celebrated and commented-upon type of gift: an object that the Dutch called "lanterns," or "chandeliers" in their diaries, although a more appropriate name might be candelabras. We'll examine the candelabras first and then have occasion to explore some of the other rather unique gifts in this category.

The two major instances in which candelabra were given as gifts are particularly noteworthy because in both cases the gifts had repercussions that dramatically affected the Company's fortunes in Japan: one positive and one negative. In order to understand the full significance of the first candelabra, we must set the scene with a somewhat extended aside involving one of the more remarkable figures in the VOC's history in Japan.

The Nuyts Incident[31]

By around 1630, VOC trade with Japan was finally beginning to pay dividends, to use the obvious pun. The Company had established a factory on Taiwan in the mid-1620s and was thereby able to finally obtain a steady if rather small supply of silk with which to trade for precious metals, notably silver. This was the trade from which the Portuguese had made a fortune with their trading post in Macao and their access to Chinese merchants. For years the Dutch officials had written in vain to their superiors that unless they could obtain Chinese silk, all of their plans in Japan would come to naught. Indeed, up until the factory in Taiwan was established, supplies of silk were largely the result of attacking Iberian or Chinese vessels, which earned for the VOC the sobriquet of pirates, something that the Dutch tried hard to counteract, but with some difficulty as they arrived at Hirado with captured Chinese and Portuguese goods in their holds. Be that as it may, by around 1630, VOC access to Chinese merchants on Taiwan was starting to make their trade in Japan profitable.

It was in this context that Pieter Nuyts was appointed to the position of chief merchant of Fort Zeelandia, as the factory on Taiwan was called.[32] Nuyts, a merchant with little firsthand experience of VOC activity in Asia, took up his post in 1627, and immediately set about both trying to increase contacts with Chinese merchants and limiting Japanese junk trade with the island, which was rather significant at this time. It was while attempting the latter that Nuyts brought disaster upon himself and temporary disaster on the Company's trade in Japan.[33]

In order to try to regulate Japanese trade and make at least a minimal profit from it, Nuyts decided to enforce a so-called "harbor tax" on Japanese ships that called to trade.[34] The Japanese did not take kindly to this proposal and pointed out, rightly, that they had been coming to Taiwan to trade years before the Dutch arrived.[35] Nevertheless, Nuyts stuck to his decision and when, in 1628, two Japanese vessels under the command of Hamada Yahyōe arrived, they were subjected to the tax, even though Hamada was ostensibly returning with two ambassadors from the village of Sinkan who had journeyed to Edo. Nuyts dealt quite harshly with Hamada and the villagers from Sinkan and threw both into prison, although Hamada was released shortly thereafter. After Nuyts refused a demand that the Japanese ships be set free from having been impounded, the Japanese, led by Hamada, stormed the governor's quarters and took Nuyts, his young son Lawrence, and Francois Caron, a future chief merchant of the Japan factory, prisoner. This stand-off lasted some time until the two sides could negotiate a resolution.[36] Essentially, the compromise was that the Japanese would be allowed to sail back to Japan with the ships and merchandise restored. To ensure good faith on both sides, the Japanese would be accompanied by the three "prisoners," including Nuyts' son Lawrence, and the Dutch would also be given a few Japanese "hostages." Once in Japan, the case would be adjudicated by the authorities. Nuyts agreed to this course of action, and thus the Japanese and their hostages made their way to Japan.

The authorities in Edo were not at all happy with this turn of events since it was perceived that an attack on a Japanese vessel was essentially an attack on the dignity of the Shogun, since the *shuinjo*, issued to legitimate Japanese merchant houses, were issued by the shogunate.[37] Seen through this lens, it makes perfect sense that an otherwise minor incident would be treated so harshly in Edo. The Shogun and his councilors ordered that all Dutch trade be stopped and that Dutch ships currently at Hirado be impounded.[38] This came at a time when the Dutch were finally beginning to realize the potential of East Asian trade through their commercial contacts with Chinese merchants on Taiwan, and now that trade with Japan was on the cusp of taking off, the Japanese shut down all Dutch commercial because of Nuyts' rash actions on Taiwan.

The Company was in a real bind as to how to placate the authorities, and so after more than two years of the trade embargo, the authorities in Batavia took the drastic measure of extraditing Nuyts to Japan for punishment.[39] Nuyts arrived in 1632 and was immediately put under house arrest in Hirado, whereupon the Japanese allowed Dutch trade to resume as before, to which the chief merchant of the Dutch factory in Taiwan wrote, "God be praised!"[40] Upon his arrival in Japan, the unfortunate Nuyts learned that his son Lawrence had died in Omura in December of 1631.[41] Nuyts would spend the next four years under house arrest in relative comfort and freedom of movement within the confines of the house. We know from Dutch sources that he spent much of his time studying and writing, and that he ran up rather large tabs for personal items such as clothing and food, a source of great annoyance, no doubt, to the authorities back in Batavia since the Company was obliged to paid these bills.

Francois Caron, Nuyts' old colleague on Taiwan and, apparently, a good friend, became a senior merchant of the VOC factory in Hirado in February of 1633, and, along with the chief merchant, Nicholas Couckebacker, continually advocated for the release of Nuyts from his house arrest.[42] The end of the ordeal for Nuyts, at least in Japan, came in the summer of 1634 when the Company sent to Japan an unusually sumptuous gift: a copper candelabra, hand-crafted in Holland, and a superb piece of craftsmanship. Company servants assembled the piece and sent it on to Edo for that year's court journey where it was presented to Tokugawa Iemitsu, third Shogun and grandson of Ieyasu. The candelabra was received with much gratitude and ceremony, and, after being displayed prominently in Edo, was shipped off to Nikkō, the newly constructed shrine to the dynasty's founder, Ieyasu, who had been posthumously raised to the level of a Shinto deity as well as an incarnation of a Buddha.

The gift of the candelabra was undoubtedly a grand occasion of deft diplomacy on the part of the Dutch, but the true significance of the gift is to be found in the specific circumstances of the time. The Shogun Iemitsu, although formally Shogun for many years, was only able to exercise authority in his own right from 1632, when his father and the second Shogun Hidetada died. Iemitsu was not an uncontested successor to his father, and was perhaps not even his father's first choice, but Ieyasu insisted that the oldest son succeed to the shogunate, and so Iemitsu, in a real sense, owed his position to his grandfather. More than that, though, Iemitsu seemed to have a real reverence for Ieyasu, and of course, by emphasizing his grandfather's greatness, he was also enhancing his own legitimacy as Shogun.

In order to honor Ieyasu to the fullest, Iemitsu conceived of a plan to enlarge the modest tomb of Ieyasu into an elaborate structure suitable for a Shinto deity. He called on the various daimyo to contribute resources to the building of the shrine, and also required that every daimyo have a branch shrine in his own domain so that the total number of these shrines at the peak of their popularity reached perhaps several hundred throughout the country. Not only was the shrine constructed on an elaborate scale, but the shogunal court made regular journeys to the shrine in which daimyo who were in attendance in Edo at the time were required to join in. On several occasions, the Dutch also joined in these processions during their yearly visit to Edo.

Thus, when the Dutch presented Iemitsu with the elaborate candelabra in 1636, he was excited not just because it was a work of fine craftsmanship, but because it was a very public recognition by the Dutch of Iemitsu's authority and power. Furthermore, by placing the candelabra at Nikkō, Iemitsu was able to further associate himself with the awesome power and prestige of Tokugawa Ieyasu, now literally honored as a *kami* and a guardian deity of the Japanese islands.

Iemitsu was so pleased with the gift of the candelabra that he immediately ordered the release of Pieter Nuyts from his house arrest, ending four years of petitions by the Company.[43] Nuyts was sent back to Batavia where, after a series of lengthy trials, he was punished with a hefty fine and dishonorably discharged from Company service and sent back to the Netherlands. A seemingly haughty and self-obsessed individual, Nuyts willfully disregarded the sage advice of one of his contemporary officials, Cornelus van Nijenroode, who wrote to Nuyts earlier that the Japanese must be treated with the utmost discretion or else disaster could result. This warning turned out the be prophetic, and Nuyts' blatant disregard of it led to the downfall of Nuyts' career, severe economic damage to the Company for a couple years, and, most cruelly, the death of Nuyts' son Laurens.

This gift in particular is illustrative of a larger truth: despite the fact that the Dutch were the foremost commercial power in Europe at the time and had a fleet of armed ships out of all proportion to the size of their country, in Japan, they were very much beholden to the laws and, to be slightly less charitable, whims, of the Japanese authorities. There was no question of a military response to the Japanese embargo on Dutch trade in Japan, nor was there any thought given to disobeying shogunal decrees. Rather, the Dutch placed themselves under shogunal rule while they were in Japan. This is in marked contrast to the situation two centuries later when Europeans did not hesitate to use military force, or at least the threat of force, to achieve their aims in Asia. For the entirely of the Company's activities in Japan, Dutch merchants adhered to shogunal authority and continued to ply officialdom in Edo and Nagasaki with lavish gifts. And on occasion, as we're seen above, those gifts could be quite lavish.

The Inaba Incident

Thirty years later, in 1665, another candelabra would have profound consequences for the VOC, although in a rather different way than the one that effectively ended the Nuyts affair. On this occasion, the VOC brought two candelabra to Japan and included them among the gifts that were given to the Shogun.[44] We know from Dutch diaries that the Shogun was pleased with the gifts, and so we can only imagine that the Dutch returned from Edo feeling very much pleased with themselves for scoring yet another diplomatic success. Little did they know, however, that these same candelabra would be the source of so much stress and anxiety for the Company.

Somehow the Dutch on Deshima lost track of the fact that the two lanterns in question were requested by Inaba Mino-no-Kami Masanori, daimyo of

Odawara and a senior counselor in the shogun's government at Edo. Inaba was a powerful figure at the shogun's court and was given the task of overseeing the Dutch. Normally the Dutch were exceptionally diligent with plying figures such as Inaba with everything that they could possibly desire, from spectacles and telescopes to exotic animals. On this occasion, however, these lanterns seemed to have simply slipped through the cracks, and the Company would pay for their oversight. Engelbert Kaempfer, a surgeon who worked on Deshima in the early 1690s, noted the incident in his history of Japan and wrote about the repercussions:

> Mino, disappointed in his expectation, thought himself offended to the highest degree, and from that moment took such a hatred to the whole Dutch nation, as without a fatal and sufficient revenge he knew would be pursued, even after his, by his descendants and relations. The Japanese in general, when once they throw a hatred on a person, know how to conceal it for a long while, till a favorable opportunity offers to take revenge for the insults and affronts they have, or fancy to have received. In like manner, Mino watched the opportunity to put the revenge he mediated to take of us in execution, and it offer'd no sooner but he gladly embraced it and chastis'd us most severely.[45]

Surely Kaempfer is exaggerating the hatred that Inaba bore the Dutch, and underrating the structural changes that were happening that led to decreased trade in precious metals, but even so, it is apparent from this account and from contemporary Dutch diaries that this oversight was a serious breach of etiquette. The diaries of the Company on Deshima tell us that Inaba really needed those lanterns, and what is meant by this is probably that Inaba himself was looking for extraordinary presents to give away, in this case most likely to the Shogun.[46] Even though Inaba was a senior counselor and a daimyo of a not-insignificant domain, sources from the seventeenth and eighteenth centuries make it clear that the bestowal of lavish gifts was an absolute necessity, and that even at the top ranks of society people competed for patronage of those above them in the social rankings. This is one of the reasons that Dutch/European exotica was so much in demand among the Nagasaki and Edo elite: they were in turn used as gifts, and the more costly and exotic, the more effective the gift.

Two years after the lanterns were given to the Shogun, the chief merchant begins to note in his diary that Inaba was quite upset that the lanterns were not given to him, and he extrapolates from this that the reason life in Japan was becoming stricter was that the current Nagasaki *bugyō* was a great favorite of Inaba's. The implication, borne out by Kaempfer more than twenty years later, is that Inaba was taking his revenge on the Company for this insult. On February

22, 1667, for example, the chief merchant complained that "everything was inspected so closely it was as if we were rogues and traitors."[47] And again the following year, we read that "we live in Japan as dumb, deaf, and imprisoned men."[48] On September 23 of that same year, the Company made a special effort to deliver costly and rare presents to Inaba in an attempt to assuage his anger: "We hope that the lanterns and the books which have recently arrived for His Honor will also be accepted by him and that his anger is somewhat placated, because he is a powerful man."[49] These gifts were in addition to an expensive medicine chest that was also given to him this year, the same medicine chest that was, incidentally, presented the previous year, but which Inaba, in his anger, had refused to accept. The fact that this time around the chest was accepted gave the Dutch hope that the affair was drawing to a close. Indeed, the following April, the Dutch report in the diary that Inaba was exceptionally happy with the medicine chest.[50]

The events related here beg the question of whether Inaba Masanori was in fact trying to make life miserable for the Dutch out of spite over the candelabra. The previous official responsible for keeping tabs on the Dutch was a man who we've met several times before, Inoue Masashige, was a great favorite of the merchants on Deshima. He was, however, forced to retire by the *bakufu*, ostensibly because of his age, but more likely because a rash of Christians were found in Japan on his watch, which was a great embarrassment to a government that had made every effort to stamp the religion out far and wide. At any rate, Inoue was much beloved by the Company officials because of the perception that he looked out for Company affairs in Edo among the power brokers of the *bakufu*, but in 1661, just before the "Inaba incident," Inoue died. Perhaps the Dutch were simply ascribing to the officials who were responsible for monitoring them character traits that happened to fit their experiences in a changing Japan. In other words, perhaps the changing Dutch condition in Japan had very little to do with the individual officials, but had everything to do with the nature of the *bakufu's* attitude toward things such as the export of precious metals.

The Dutch found that the profits from their trade in Japan had gradually begun to taper after the midpoint of the seventeenth century. Added to this was the disappointing loss of Taiwan to the forces of Zheng Chenggong as well the shogun's insistence that the Dutch could not attack Zheng ships in retaliation for the loss. On a couple occasions, as Adam Clulow points out in his study of the VOC in Japan, the Dutch frustratingly found themselves at odds with the *bakufu* over their attempts to wage war on the Zheng family, and risked their trading activities entirely by continuing to attack Zheng ships And lastly, and perhaps most seriously, the *bakufu* began to curtail the amount of silver that could be exported before banning silver exports outright in the 1660s.[51] Each of these considerations could entail a monograph of their own, but suffice it to say that the Dutch situation was changing rather radically both inside and outside Japan, and many of these changing situations led to a more constrained commercial relationship, regardless of who was in power or what official happened to be assigned to oversee the Dutch.

This is not to diminish, of course, the role that a powerful antagonist could play in Dutch affairs in Japan. But reading the diaries over the grand sweep of the seventeenth century, it seems that there was simply not a lot of substantive change in the Dutch situation in Japan, certainly after the move to Nagasaki in 1641. It is true that the volume of trade decreased gradually to the point where official trade was barely profitable, and it is true that the Dutch lived lives of seclusion and heavy regulation, but the former was a response to the changing commercial situation within and outside Japan, and the latter was not that different from the previous Dutch experience on Deshima. The Dutch had reason to hope that their gradually declining situation in Japan would change, and in fact their diaries are filled year after year with expressions of such hope, but in the end, the situation never did change. It is somewhat pathetic in the true sense of that word to read year after year about the lavish gift-giving that was supposed to curry favor and allow an expanded trade, only to realize that decade after decade, the expected "return on investment" never materialized, and that by the mid-eighteenth century, trade had slowed to a trickle. Perhaps this is what led Donald Keene to treat so dismissively Dutch life on Deshima as he lambasted the officials for their greed and corruption. In a world in which all attempts to increase the Company's trade in Japan failed, save for a few gifts of magnificent stallions, perhaps it made sense to concentrate on the private trade, both institutionalized and covert, as this was the one area of trade in which Company servants could have real hope of success.

While the candelabra are certainly the most celebrated item in the category of metalworking, we can also see a number of other rarities that were imported as gifts and that undoubtedly caused a sensation in Edo and Nagasaki. In 1668, for example, the Dutch mentioned that among the gifts for the Shogun that year was "a copper lion which had stood here in the Company garden for some years and weighs at least 150 pounds." Chief Merchant Ranst elaborates that "the governors have ordered that is should be used as a gift for the Shogun because it is old and rare."[52] In September of 1647, we read that the Company brought copper horses for the Shogun as part of his gift. Interestingly, in a diary entry on the last day of the Company's stay in Edo, we read that as the Dutch were packing up to leave, they gave the son of their landlord "five copper animals."[53] We've seen that the world map presented that year was rejected by the Shogun because Japan appeared so small compared to other countries, and so perhaps the copper horses were rejected as well? This might explain why the Company happened to have copper animals just lying around at the end of the intensive round of gift-giving in Edo.

Although we will deal more extensively with timepieces in a later chapter devoted to European technological goods, suffice it to say that many of the clocks given to the Japanese were also examples of fine metalworking. M. E. van Opstall relates the story of a series of rarities that were taken out of storage when Tokugawa Yoshimune became Shogun (Yoshimune was quite curious about European material culture, and resumed the import of books to Japan after they had earlier been banned lest any Christian material enter Japan surreptitiously).[54] One of the items was a silver clock that was given as a present years before. The clock was made by Quirijn Oosterwijk in the Hague and given as a present to an earlier Shogun, whereupon it was packed away, only to be brought back out when the new Shogun took an interest in such things. Although this is an isolated item, many gifts spanned across the artificial categories I have created in this book, clocks, for example, were at once technological marvel, scientific instrument, and example of fine artistry and craftsmanship.

The last example of fine metalwork is a "silver ship" that was brought to Japan in the autumn of 1648 with the arrival of that year's trading vessels. Inoue Masashige sent for the ship, which the Dutch describe as quite large and quite labor intensive to set up, which meant it must have consisted of several pieces. On this particular occasion, however, Inoue fell ill and thus was not able to view it and returned it unassembled, although a few days later the Dutch state that local dignitaries came by the Company's lodging specifically to view the ship.[55] On June 21 of the next year, the chief merchant writes that several important people came around to the Company's lodgings on Deshima: "I took them to the garden, and the billiard table, and then to my house. I showed them the silver ship and all other rarities. In the meantime, the ship was prepared to sail. I treated them to as many fruits, confitures, and *sakana* as could be prepared at this short notice." Later, the chief merchant reports: "The ship was ready and they heartily applauded it. They spurted water at each other and had a jolly time."

The next we hear of the ship, it had been taken to Edo as part of the yearly audience with the Shogun in 1650. As usual with such exotica, several people viewed the piece and commented on its suitability as a present for the Shogun, although on January 22 of that year, we learn that the ship was designated not for the Shogun, but rather for his son, the heir to the shogunate. On the day of the audience, April 7, we learn that after the customary ceremony was over, a Dutch corporal and a silversmith stayed behind "to teach someone how the ship should be sailed, as he had shown the councilors before." The audience over, the silver ship sails out of the records of the chief merchant and presumably into the household of the heir to the shogunate, although the ship did achieve some notoriety hereafter through Arnoldus Montanus' *Atlas Japonnensi*, published in 1670. Montanus describes the silver ship and records that a Dutch jeweler instructed the Shogun, or more likely his officials, how to operate it.[56] Needless to say, this must have been a special ship to have commanded so much attention on two continents.

In the same way that metalwork was used as an exotic gift at the shogun's court, glassware of various types was also often used as gifts in Edo and at Nagasaki. Probably the most common type of glassware so designated were European mirrors. Mirrors have long had a special place in East Asian culture as a symbol of advanced technology and culture. The most prominent example of mirrors in ancient Japanese mytho-history is the mirror used by the associates of the sun-goddess Amaterasu to lure the brooding goddess from the cave inside which she had hidden herself in response to a slight by her mischievous brother Susano-o.[57] Because the world had been plunged into a crisis of darkness, the other divine beings, being at a loss and out of options, tried to lure Amaterasu out of the cave with jewels and a mirror. The legend relates that when Amaterasu peeked out of the cave and saw herself in the mirror, she was momentarily dazzled by her own reflection, and the other gods were then able to draw her out of the cave and set the world to right. The mirror, along with the jewels and a sword, subsequently became known as the three imperial regalia that together acted as symbols of the imperial family, linking that family physically and symbolically with the gods.

A more historical association of mirrors with ancient Japan occurs in the early years of the emerging proto-state known as "Yamatai." In the third century, we read in the Chinese chronicles of the Wei dynasty about a female ruler of the proto-state named Himiko. The records indicate that in 239 CE, Himiko sent a diplomatic gift to China, no doubt interpreted by the Wei as an early form of tribute, and in return, the Chinese dynasty sent the queen a return gift of one hundred bronze mirrors.[58] These mirrors would have symbolized a form of legitimacy as Himiko undoubtedly strove with other contenders to rule the nascent state. That the Wei dynasty, the most technologically advanced state in East Asia in the third century, sent these objects that were already associated with Japan's mytho-historical past was a powerful political tool that Himiko could use to bolster her authority over the realm.

Although perhaps not imbued with the same connotations of power and legitimacy as Chinese mirrors in ancient Japan, the Dutch brought mirrors at quite regular intervals to use as gifts both in Nagasaki and in Edo. Both in 1647 and in 1648, for example, the Dutch brought mirrors to Edo as gifts. On several occasions in 1647, while the Dutch were in Edo, the chief merchant notes that many Japanese officials came to the Company's residence and enjoyed having a look at the rarities, including the mirrors. In 1648, we are told that the Dutch had brought "a beautiful square mirror" to Edo, but were unable to use it as a gift that year, and so left it with their landlord's sons for next year's gifts, mainly to prevent breakage on the way back to Nagasaki.[59] A few years later, on May 5, 1652, the daimyo of Hirado was passing through on his way to Edo and when he arrived in Nagasaki, sent a servant to Deshima to fetch a few small things that would be interesting to see. The chief merchant writes that the daimyo requested compasses, small mirrors, and anything else that was rare, and in response, with perhaps a slight touch of resignation, he wrote that he "gave him as many things as possible." Two days later, as the *bugyō* prepared to leave Nagasaki, he again sent for some rarities to marvel at, and this time the Dutch included "the company's ebony and large illuminated mirror . . . which he returned after a while with many compliments of gratitude." And finally, in 1654, we read that the Dutch, in gratitude for the ongoing patronage of the Nagasaki *bugyō*, gave him "a clear mirror in an ebony frame, which had caught his eye." Directly after this, the chief merchant adds, by way of motive, "Such a small gift might contribute to his good feelings towards us."[60] It is quite possible that this was the same mirror that the daimyo of Hirado had admired two years previously.

In 1652, when that year's ships arrived at Deshima, a servant of the Lord of Arima came to the island to request that four mirrors be set aside for the daimyo. We can only assume that this was an important matter since the chief merchant writes in his diary that "the governors had advised us to look for the mirrors beforehand." In February of 1656, we read in a diary entry that as the Dutch were writing out the list of presents for the shogunal officials for that year, the chief merchant wanted to know if he could include pistols, spyglasses, reading glasses, and mirrors in the lists, noting that he had brought ample supply of these things.[61] In the case of the mirrors, we are told that they serve as playthings for the children of the shogunal officials. Reading through the Dutch diaries, it seems that this was the strategy that the Dutch used in Japan: to bring along as many of these small but rare items as possible so as to be able to shower patrons and potential patrons with gifts at every opportunity. In the same year of 1656, while the Dutch were in Edo, an official's servant came by the Company lodgings to ask if there were any more mirrors left in order to please the officials' children. The Dutch were happy to oblige, writing, "This trivial thing is now a novelty and more appreciated that something large and costly."[62]

In 1657, Inoue Masashige expressed gratitude for "two large beautiful mirrors." A few days later we read in the diaries that the mirrors were actually sent to Japan as presents for the Shogun, but that he wished to keep them for himself. Writing of his ulterior motive, the chief merchant states: "Later, he would present them to His Majesty, but he would keep quiet about it and hide them from others."[63] From a close reading of the diaries, it seems that this was the motive of many of the officials to whom the Dutch presented gifts. They wanted in turn to present these exotic goods to their patrons, or to the Shogun, and in so doing, curry favor in exactly the same way the Dutch hoped to do.

In 1670, we read of an interesting request on the part of the Nagasaki *bugyō*. When the Dutch sent this year's gifts for the Shogun to be inspected, as per yearly custom, the *bugyō* sent the mirrors back "with his orders to have the backs of the mirrors and the frames lacquered over and covered with gold foliage."[64] Perhaps this in an indication that the decades of bringing mirrors to Japan were making this particular gift somewhat commonplace and so measures had to be taken to make these mirrors more novel than they were in and of themselves. It may also have been that the value of gifts was judged too low for that year and so by enhancing the mirrors, the value would have been increased. It's impossible to know, but there is a certain attraction to imagining the *bugyō* receiving wearily yet more mirrors as gifts for the Shogun and perhaps, in their exasperation, requesting the Dutch to make the by-now commonplace exotic once again.

While mirrors were far more common as gifts, other types of glassware also make an appearance in the diaries. In April 1661, for example, the chief merchant notes that he sent some glassware to the son of the recently deceased Nagasaki *bugyō*, and to yet another official, the Company sent glass dishes and cups on the same day, with which gift, apparently, the official was well pleased.[65] This all came on the eve of the Company's departure from Edo, and so perhaps the Dutch were trying to get rid of some of their unwanted baggage, and so rather than junking the glassware, they chose instead to give it away as an exotic gift and earn a bit of political capital in the process. We can infer that the glassware that the Dutch used was of no real value because in 1660 the Dutch report that there was a fire in Edo, and in the haste of packing up, some of the glassware was broken, but that these were things of little value.

On July 1, 1656, the chief merchant writes that the Nagasaki *bugyō* came to visit the island with a

> large train of servants. I went to welcome them at the gate and led them to my house. There I treated them to some pastries and drinks. The governor was very friendly and affable. He . . . drank a cup of tent wine and looked at some things that we still had in the factory, including some glasses, of which he selected a beer glass, which he liked. I accompanied him to the garden and he enjoyed himself at the billiard table. He thanked me for the hospitality and, evening approaching, he said goodbye.[66]

For those of us who are barflies, it is always tempting, at least in the moment, to consider trying to come into possession one way or another of a beer glass to commemorate the night's festivities, the more so if the glass is distinctive in some way. It is heartening to observe that the same was apparently true almost four hundred years ago.

Needless to say, there are many other instances in which the Dutch brought glassware as gifts, usually for the shogunal officials rather than for the Shogun himself. Apart from glassware, other prominent types of glass were glass phials for the "medicine" that became such a prominent gift, glass beads, and glass bottles, either empty or filled with the spirits and wine that were usually brought to Edo in rather large quantities. And finally, Timon Screech tells us that glass panes became a highly valued commodity in the late eighteenth century, and that on occasion, such glass would be stolen from the Dutch factory on Deshima. Screech also tells us that one daimyo was so taken with glass that he had many glass panes obtained from the Dutch installed in his residence.[67]

As the relatively limited examples given here demonstrate, the gifting of objects of beauty, artistry, and craftsmanship played a role in ensuring the Dutch relationship with the Japanese remained cordial, the more so since especially in the case of metal and glasswork, these were the types of objects that seem to have been liberally bestowed on several of the shogunal officials and even their children. Even when these items were not specifically given as gifts, there are dozens upon dozens of references in the diaries of Japanese officials who came to the Dutch residence to be liberally entertained with food and drink while they either rifled through Dutch belongings or were shown them as a form of entertainment. In 1655, for example, we read of Japanese officials who came to the Dutch residence in Edo and took away even personal belongings to show to others. In that year apparently, some servants ripped the blanket right off of a bed and carried it away to show their masters. In a spirit of resignation, the chief merchant writes that the Dutch must bear all of these indignities with a smile, and serve the Japanese who came to visit sweetmeats all the while![68]

The diaries make clear that the VOC's strategy for incurring favor with Tokugawa officialdom was to liberally bestow gifts both in Edo and at Nagasaki, and to entertain the elite at the Company lodgings, even when such entertainment was clearly an imposition. In April, 1666, for example, the chief merchant writes with grim stoicism, "Every day we have been receiving many visits from curious spectators who came to have a look at the Dutchmen . . . for this crowd we have to sit up and be on show like a party of fools, to our disgruntlement."[69] The chief merchant alludes to this strategy when he states that the Company intentionally stocks the warehouses with rarities and curiosos in order to be able to curry favor with officials even above and beyond the official gifts presented each year.

The personal ties forged in the complex ritual of gift-giving, both on the court journey as well as in the many informal encounters that happened almost every week, cannot be trivialized, despite the fact that the Dutch treated the objects that were given away as often trivial in nature. The Dutch realized very early on that in order to maintain these personal ties and to curry favor with strategically placed patrons, they must, to quote Engelbert Kaempfer, make every effort to use the "most exquisite curiosities of nature and art" as presents.[70]

4

Rarities and Curiosos: Scientific Paraphernalia as Gifts

On February 21, 1656, the Nagasaki *bugyō* inquired of the Dutch why the "fire hose" that he had apparently ordered the previous year did not arrive on the ships that year. The Dutch replied that the machine was broken, the only person able to fix it had been ill, and, because of the prevailing winds that brought Dutch ships to Japan, they could not wait and so the contraption would undoubtedly arrive from Batavia next year.[1] However, in October, when the next batch of ships arrived, an interpreter arrived as the Dutch were unloading the ships to ask if "the long-requested fire engine had now come," to which the Dutch were forced to answer in the negative. Again, on February 25, 1657, nearly a year since the first mention of the contraption, an interpreter again asked why the fire engine had not arrived, and all the Dutch could do was to give assurances that it would surely arrive the next year. Sure enough, the next mention of the fire engine is in October 1657, when that year's ships arrived at Deshima. The chief merchant writes that when an important daimyo came to visit the island to see some of the newly imported rarities, he was shown, among other things, a fire engine, which means that the long expected and apparently highly anticipated request of the Nagasaki *bugyō* had finally been answered.

On October 1, the chief merchant notes that "in the afternoon, both governors and shogunal intendant came with a large suite and interrupted us in the midst of our work. They said that the sole reason of their visit was to see the fire engine, which had recently arrived from Batavia for [Inoue Masashige], in operation." The next month, Inoue wrote from Edo to say that he was very pleased the engine had finally arrived and that the Dutch should pack it carefully for the court journey and show it to no one, which, of course, was totally unrealistic given that the month before several people had been around to gawk at the machine. In fact, the very day after the Dutch received the instructions to squirrel the engine away so that no one could see it, we are told that a prominent daimyo, with a large retinue no less, came to visit the island and was shown the fire engine, including a demonstration of how it worked. One can only imagine Inoue Masashige's feelings if he knew that all and sundry were gawking at the fire engine that he had so longingly ordered and expectantly waited for from Batavia. On February 5, 1658, the very day that the Dutch arrived in Edo after the arduous court journey, the chief merchant recounts:

> [Inoue Masashige] sent his interpreter to fetch the fire engine, which had not even been unpacked. We had to assemble it this same evening, but when the interpreter saw that it entailed a lot of work, and that he did not have enough bearers, he took only the main parts. In the morning, [Inoue] sent for the remaining parts of the fire engine. He also wanted someone who could assemble it and who could explain its use. I sent assistant Nicholaes de Roij, who is familiar with it. When he returned in the afternoon, he said that it had been assembled, and in [Inoue's] presence he had sprayed around with it in his garden. His Honor had looked at it with wonderment, and was exceptionally pleased with it, being an instrument that was most useful here.[2]

It seems that everyone was quite pleased with the fire engine that had been brought that year, although it emerges in the diaries that this was not the first of these machines to be brought to Japan. In previous years, two other fire engines had been brought as gifts, although, in a supreme irony, both of them had been destroyed in a fire, leaving only the one that the Dutch brought on this occasion.

One can imagine why the Japanese would be so interested in the latest technology for fighting fires as fire was a perennial hazard in Japan, especially in the dry winter months when every household had a brazier going and entire cities were essentially made of wood and paper. Perhaps the most notable fire of the early modern era occurred in March of 1657 in the city of Edo and is known as the Great Meireki Fire, so named because of the imperial era in which it occurred.[3] Over the course of three days, several tens of thousands of people were killed and much of the city was destroyed.[4] Although this fire stands out for its destructive ferocity, according to Matsukata Fuyuko, Edo experienced 1,798 fires between 1601 and 1867.[5] Interestingly, the fire engine that the Dutch gave as a gift arrived in Edo one year after the Great Meireki Fire, and, in fact, the Dutch record another rather large fire in Edo that year, one that forced them to evacuate their house, although in the end it was nowhere near as destructive as the Meireki fire the year before.[6]

The tale of the long-awaited fire engine is one example of a category of gift that I shall call here "scientific instruments," but which in reality will readily overlap with several other categories, including the previous category, namely, gifts of fine craftsmanship and artistic works. "Scientific instruments" is necessarily a broad grouping that ranged from the truly unusual, such as our fire engine, to the mundane, examples of which are the dozens upon dozens of spectacles that were brought year after year and distributed liberally to Tokugawa officialdom (in October 1649, the chief merchant writes somewhat hyperbolically in his journal that the Japanese desire only spectacles, even more so than costly jewels).[7] The category includes all lens-based gifts, including spectacles, but also extends to telescopes, spyglasses, and burning glasses. It also includes medicines and navigational instruments, mainly compasses, but also astrolabes and timepieces, including smaller personal pieces as well as larger clocks. In the same way that artistic objects were used to demonstrate in an ostentatious way the power of the Shogun vis-à-vis other daimyo, so these marvels of human inventiveness were also larger symbols of the fact that the very finest in European technology was voluntarily brought over huge distances simply for the enjoyment of the Shogun and his officials. In as much as they were exotic and representative of a foreign culture far beyond the shores of Japan, these "scientific instruments" were outward and visible symbols of the inward power and prestige of the Tokugawa family.

One of the most ubiquitous items brought to Japan as gifts or quasi-gifts was the telescope, sometimes referred to as a "spyglass."[8] Among the gifts accompanying the very first English mission to Japan under Captain John Saris was a silver telescope intended for Ieyasu as the English sought the establishment of a trading factory in Japan.[9] This particular telescope has been lost to history, but we know that Saris' embassy was a success, for the English were granted a trading charter as well as given return gifts by the retired Shogun.

Items such as the English telescope blurred the lines between implements of war, utile scientific instruments, and works of art, as demonstrated in the several instances in which the Japanese requested these items and were rather specific about how they wanted the tubing to be decorated. It seems that no matter how many of these items were brought for the Shogun, there was always a demand for more. In 1644, for example, the Dutch were told while in Edo that the Shogun was quite curious about telescopes and the Dutch should take care to bring him instruments that were of extraordinary craftsmanship and beauty.[10] Although the Shogun was in possession of many telescopes, and not just ordinary ones, but ones whose tubes were constructed from finely crafted gold, in this case it seems that the lenses were less than perfect and so a request was made to bring a telescope next year that was of better quality. Indeed, three years before, the Dutch were told that the Shogun wanted a telescope "with a clear lens, offering a perfect view, from Batavia or Holland," and not to worry whether the tube of the instrument was artistically crafted, but to make sure that the lenses were of high quality. Interestingly, the Dutch were told, almost parenthetically, not to spread these types of rarities around, but to reserve them for the shogunal court so that they would remain precious.[11]

In a similar vein, we read in a diary entry for January 9, 1647, about the following exchange with Inoue Masashige:

> "Your gifts with the inclusion of many rarities have pleased His Majesty, which is good for the Dutch and a great honor for you." He added the late Shogun was once given a telescope by the Dutch, and its likeness had never been seen again, and it had been lost in the fire. He asked if I had brought any good telescopes. I told him that I had not, although I had given the Governor of Nagasaki an excellent one. However, this has to be kept quiet to avoid envy. He asked me to obtain the best possible one from Holland for His Majesty. He said that His Majesty had received some costly telescopes recently, but their focusing was not good. This is His Majesty's prime requirement. We should not bother much about the costliness of the tubes, but more with the excellence of the lenses. It did not matter if the tubes were of indifferent quality. I should do my very best to obtain them. It is in the company's interest to oblige him. This is what the Shogun himself wishes, and [Inoue Masashige] has ordered.[12]

Inoue reminded the Dutch yet again about the telescopes on December 1 of the following year, but despite these several exhortations, a suitable one had not arrived. On October 8, 1649, several telescopes arrived in the hulls of that year's merchant vessels, but the lenses were all cracked and darkened, and thus, presumably, they were unsuitable as a present for the Shogun.[13] Again on November 15, 1650, the Dutch were asked, with even more urgency, to bring "extraordinary, beautiful, sharp spyglasses to be presented to His Majesty . . . for he was very eager to have them and had already asked for them several times." The same request was submitted on April 1, and again, the Dutch were reminded that the Shogun had requested the telescopes several times to no avail. The following year, on July 23, 1652, we read that the Nagasaki *bugyō* had also been ordering telescopes for several years in a row, again to no avail, although among the cargo for that year were in fact several spyglasses. Finally, on August 17, some large spyglasses were sent along for inspection, so we might surmise that the Shogun and the *bugyō* may have had his wishes fulfilled, at least in regard to the telescope. Two days later, the chief merchant notes that he was extremely pleased with the telescope and said he had never seen one of such fine quality.

The *bugyō* might have been satisfied, but alas, on February 19, 1656, the chief merchant noted in his diary yet again that Inoue was unhappy that "the telescopes, which had been ordered four years ago, had not yet arrived. Could they be made? The telescope which Captain Coyett had given him in 1648 was fine, but too small to see the moon in its entirety when it was full moon."[14] This was despite the fact that just over a year ago, the old patron of the Company had "expressed his satisfaction that several rarities, such as spectacles, spyglasses, prints, and earthenware, which he had ordered several years ago, had now arrived. He was looking forward to the [chief merchant] bringing them to Edo." These lenses were apparently not to his liking.

On August 27, 1654, we are given a slight clue as to why the telescopes ordered for Inoue might not have been reaching him, even though Company records indicate that the very items in question were often aboard the ships arriving at Deshima. The chief merchant writes:

> Apparently [Nagasaki officials] will take some of these goods for themselves, or for other gentlemen to capture their favor, although they are well aware that most of the things have been ordered expressly by [Inoue Masashige]. The interpreters dare not mention this, and we have to comply. It seems that there is a great deal of jealousy among these gentlemen. Each tries to oblige the high officials with rarities to try to win their favor.[15]

The Dutch mention on several occasions this practice of ordering rarities so that the shogunal officials can then use them as gifts for their patrons or those who are higher in rank than them, including of course the Shogun himself. In short, gift-giving in premodern Japan was so pervasive, and it was not only the Dutch who used gifts to curry favor with officialdom but also the gifts seem to have been a social lubricant that more or less facilitated interpersonal relationships in Japan at every level of society.[16]

When the Company received yet another request for a beautiful telescope, as well as for several other items, the Dutch apparently took this opportunity to try to explain to the Japanese that orders in any given year often took several years to fill because of the vicissitudes of sea travel and the long distances involved:

> When the gentlemen, who did not know the situation, and the great distance between our countries, were to ask for something this year and did not receive it next year, they might easily turn against the company, making out its servants for liars. This would not bear any good, but only hate and envy. . . . He should also ask his honor to consider the distance between our countries and the hazards of the sea which often caused a delay in the delivery of the goods, or

even an inability to do so. Therefore, at the best it would take two years to supply them, and sometimes 4–5 years. In those cases it should not be attributed to the unwillingness or the neglect of the Dutch, who have always been willing to serve Japan, and especially the high officials as best they could.[17]

The diaries of the chief merchant are filled with these sorts of entries, which are a cross between an accurate assessment of the situation and a diatribe against the Company's travails in Japan.

One can easily understand the frustration of the Company officials, especially as the diary entries for the entirety of the seventeenth century are filled with accounts of officials coming to Deshima, rifling through personal belongings in order to have a look at the rarities, even borrowing clothes to take back to their residence, presumably to show visitors, and coming around constantly to be entertained. This is to say nothing of the steady stream of requests the Company received for these goods from on average about a dozen officials a year. And some officials, notably Inoue Masashige, requested many more goods on a much more frequent basis. In fact, when reading the diary entries, especially during the court journey and other times of social obligation, it is easy to lose sight of the fact that the VOC was the leading commercial enterprise of the seventeenth century, tremendously powerful and far reaching in its commercial and military activities. Rather the impression one gets is of a vehicle for the importation of curiosities into Japan for the Tokugawa elite or, at the very least, a means whereby the Tokugawa gained access to the culture and knowledge of Western Europe. Obviously, the Company made a good profit in Japan, especially in the seventeenth century, and of course the Tokugawa used the Dutch for much more than simply a mail order catalog, but nevertheless, on a personal level, it was clear that the chief merchants found the constant demand for rarities annoying and probably not a little exhausting.

Another such diatribe, illustrating nicely the daily grind of the trip to Edo, is found on February 18, 1657. On that day, Inoue sent a rather curt message asking why it is the Dutch had not packed up the shogun's gifts and sent them to his very own fire-proof warehouse he had earlier offered the Dutch. The Dutch took this occasion to vent just a little, writing:

> Yesterday my attention had been diverted from the intended task in hundreds of ways. Had I been able to set a foot out of my room, when all day long visitors were there looking at things, coming and going, fetching and bringing, let alone had I been given a chance to apportion the gifts? It had not been because of my carelessness or negligence, but because of the callers who had been in the way. [Inoue Masashige's] own sons had even been the most bothersome.

Surely the chief merchant didn't respond to their patron in this manner but reserved his frustrations for that evening's pen and paper session. In the same entry the chief merchant noted that after managing to have a couple hours to himself, another worthy came round immediately afterward and began to "rummage through [my belongings] like a pig." He then goes on to say that the long-suffering Dutchmen must keep this all to themselves, because if Inoue heard of it, then he would have to crack down on the visitors, especially his sons, and of course he would become quite angry and the Company would probably be the worse off for it.[18]

Inoue Masashige was relieved by the Shogun of his duties, according to the Dutch "on account of his advanced age and failing eyesight," but probably also because the *bakufu* had continued to discover pockets of Christianity throughout the country. Accordingly, the Dutch note on April 5, the day after their arrival in Edo, that this would be the last time the Company would bring gifts for the Company's old patron. It must surely have been with mixed emotions that the Dutch handed over that year's gifts, for he had been a great friend to the Company over the many decades since he had begun facilitating Dutch activity in Japan. Interestingly, the Dutch mention that on that very same day, they went to the mansion of the new overseer of the Company, Inaba, and presented him with a large telescope.[19] While there were many spyglasses and telescopes brought to Japan over the years, it seems that the high-quality telescope that Inoue had ordered year after year, for almost a decade, had never arrived, or if it had, we have no specific mention of it. It would be a great irony if the large telescope that Inoue had been pining over these many years finally arrived in the year that he was stripped of his offices and went instead to another high-ranking official.

Telescopes remained an important gift item well into the nineteenth century, probably because of their functionality, but also because as we've seen indirectly in the diaries, they had the ability to be superbly crafted and gilded with precious metals, making them inherently valuable. Probably the most famous depiction of a telescope is in the Western-style painting by the Japanese artist Kawahara Keiga entitled *Arrival of a Dutch Ship*.[20] In the painting, the noted physician Phillip Franz von Siebold, along with his mistress and young child, can be seen on a lookout platform observing the arrival of a Dutch ship. Siebold is observing the ship with a long, black telescope as the ship is towed into Nagasaki Bay by several Japanese boats.[21] Telescopes would undoubtedly have been useful for the several Western daimyo who the Tokugawa charged with maintaining the coastal lookout posts on the island of Kyushu, but beyond their utility, these items were symbols of fine European craftsmanship, and of course ultimately of

Tokugawa power and prestige as they were brought year after year as gifts for the Shogun and his officials.

Related to telescopes were helioscopes, which were imported with much less frequency than telescopes, but enough to warrant mention here. On April 10, 1766, the chief merchant writes that the Dutch brought twenty such instruments for the Shogun that year "of variously colored glass, one Japanese inch, which is 1¼ Dutch inches, square or in diameter."[22] These must have been quite in demand for we read that the next year (August 8, 1767) twenty more helioscopes were ordered from Holland.

Another ubiquitous gift in this category was spectacles, a gift that was liberally bestowed on all sorts of officials both at Nagasaki and at Edo. As we have seen with the telescopes, the official that most requested these particular "rarities" was the company's patron, Inoue Masashige, at least through the middle third of the seventeenth century. In 1647, for example, he requested that the Company send to Japan "some spectacles with excellent large glasses for people of different ages," and he further specified that they "have to be stored separately in single cases."[23] This last provision was probably because the spectacles had a habit of arriving in Japan broken or cracked. Another reason might have been that if the spectacles were shipped en masse in a large container, the Japanese might have devalued the goods as being commonplace, whereas if they were housed each in their own special case, the perception of rarity and value could be maintained. This last point must necessarily remain in the realm of speculation, but the former point is well attested in the diaries, as it was not uncommon to read of the lenses in spectacles being cracked on arrival.

An illustration of the travails of long sea voyages on finely crafted crystal lenses can be seen in a diary entry for October 8, 1649:

> Today we inspected the spyglasses and spectacles which have arrived. We found them to be badly damaged. The costliest spyglasses and spectacles, for which people here are most eager, were for the most part darkened or cracked, just like the crazing on thin ice. We judged that this had not been caused by falling or rough treatment, but because the crystal of the glasses had cracked of itself, after having lain too long, for they all looked as if they had all been covered with flour. We found the faults to be such that they cannot be presented by using a preservative. Therefore, no crystal spectacles or tubes should be sent in future, but the very best common glasses, which are not subject to this kind of deterioration. I have elaborated on this point because this nation is so desirous of these articles, not caring for expensive jewelry, but only for the glasses.[24]

This entry further reveals the nature of the diaries that every chief merchant was obliged to keep while in Japan. Rather than being personal thoughts and reflections, the diaries were treated as official Company property, and were read by successive chief merchants. It is clear from many diary entries that chief merchants often went back into the journal records to retrieve information, and of course entries like the one given here make it clear that chief merchants expected others to read the journals and to heed the advice therein. In fact, the very fact that the official VOC journals give such prevalence to gifts is in itself an indication of how much weight the Company put on bringing rarities to Japan to be used as gifts or quasi-gifts.

An indication of how seriously the Dutch attended to providing their patrons with high-quality goods can be seen in an extended diary entry for January 31, 1652, about a week after the Company representatives' arrival in Edo for the yearly journey to court. In this entry, the Dutch note that "not a single one" of the spectacles were of the quality that Inoue had ordered a few years back, and so rather than provide him with substandard specimens, the Dutch decided on the strategy of telling him that because the lenses were not up to snuff, they had been sent back and that they "expected that improved ones would arrive next season." This was most likely a white lie; certainly, the diary entry carries the connotation, at the very least, of misdirection. The chief merchant goes on to lament that "if it had been possible to actually hand them to him now, His Honor would undoubtedly have been highly pleased and would have appreciated these small things more than anything more sizeable."[25] That an entire diary entry is essentially devoted to strategizing about what to tell the Company's patron concerning a few spectacles, especially in light of the many, many other gifts that he was routinely given, speaks volumes to the weight the VOC put on filling Tokugawa officialdom's orders for goods.

In the same year, 1652, the Dutch note that they received several orders for rarities from various high officials, among which were: "five fine spectacles of the same shape and size as the ones ordered for [Inoue Masashige] in the past and of which a model has been provided, for people aged sixty to seventy years"; "ten fine spectacles with their cases for persons of fifty to sixty years old"; "three fine pairs of spectacles for persons of fifty to sixty years of age"; "fifteen fine, clear spectacles for people of sixty to eighty years old"; and finally "twenty spectacles, namely eighteen for people of the same ages as mentioned before and two for fifty year olds." In total, the orders from high-ranking officials for that year included fifty-three pairs of spectacles, and this is on top of a whole host of other goods, including a few "reading glasses" that we will have occasion to discuss further.²⁶ Even this number was nothing, however, compared to the order for 1668 when, as the Dutch were about to depart from Edo, an order was submitted for "300 fine, Dutch spectacles with their cases, for people of various ages. This is a repeated request from the councilors (who are all old men, aged 45, 50, and 60). Hence it is imperative that we take good care to supply them."²⁷

In the introduction we noted that as part of Inoue Masashige's role in facilitating Dutch-Japanese relations, he would routinely inspect the gifts that the Company brought that year for the Shogun and his officials, and would often make recommendations on how to improve the gifts. Such an example can be seen in February 1656, when the chief merchant and his compatriots were unpacking the gifts after having arrived in Edo for that year's court journey. Once the gifts had been sorted by recipient and a list drawn up and translated, Inoue recommended that "the pistols for the counselors [be replaced] with two fine, large pairs of spectacles for each—which His Honor had previously ordered for himself and which have now been brought."²⁸ One wonders, given the sheer number of spectacles brought on a yearly basis, and given that by this time in the seventeenth century the weapons that were imported were usually quite elaborately crafted, whether Inoue rather fancied the pistols for himself and so proposed the swap for personal reasons. We cannot know, of course, but it does seem that he was quite a collector of rarities, and of course we know that he had ordered lots of spectacles, and that pistols were quite a bit rarer. One particularly interesting firearm was a walking stick with barrels that shot bullets out of the end like a gun! The weapon was apparently a hit in Edo for we are told that a courtyard was prepared for a demonstration of the weapon. The demonstration caused a sensation, and there must have been great demand for further test firings, because a couple days later we read that some lead implements were melted down so as to make more bullets.²⁹ Ultimately the walking stick ended up in the list of presents for the Shogun that year. This was the first year the new Shogun received gifts as a Shogun, and we know that Japanese advisers suggested the gifts be of special quality on such an occasion, so perhaps the walking stick was in response to this suggestion.

There are many other instances in which spectacles were used as gifts both in Nagasaki and in Edo; so many in fact that it would quite belabor the point to illustrate the matter further, except to note that while it is impossible to know the state of mind of the writers of the Dutch diaries, it is at times possible to get a hint of sarcasm, or perhaps sarcasm mixed in with a measure of frustration. In April of 1667, for example, when the Dutch were getting ready to leave Edo, a high official came to see the Dutch and told then to do their best "to ensure that next year a goodly number of spectacles be brought to Edo, because many great gentlemen were in need of them." The chief merchant added that he "gave them [his] assurance, thanked them for their fatherly care, and returned home."[30] The fatherly care did not extend, one presumes, to the facilitation of more precious metal, or the easing of trade restrictions, or any of the other things the Dutch routinely and fastidiously complained about in their diaries. About a week later, on the evening before the Dutch departure back toward Nagasaki, the chief merchant recorded in his journal that "the commissioners strongly recommended that I see to it that the Shogun be supplied with some rarities next year, because there had been comments at Court that the Dutch did not make much effort to please the Shogun (for they no longer brought any rarities). Furthermore, several councilors needed spectacles, and we should also take care of this." One wonders if indeed the Dutch had not been bringing as many "rarities" to court or if the several decades of bringing the goods had caused the rarities to become, well, less rare. It's difficult to tell, although it certainly seems that the usual bewildering array of goods had been brought to Edo more or less consistently over the past several decades, although it is true that Dutch trade began a slow but steady decline in the third quarter of the seventeenth century.

Another instrument that could substitute for spectacles are what were called "reading glasses." These seemed to be what we might today call magnifying glasses and which can still occasionally be seen when people with poor eyesight read small-print media, such as newspapers, or God forbid, the miniscule print on medicines that warn of possible dire consequences, all of which naturally far outweigh the benefits of the medicine. This interpretation is further reinforced by the fact that these lenses were occasionally also referred to as "burning glasses," and as every schoolchild knows, magnifying glasses can be used on a sunny day to focus the sun's rays to the point where one could potentially cause any amount of petty mischief.[31] In April 1647, for example, the chief merchant writes that a senior official

> sent a letter requesting some glasses from the Dutch. He could not specify exactly what was meant, but they thought reading glasses. I sent two large ones to the governor. On one side they are ground concavely and they can be used instead of spectacles. He was very pleased with them. Because they have to be given under the pretext of a sale, [we] proposed a very low price. His excellency was pleased with this.[32]

This quote again demonstrates what we have above termed a "quasi-gift." On many occasions, the Dutch make it clear in their diaries that goods that were given to Tokugawa officials were indeed sold to them, but that the prices were set so low as to effectively be a gift. In other words, even if the price of the good was at cost, the additional amount spent shipping the goods made it so that the Dutch invariably lost money on the items, which is, of course, one of the defining features of a gift. In one passage in the diaries for 1655, we are given a sense of how much of a discount these "quasi-gifts" entailed: the chief merchant calculates that the true value of the luxury goods given away was 220 gulden, but that in Japan they "sold them for 57 gulden," or 25 percent of their true value.[33] A bit later, the chief merchant also notes the price of goods "sold" in Edo was even more of a loss for the Company than those in Nagasaki because the Company had to pay for the goods to be transported, a factor not accounted for in the sale price.[34] As we saw in the introduction, the gifts given to Inoue were always quasi-gifts as the Shogun forbade him accepting outright gifts, probably because of his position as a regulator, a practice that even today is a hallmark of conflict of interest clauses across the land. More than anyone else, until his retirement, Inoue was responsible for facilitating Dutch interactions with the *bakufu*, in addition to his role as "inspector of religion," in which he was charged primarily with rooting out all traces of Catholicism from the country. Because of the sensitive nature of this job, and the fact that he was a direct intermediary between the Company and the Shogun, it would surely have been at least unseemly if he were to accept gifts from the very group he was meant to oversee. Therefore, by using quasi-gifts, the Dutch were technically able to adhere to shogunal policy while still being able to shower their patron with gifts.

Another item in this category of "scientific paraphernalia" is the various types of "medicines" that the Dutch brought to Japan and used occasionally as outright gifts, but mainly as what we have been calling "quasi-gifts." In January of 1651, the chief merchant relates that Inoue Masashige inspected the medicines that were brought for that year and recommended that they be presented to the Shogun as a gift. He also exhorted the Company to bring additional medicines the Shogun asked for, but which had not arrived on that years' ships. According to the diaries, the Shogun "had now seen and experienced some fine examples of Dutch medicine. This had led to the Japanese appreciating and esteeming it more than before."[35] This entry also illustrates a common procedure when medicines were brought to Japan: invariably the Company surgeon would be sent for and asked to write descriptions and uses of the medicines, which would then be translated into Japanese. On May 7, 1644, for example, the Dutch were asked to bring for the Shogun "various kinds of medicines, drugs, balms salves, and some oil, with a memo, what they were used for, and the containers."[36] Two years later, the Nagasaki *bugyō* was given a chest of medicines, each one explained in Japanese, and we are told that he was happier with this gift than he would have been with a far costlier one.[37]

As an example of how complicated the issue of "quasi-gifts" could be, in April of 1669, Inaba sent the sum of twenty gold *koban* to the chief merchant as a "return gift" for two medicine chests filled with "medicines, essential oils, and precious spirits" that had been given him last year. As Chief Merchant Daniel Six relates:

> This is 220 guilders less than they cost the company according to the accounts, if one sets a *koban* at 5.6 taels. Although I expressed my dissatisfaction to the interpreter, I could not make him communicate that, but on top of this I was forced to refuse the *koban*, because the interpreter claimed that [the previous chief merchant] had given the chests to the councilor as a gift. But because the [servant] had riposted that his Lord would return the chests if I refused to accept the *koban*, honor was preserved and expenses saved. Still, in order to show that the Lord had not sent these *koban* without having given due thought to paying for the chests, what they were worth, the doctor said that Mino-no-Kami had ordered him to tell me that five years ago, Willem Volger had also handed him two chests with medicines and at that time, His Honor had given Volger 20 *schuiten* of silver. But because His Highness considered these chests to be of greater value, he had sent me 20 *koban* as a gift.[38]

This passage nicely illustrates the way that even goods that were not necessarily meant to be gifts eventually seemed to become gifts! The costs that Six estimates probably don't take into account the expense of shipping the chests to Japan, and so the disparity in value between the "present" and the "return present" was most likely even greater. There are several instances in the diaries of chief merchants noting that the return gifts given for a particular item, or the payment for ordered goods, was significantly less than the value of the item, but in almost all cases, the chief merchant chose to overlook it and write off the disparity as a gift that would continue to stand the Company in good stead in Japan. If anything, this particular case is one of the few times in which we encounter a chief merchant actively challenging "payment" for an item given to an official.

As we noted earlier, some officials were not technically allowed to accept gifts, and the Nagasaki *bugyō* fell into this category, and so as with Inoue Masashige, they were supposed to pay for their gifts, although as we know from several diary entries these were essentially token payments rendering the items handed over gifts in all but name. Medicines seem to have been an exception to this rule.

On November 23, 1646, for example, the Dutch gave the *bugyō* a chest filled with essential oils and medicines. The chief merchant states that

> he was very grateful. He returned the notes with the names. I had the potency and efficacy of each written in Japanese and sent them back to him. He sent the interpreters to thank me. He let me know that he did not accept any gifts, but he could accept medicines. According to the interpreters, he was more pleased with this that if he had been given a grand gift.[39]

It is not clear whether the *bugyō* could not accept gifts at any time, or whether he refused to accept gifts other than the official gifts earmarked for him at the appropriate time. We do know from the diaries that the Nagasaki *bugyō* were routinely given items from the Dutch, and they are usually called gifts, but whether they "paid" for them in order to preserve the fiction that they did not accept gifts is unclear.

Less than two months later, the Company again presented a medicine chest, this time to Inoue Masashige, and ordered his servant to tell him that it cost three *taels*. The chief merchant records that Inoue laughed heartily because he knew that the chest was actually worth much more than that, but when he confronted the Dutch, they told him that they insisted on this price in order to demonstrate that they valued his patronage and because they knew that he couldn't accept gifts. We are then told that he was well pleased with this response, but that he wanted to pay more. Whether he did end up paying more is an open question as the sources are silent on that matter.

One of the most bizarre medicines consistently mentioned throughout the diaries in the seventeenth century is what were called "bezoar stones."[40] These were masses that were found in the stomachs of goats and were believed to have curative properties, especially as antidotes to many kinds of poisons.[41] They apparently made for excellent gifts in Japan and were consistently in demand throughout the seventeenth century, although they seem not to have been brought in any great quantity. In April of 1650, for example, Inoue was given bezoar stones, and in response, his secretary told the chief merchant that "the bezoar stones, being rare medicine, really pleased him."[42] Similarly, in 1655, we are told two separate times in the diaries that the Shogun was particularly pleased with a set of pistols and bezoar stones that had been part of that year's gifts.[43]

In 1650, the Japanese requested that the Company surgeon remain in Edo after the rest of the party returned to Nagasaki, and from what we can gather, he was quite busy attending to many officials in Edo: the Dutch were exhorted to "send various medicines for the surgeons, for [he] is treating many officials." On this occasion, the surgeon was also accompanied by a "pyrotechnist" who spent his time instructing the shogunal officials how to fire mortars and demonstrating some of the artillery that the Dutch had previously brought to Edo as gifts.[44] The Dutch included a note in the journal that the Shogun was footing the bill for the room and board of both of the VOC officials in Edo. This year was not simply an ordinary year for the annual Dutch journey to court, but it was the occasion of a special embassy to the capital in order for the Company to officially thank the Shogun for his care of several shipwrecked sailors aboard a Dutch ship called the *Breskens*. The shogunate was quite obstinate in its demand that the Dutch send an embassy specifically for this purpose, and after many years of negotiations (the *Breskens* "incident" happened in 1643), the embassy arrived in 1649 and was received in the beginning of the following year.[45] Thus it was not the norm that Dutch officials were left behind in Edo, although it became normal for the Company's surgeon to be a much sought after person in Edo. In an interesting diary entry for February 2, 1655, the day after having arrived in Edo, Inoue Masashige ordered:

> Our surgeon should go to his house to discuss some medicinal herbs with the Japanese doctor. Notwithstanding the shogun's edict, or rather that of the councilors—for no edict of the shogun can be violated—that no one ranking below the high nobility use a *norimono* in Edo (a palanquin), in particular within the confines of the castle, for the reason that sons of several nobles had smuggled in whores in this way, the commissioner had ordered our surgeon to go there in a *norimono*. Should anyone stop him, he should say that it was on [Inoue's] order.[46]

Clearly the surgeon was an important personage in Edo during the *hofreis*, as evidenced over the years by the high-ranking officials that he routinely attended to.

According to Stephen Gudeman, a gift does not necessarily have to be an object, or something tangible, but rather can be a service or, in the case of Japan, knowledge of Western medicine, Western scientific advances, or global intelligence.[47] According to Suzuki Yasuko, "the shogunate continued to trade with the Netherlands partly because it had to carry on traditions established in the founding Shogun Ieyasu's times, and party because it was impelled by the need to gather foreign intelligence and import European scientific knowledge and technology."[48] Likewise, Nagazumi Yōko sees the value of the Dutch shift from a trading partner from the sixteenth to the mid-seventeenth century to a source of information thereafter.[49]

As for the surgeons, they were required to not only tend to the sick and dying Dutchmen on Deshima but were also routinely called upon to examine high-ranking Japanese patients not only at Nagasaki but also in Edo. We often read of small gifts that Japanese worthies would send to the physician in return for tending to them. In 1648, for example, we read that a high-ranking daimyo sent the surgeon three silk "gowns" and seven *katabira*, or summer robes, to the surgeon in thanks for having been healed under his care.[50] A couple years later, we read that the surgeon was given a duck for having healed a burned leg.[51] Later the surgeon was routinely asked to be a tutor to Japanese physicians whose daimyo asked them to study Dutch medicine to complement the traditional Chinese-style medicine then prevalent in Tokugawa Japan. It is not an accident that some of the best-known Westerners on Deshima were surgeons: Caspar Schamberger, Engelbert Kaempfer, Carl Thunberg, and Phillip Franz von Siebold.[52] As early as the seventeenth century VOC surgeons instructed Japanese in the art of Western medicine, as Kaempfer notes in his description of his time in Japan.[53] In 1650, as noted earlier, Schamberger was required to stay in Edo much longer than his Dutch counterparts, presumably to treat high-ranking patients and to instruct shogunal physicians in Western medicine.[54] Schamberger was so influential that when he left Japan in 1651, a style of medicine was named after him, the *kasuparu-ryū geka*.[55] Western-style medicine grew so popular that by the nineteenth century, Siebold had a gaggle of students to whom he formally taught Western medicine at his private academy called the *Narutaku Juku*.[56] It seems the Dutch were not always glad of the Japanese students hanging around all the time; Chief Merchant Reijnhouts writes in 1760 that several shogunal physicians were on the island and that he was being continually bombarded with "bothersome questions."[57]

In the diaries, we read of countless instances in which the surgeons were summoned to treat patients, and even more instances in which Japanese came to the Dutch lodgings to learn from the good doctors.[58] On one occasion the chief merchant writes with obvious exasperation that Japanese officials have been asking the surgeon even to attend to animals: "First a skinny bitch, now a monkey, after this it will probably be a cat or an owl. But we shall oblige this touchy big cabessa in every way, even if he were to send injured billy goats, buffaloes, and pigs to us."[59] These services should also be thought of as gifts, just as much as the finely wrought telescopes or the megafauna that were brought to Japan.

Perhaps one of the more profoundly impactful types of gifts given the Japanese was the gift of books. Imported books were banned in the early seventeenth century when the first three Tokugawa shoguns clamped down severely on Christianity. This ban held firm until 1720 when the Shogun Tokugawa Yoshimune allowed their import, provided they be rigorously searched by censors who would ensure that no Christian propaganda entered surreptitiously. Yoshimune himself was quite curious about Western knowledge, and he encouraged a closely scrutinized group of scholars to learn about Western science, especially medicine. Books were a prime vehicle by which *rangaku* (literally "Dutch studies," but more accurately translated as Western studies), was spread through what Terry Jackson describes as a network of salons among early modern Japanese scholars.[60]

As early as 1659, a copy of Rembert Dodonaeus' *Cruijdeboeck* (published 1618) was presented as a gift to the Shogun, and after 1720, the number of books that were brought as outright gifts or as "quasi-gifts," grew steadily.[61] Yoshimune himself ordered several hundred texts and made sure that one of his scientists learned Dutch in order to be able to read the newly imported books.[62] Yoshimune also engaged the Nagasaki interpreters to question the Dutch about a variety of books that were of interest to him, and through these interviews, early Japanese *rangaku* scholars were able to piece together translations of these books.[63] Peter Kornicki notes that while imports of books were somewhat limited, over the years, some impressive collections were accumulated, notably by the Nabeshima daimyo family on Kyushu.[64] One incident involving a book is a good illustration of how exacting the Japanese could be regarding the goods that were brought for officials. On April 8, 1659, a book was among the items selected as gifts for the Shogun, along with a telescope. We read two weeks later that the book and telescope had been rejected because the quality was not good enough, which prompted the chief merchant to include this diatribe in his diary: "Oh these poor people! How little do they know of the excellence of such or other kinds of books, for they think that such books are available in many kinds, such as shoes in the shop of a shoemaker!"[65] While gifts of books were not as ostentatious as, say, camels or Persian horses, nonetheless they were exceptionally impactful, especially in the eighteenth century when books ceased to be objects of curiosity and became, rather, objects of serious study.

The final type of gift in this category consists of navigational tools, mainly compasses and astrolabes, and timepieces, either personal timepieces or clocks.[66] Of these goods, compasses were the most commonly used for gifts or quasi-gifts. In the year 1660, for example, there are twelve mentions of the Dutch giving away compasses, and even allowing for some overlap in the diary entries (for example, one entry refers to the compasses previously given as noted in another entry), there still would have been no less than eighteen compasses given away in that year. Of course, for a group of people who by their very profession were seafarers, it's not surprising that there should be a number of these instruments at hand, or that every VOC ship should be supplied with these essential instruments of navigation. An indication that these were somewhat common for the merchants on Deshima is that the chief merchant often times refers to them as "small things," or "trifles," although in February of 1656, we read about three "ivory compasses," which surely must have been at least passingly valuable commodities.

An interesting incident involving a timepiece occurred in 1670, at a time when the *bakufu* had temporarily banned the import of rarities into Japan, and so to get around this, the Dutch saw fit to bring a drawing of an elaborate clock in order for the Nagasaki *bugyō* to decide if this should be included in the lists of banned goods. The drawing arrived on August 3 aboard the ship *Schermer*, and the *bugyō* requested that the Dutch explain the description and drawing to an interpreter in order to have it translated into Japanese. The next day we read:

> It was impossible for the interpreters to understand the description of the timepiece and it is no wonder, because they are unable to understand even minor matters. They are absolutely incompetent in understanding and translating anything difficult. Hence all I could tell them now was that it was a costly piece which needed winding just once a year and shows the day of the month and the hour of the day and the night.

The next we hear of the clock is three weeks later when the chief merchant relates:

> A timepiece which had been ordered some years ago as a gift for Japan had arrived in Batavia from Holland, but, because the import of timepieces, and all rarities was banned in Japan, their honors had sent a drawing of it to show to the governor and ask his opinion about whether or not it could be sent next year.

The denouement of this episode came on November 1, almost three months after the drawing was sent to the *bugyō*. They told the chief merchant the Shogun had ordered that the clock not be used as a gift next year after all, but that they were pleased that "an experienced herbalist had been ordered form Holland" along with a number of scientific instruments.[67]

Clearly, all gifts were not banned from Japan, because we can see throughout the remainder of the seventeenth century and through to the "opening" of Japan in 1854, gifts continued to be sent to Edo for the Shogun and his officials. So what are the Dutch referring to in the above incident in 1670? The answer probably lies in the fact that in the second half of the 1670s, the *bakufu* became increasingly concerned about the Japanese economy. It was precisely at this time, mainly at the behest of Arai Hakuseki, that silver was banned for export, thus beginning a decades-long struggle to limit precious metal outflows from Japan aboard Dutch and Chinese ships.[68] It was also at this time that the *bakufu* uncovered an enormous smuggling operation in the Korean trade that involved illegally exporting Japanese weapons to Korea. And finally, as Kaempfer points out in his *History of Japan*, the Dutch came to be increasingly involved in what was charitably called the "private trade," some of which was legal, but much of which was in reality smuggling. Kaempfer accuses even the chief merchant of being in on this trade, a charge that is highlighted by Donald Keene in his *Japanese Discovery of Europe* in which Keene states:

> In Japan, where strict regulations curbed the elán of the Dutch merchants, there was nevertheless considerable smuggling. Indeed, as the eighteenth century advanced, and there was less and less profit to be derived from the legitimate trade at Deshima, the chief excuse for maintaining the factory was the private smuggling in which the Dutch engaged . . . . Their sole purpose was to make money, and to this end they devoted themselves with unbounded energy and complete ruthlessness.[69]

Interestingly, the issue of private trade, which was anathema to the VOC for many, many years, was brought out into the open in Japan when Edo officially recognized the private trade that had been happening for years at Deshima as a form of legitimate trade.[70] And because Edo recognized it, and because the economy of Nagasaki was, to a certain extent, reliant on foreign trade of all types, including private trade, the VOC was forced to recognize it, at least in Japan, a few years later.[71] Private trade was so lucrative on Deshima that it appears the chief merchants had taken to paying bribes to the authorities in Batavia in order to secure the position. But even allowing for a certain amount of private trade, there is no doubt that Dutch merchants, perhaps especially the chief merchant, routinely exceeded the limits put on this trade so that it is still possible, to return to Keene's earlier allegation, to speak of smuggling on Deshima.

To return to the scientific paraphernalia that was brought to Japan as gifts, we could, of course, add a plethora of other objects that were brought and that would fall under this category, including microscopes, camera obscuras, and a host of other objects that found their way to Japan from Europe, but the objects described in this chapter represent the major categories of gifts that were consistently used decade after decade in Japan as gifts or quasi-gifts.[72] All of the objects, from the spectacles to the medicine chests, represented the essence of foreign technology and knowledge, and as such became a valuable commodity in the "gift economy" precisely because the owners of such objects were able to participate in the ostentatious consumption that served as a status marker. The daimyo were able to employ their own Dutch scholars who could use the daimyo's privileged access to Western knowledge to study, and this patronage itself was a form of ostentatious consumption. In the end, these gifts, as well as all of the gifts detailed in this book, were valuable because they demonstrated by their very foreignness, their "rareness," the power the Tokugawa shogunate wielded over foreign relations, a power that extended even to the Dutch, representatives of a distant and advanced European culture. The fact that these red-haired barbarians trudged their way through Japan bearing the symbols that reinforced the Tokugawa in their position as legitimate arbiters of power in Japan; and the fact that European material culture continued to flow to the upper echelons of samurai society only served to reinforce that power in every pair of spectacles a daimyo held in his hand, or every time a daimyo's courtesan gazed through a telescope or lifted a glass of Spanish wine to her lips.

5

A Taste of the Exotic:
Food and Drink as Social Lubricant in Early Modern Japanese-Dutch Interactions

The gifts that command the most attention in scholarly and popular works on early modern gift-giving are usually exotic and costly gifts. Most of the gifts that have been studied in the context of the Dutch East India Company in Japan are no exception. Most, if not all, of the major studies deal with, for example, Persian stallions, exotic birds of paradise, ostriches, and other large animals, or, on the other hand, European manufactured goods such as we have just examined: telescopes, camera obscura, finely crafted metalwork, and so on. Most of the gifts that were exchanged between the Dutch and various Japanese officials, however, were smaller, more mundane gifts, although even these could be considered exotic to the Japanese. These gifts usually took the form of food and drink, liberally given upon request (although occasionally sold), and the Dutch also accepted small gifts of food and drink as return gifts as well. This chapter will examine these smaller gift items of food and drink and, in the process, we will be able to catch a glimpse of daily life for the Dutch in a way that we are not necessarily able when examining the more "charismatic" gifts.

Gifts of food are some of the most studied exchanges in history and anthropology, probably because gifts of food are so ubiquitous across societies, and yet so laden with meaning.[1] Food is not only central to survival in a biological sense, but is also at the very center of many of our most sacred and communal rituals. It's telling that the central observance of the Christian faith is a highly ritualized meal in which the elements, that is to say the bread and the wine, are referred to as gifts, and the ritualized presentation of the bread and wine to the altar is called an oblation, that is to say an offering. Similarly, food plays a central role in many religious observances in Judaism (Passover) as well as in Islam (Eid al-Fitr). Food serves as a means through which community is formed, whether around the family dining table, around restaurant tables, or in mess halls and cafeterias. And in Japan, food plays a central role in the rituals surrounding the commemoration of ancestors and gods in the Shinto worldview. It is not uncommon in modern households to offer up gifts of fruit, rice, or sake on family altars in a custom known as *naorai*. As Harumi Befu relates:

> *Naorai* is now commonly understood to refer to the feast held after a religious ritual proper, but this is evidently a later modification. In the original form of *naorai*, offerings to gods were gifts to gods, and these gifts were returned by gods as their gifts for mortals to share with them, so that the mortals might partake of the divine power of the gods to whom gifts were originally offered.[2]

Gifts of food serve as what Furubotn and Richter call "symbolic, low-cost investments."[3] Food and drink are ubiquitous as symbolic gifts, from the literally tons of chocolate given away at Valentine's Day to bottles of wine that are handed over upon visiting someone's house to the Midwestern casseroles that are exchanged at housewarming parties and at the birth of children (my church in Wisconsin, for example, had a casserole brigade that would send over creations every couple of days when our first child was born). These gifts are laden with meaning, and they serve to create lasting bonds in the community in part by weaving a web of reciprocity that must be repaid either in kind at a later date or in some other equivalent, but approximately equal, form of social currency.[4]

Gift-giving in Japan is a well-studied phenomenon and is almost immediately experienced by visitors. As the noted anthropologist Harumi Bepu notes, "gift-giving is a minor institution in Japan, with complex rules defining who should give to whom, on what occasion he should give, what sort of gift is appropriate on a given occasion, and how the gift should be presented."[5] And food is a central part of gift-giving culture. Foreigners are often struck by the Japanese penchant for selecting and presenting the perfect piece of fruit as a gift, and by how expensive this perfectly grown fruit can be.[6] Similarly, food items bought as gifts are as often selected because of their exquisite wrapping as they are for the actual food inside.[7] In short, presentation is part of the ritual of giving gifts of food, and the same generally held true for Japanese gifts of food and drink to the Dutch. And the Dutch, for their part, often took pains to wrap the gifts for the Shogun and his officials in a comely way, particularly bottles of wine, which were often packed in decorative (and utile) cases.

And finally, this chapter will examine not only tangible objects as gifts (such as bottles of wine or Dutch food items) but also intangible gifts such as invitations to dinner, which occurred regularly on special occasions such as the Dutch New Year, invitations to partake of sweets and liquor when officials visited

Deshima or the Dutch quarters in Edo, and, somewhat interrelated, instances when the Dutch entertained Japanese guests by allowing them to observe Dutch entertainment such as billiards, musical performances, and the generally foreign way of life, including showing them objects of Dutch material culture.

On May 10, 1657, the Dutch invited a number of Japanese guests to the island of Deshima to partake of a feast. The chief merchant records that he served his distinguished guests "a well-prepared, young, fat billy-goat," but that the Japanese didn't seem to like it, preferring instead "bean soup and lean greens." Here the matter may have rested but, as we have seen in other chapters, although the Japanese always responded to being entertained with a small token of appreciation soon after, on this occasion, only one of the ten guests sent a word of thanks to Deshima, and that was the young son of one of the interpreters. The chief merchant likened the other nine guests to the nine lepers whom Jesus healed in the Gospels but who couldn't be bothered to come back and thank Jesus for his efforts on their behalf (although likening the chief merchant to Jesus doesn't seem really in keeping with Dutch Reformed piety!). Be that as it may, the chief merchant goes on to write that this is against all good manners and custom, and speculates that perhaps it's because the Japanese didn't like the goat: "If this is true, I think these fussy men should be treated to a young roasted donkey."[8] He goes on to note, probably with some pent up bitterness, that it would rather be to the Company's advantage if the Japanese guests wouldn't come round so much to be entertained as it would surely save the Company a pretty penny.

The aforementioned feast was not a rare occasion on Deshima. We read of several occasions when the Dutch entertained their Japanese hosts with a formal meal, and even more occasions when Japanese officials called at the island and were invariably entertained with food and drink. In short, much like today, food and drink served a number of functions depending on the occasion: sharing a meal could serve as a social lubricant between people who were of very different social and economic classes, not to mention from totally separate cultural worlds; food and drink could serve as an expression of gratitude for service rendered, or, in other words, a thank-you gift given either by the Japanese or by the Dutch; a shared meal could serve as a venue in which to discuss matters both personal and professional; and finally, food and drink were often used by both the Japanese and the Dutch as formal gift items, both between individuals and between the Company and the shogunal officials in Nagasaki and Edo.

Food and drink served as gifts on a variety of occasions, both formal and informal. Perhaps the true value of looking at food as a gift, however, is its role as a social lubricant. There were never more than a dozen Dutchmen on the small island of Deshima, and they were constantly subjected to almost daily negotiated interactions with Japanese officialdom, including the two Nagasaki *bugyō*, the interpreters, both senior and junior, the guards, the local officials in the city, and the merchants.[9] This is quite apart from the many Japanese daimyo and their kin who consistently visited the island and who all expected to be entertained or who came to request food or drink in varying quantities at Company lodgings in Edo. In short, food and drink served then, as it does now, as a social lubricant, making these daily interactions more pleasant and facilitating the business that was transacted between the Company and the Japanese.

In a fascinating study published in 2017, psychologists showed a correlation between groups of "strangers" who ate a meal together and the level of trust and cooperation that was developed between the two groups.[10] Of course, we know of this phenomenon from personal experience, but it is interesting that, at least according to this research, eating at the same table and of the same foods can make somewhat tense social situations smoother. In the case of the Dutch-Japanese interactions, the relationship was always tense, no matter how close the individuals involved might be, especially in the environment of scarcity from the last years of the seventeenth century onward. The Dutch continually demanded more precious metals and resented the many rules and regulations they were subjected to, not to mention the stifling role that tradition could play in negotiations. The Japanese officials in Nagasaki seem to always have been conscious of their role in making sure that everything went smoothly, and even slight aberration from routine could be viewed in Edo as a failure to protect the honor and dignity of the Shogun. Food served to build trust and engender cooperation in these tense relationships, and also served as an outlet after the negotiations were done.

As mentioned earlier, there are three instances in which food and drink can be considered gifts. The first involves the giving of food and drink to Japanese officials when they specifically requested it of the Dutch, almost always through their "secretaries." The second is when the same Japanese officials invariably sent the Dutch a "return gift" in thanks for having entertained them. These gifts almost always took the form of food and/or drink. And the third occasion when food and drink can be considered a gift is on the many occasions the Dutch entertained Japanese officials on Deshima. This entertainment happened on the several tours of inspection that the officials made, at times when the Dutch invited Japanese officials to Deshima for a formal dinner, or when officials and powerful daimyo happened to stop by, either alone or, more likely, with a retinue of family or retainers. In every case, food and drink served to fill the gap between Japanese officialdom and the

Dutch merchants, and served to make the everyday existence of the Dutch more bearable and probably the Company's activities in Japan more profitable.

We first turn our attention to instances in which food and drink were requested of the Dutch. On February 4, 1656, four "catties" of butter were sent to a Japanese official who requested butter of the Dutch. Just six days later, another official came round to the island and was given ten more catties of butter.[11] A catty is roughly a pound and a half, and so in the space of a week, twenty-one pounds of butter were given away to Japanese officials. One naturally is compelled to ask what these Japanese officials were doing with so much butter. A clue may be forthcoming in the chief merchant's entry for February 4 in which he states that the butter was almost certainly sent to Edo. This means that the butter was probably being used as gifts by the Japanese officials for their patrons in Edo, or perhaps even for the Shogun, although there is evidence that butter was thought to be a cure for various intestinal ailments as well as bites and stings when mixed with mummia, and we know that mummia was also a medicinal item also imported as a gift for the Shogun and others.[12] The Dutch suspected this in other contexts as when, for example, their patron, Inoue Masashige, ordered all kinds of "curiosos," and then apparently distributed them as gifts to his patrons in turn. It's logical to conclude that the same was happening with these large orders of foodstuffs, for I think we can all agree that fifteen pounds of butter, save for the raw material for a butter sculpture of the Shogun, is a bit excessive.

In the abstract, so much butter might boggle the senses, but we should bear in mind that the quantities of provisions sent on ships was often staggering, and the same was surely true for the Dutch outpost on Deshima. According to Dirk Barreveld,

> In 1636 the Admiralty in Amsterdam ordered that everyone on board was entitled to a half pound of cheese, half a pound of butter and bread to a weight of five pounds a week, with double this amount for the officers. In order to feed one hundred men, the ship had to carry for each month at sea: 450 pounds of cheese, five metric tons of meat, four tons of herring, one and a quarter tons of butter, five and a half tons of dried peas, two and a half tons of dried beans, half a ton of salt, 35 barrels of beer in winter (42 barrels in summer) and French and Spanish wine.[13]

Given these proportions, it's logical to assume that Deshima would also have similarly large stores.

Butter was usually an item requested by various daimyo or officials at Nagasaki, but occasionally we read of butter being sent as a gift specifically for the Shogun. Grant Goodman relates an episode in April of 1725 in which the Shogun Yoshimune requested butter of the Dutch. Because it was a gift to the Shogun, it seems they took special care to package the butter, putting it in jars, wrapping it in paper, and tying the package with cording.[14] On that occasion it seems the Shogun was curious about Dutch provisions, as he was about so many things, and so the Dutch also sent him samples of pickled and smoked meat.

The Dutch must have had quite large stores of food such as butter because we often read about rather large quantities being handed over, and yet almost nothing about shortages. However, on rare occasions so many Dutch provisions were requested that the merchants did worry about running low, or running out completely. In 1657, for example, we read that the Dutch were running precariously low on olive oil and butter because so many Japanese officials were requesting samples. Similarly, we read on a couple occasions that the Dutch had to send to Deshima for more wine as they ran out on their yearly trip to Edo.[15] It is certainly the case with wine, and it is almost certainly the case with butter, that the Dutch packed these provisions specifically to use as gifts. The fact that the four Dutchmen in Edo had twenty-one pounds of butter to spare tells us that this must have been the case. As we'll see with wine, the bottles that the Dutch packed as they prepared for their trip to Edo were done so with the specific intention of giving them away as gifts. Nevertheless, we read the occasional complaint about having to hand so much over. Thus, for example, in 1654, the chief merchant writes, "Every day the governors and other great lords, even the interpreters, indiscriminately, without caring whether we are well stocked or not, keep sending for some butter."[16] On that day, we are told that an official came round to tell the Dutch specifically to make sure to pack a goodly amount of butter for the court journey that year, advice that the chief merchant says he will follow in order to keep the favor of the Japanese at court.

Another foodstuff that was given away in relatively large quantities was almonds. On February 12, 1654, the secretary for the daimyo of Owari came around to fetch two catties of almonds, or roughly three pounds. The daimyo must have enjoyed the almonds, because exactly a year later, on February 12, 1655, he requested five catties of almonds, which were, as usual, handed over. An even larger quantity of almonds was handed over on November 15, 1658, when the Nagasaki *bugyō* requested ten catties of almonds, or roughly fifteen pounds. He also, incidentally, requested twelve liters of butter and half a cheese, as one does, of course. All of these requests the Company fulfilled, and also threw in a ship's compass and a piece of Guinea cloth for good measure. As with the butter, we must assume that officials such as the Nagasaki *bugyō* were not taking fifteen pounds of almonds home with them and bingeing on; rather, they were most likely parceling the almonds into smaller packages and using them as gifts for their own patrons. One can imagine the *bugyō*, upon arriving for his yearly visit to Edo, presenting the Shogun with exotic gifts that he obtained from the Dutch, including almonds. The Dutch also presented the Shogun with almonds from time to time. In May of 1644, for example, the Dutch were told that the Shogun would like three or four piculs of fresh almonds that are not old or stale, which begs the question of whether previous gifts of almonds were less than satisfactory, or perhaps somewhat cynically, whether the Dutch were using gift-giving as a way of offloading stale nuts.[17]

It should be said that in most of the diary entries, there is little complaining or overt disbelief over these requests, but rather just a notation, similar to a note that one might put in a yearly ledger for supplies. This leads me to believe that the Dutch didn't think twice about handing out these goods as gifts, and perhaps even began to store them in great quantities in anticipation of handing them out. If the chief merchant thought of these requests as an imposition, he would have almost certainly not been shy about writing so in his journal. In several other places and about several other topics, there is no end to complaining. About the great quantities of food and drink that the Company was obliged to hand over, however, there is no complaining at all. This is perhaps because the Dutch in Japan understood the value of a good meal and good wine, and so didn't begrudge Japanese officialdom a few almonds and a few bottles of wine, or more probably, these were understood as gifts that cost the Company little and were simply factored into the cost of business in Japan. In fact, in a few entries, the Dutch attitude toward handing over these goods is explicit, as we have seen before. About the Company's strategy of currying favor with Japanese officials through gifts, the chief merchant writes: "It only costs the company a handful of spectacles, some telescopes, butter, tent wine, almonds, cheese, and other such trifles." Again, the chief merchant, writing about maintaining a good working relationship with the interpreters, notes: "We have to treat them all with affection and friendship, which can be promoted by presenting them with a few trifles now and again."[18] Seen in this light, we might even conclude that the regular giving of relatively small gifts such as butter and almonds was more important to the long-term success of the Company in Japan than the delivery of the larger gifts such as live animals since the giving away of common foodstuffs involved many more people with whom the Dutch were obliged to work closely.

Aside from butter, another dairy product the Japanese seemed to take an interest in was cheese. The same year in which the Dutch were transferred to

Nagasaki (1641), several officials came to visit in October after the departure of the ships, or in other words, once the frenetic business of finalizing sales, delivering merchandise, and loading the ships calmed down. The high-ranking personages were entertained with a variety of treats, as was the custom when visitors came to the factory. On this occasion, we catch a glimpse of what sorts of treats the Dutch provided for their guest because the chief merchants relates in his diary that the guests had many questions about the wine, liquor, cheese, butter, and other items the Dutch served them.[19] The Japanese made much ado about these foreign treats, although we don't know explicitly if they enjoyed them or not. Here, we can read about one of the first occasions the shogunal officials were formally visiting the Dutch "prison" island, and the insatiable Japanese curiosity about Dutch material culture. This curiosity would lead officialdom to consistently request the very things that they sampled on this occasion, including cheese. In 1656, for example, we learn that a Japanese official wanted five catties of cheese and that the Dutch, as they always did, obliged him, in this instance giving him half a cheese. A year later, the Nagasaki *bugyō* was also given a half cheese, presumably of roughly the same weight. On these instances Japanese officials received roughly seven and a half pounds of cheese, a not inconsiderable amount; certainly enough for an evening's entertainment given enough wine, but more likely to be parceled up and used in turn as exotic gifts.

Perhaps the most interesting, albeit tangential, story involving cheese occurred on February 19, 1655, while the Dutch were in Edo on the yearly court journey. One of the Dutch timepieces was not working properly, and so an elderly Japanese man of about sixty years showed up to fix it. While he was tending to the watch, the old man confessed to the chief merchant that he was a Christian and that thirty years ago he had journeyed to Batavia, perhaps as a hired sailor on a Dutch ship, something that was relatively common in the early days of Japanese-European interaction but that was explicitly banned by the shogunate early on in the Tokugawa period.[20] He related, in Portuguese, that he was now in prison and had been for eleven years on account of his religion, and that the only reason he was kept alive was because he was a superb craftsman. He went on to say that there were other Christians in prison who were kept alive for similar reasons. The chief merchant treated the man to fresh fruit and, when he left he put some butter and cheese in his knapsack in order to share them with five other Christian prisoners who had been arrested with him. We know nothing else of this interaction other than what is recorded in the chief merchant's diary, but we can surmise, given Tokugawa paranoia about the Christian religion, that this was a risky move on the part of the Dutch.

As we've seen earlier with the Shogun Yoshimune, Japanese officials occasionally requested meat prepared in the Dutch fashion, usually smoked. The chief merchant tells us, for example, that Inoue Masashige was a great lover of meat and often sent requests for samples of Dutch victuals.[21] Ironically, given the demand for Dutch provisions then and afterward, when the Dutch were originally moved to Deshima after the Portuguese were banned from the country in 1639, the Japanese tried to eradicate anything associated with the Portuguese, and so banned not just the practice of the Christian religion but also Western-style food (with the exception of the Dutch on Deshima, of course). The chief merchant notes as much on the occasion of the arrival of the first Dutch ship at Deshima: "No meat, bacon, arrack, French and Spanish wine, olive oil and other foodstuffs—which the Christians are accustomed to eat—that have been brought here on the first and second Dutch ships this southern monsoon may be sold, presented, bartered or given to anyone of that nation to any Japanese, Chinese or foreigner."[22] This was exactly at a time when the Japanese were groping for a procedure to welcome incoming Dutch ships, an era in which paranoia about Portuguese retaliations for the execution of several Portuguese sailors was running quite high. Needless to say, this particular order was either rescinded or simply disobeyed as within a year several high-ranking officials, including the Nagasaki *bugyō*, were routinely requesting Western food and drink. Most likely the order was rescinded because we know in several other such cases shogunal rules were strictly obeyed for fear of punishment. An example of this is in the acceptance of gifts from the Dutch. Japanese officials were not allowed to accept formal gifts unless the Shogun was first presented with his gifts, and this protocol seems to have been strictly adhered to. On occasion officials could get around this provision by paying for the goods and being charged a ludicrously low amount, but nevertheless it is telling that the protocol itself was important for officialdom.

Perhaps the most ubiquitous gift given to their Japanese hosts was wine in its various forms. This is certainly true for sheer breadth of time as wine was a consistent gift from the early seventeenth century all the way down to the end of the *sakoku* period in 1854. The most common forms of wine were "tent wine" and Spanish wine, although on occasion other wine is explicitly mentioned in the sources.[23] *Tint wijn*, deep red in color, came principally from the regions of Malaga or Galicia in Spain and was a great favorite of the Dutch and, from what we can gather from the sources, the Japanese as well. *Spaanse wijn* was most likely a white wine, according to noted food historian Nozawa Joji, who also notes the seeming paradox of the sheer quantity of Spanish wine in Dutch possession in the early seventeenth century given the fact that the Spanish and Dutch were locked in a bitter war for independence that was not resolved until 1648.[24] This is undoubtedly a reflection of the fact that Spanish merchants desperately needed Dutch shipping, especially in the lucrative trade with the Baltic countries, a trade that saw large amounts of grain shipped to Spain in exchange for luxury goods such as wine and olives.

The Dutch brought a lot of wine to Japan. Nozawa calculates that between 2,000 and 3,000 liters of wine were brought to Deshima every year from the 1640s to the end of the seventeenth century.[25] At any given time, there were about a dozen Europeans on Deshima, and so even if each member of the party were able to drink a prodigious amount of wine, which was undoubtedly true for many of the Company's servants, that still leaves hundreds of liters of wine for use as gifts in one form or another, or for sales. Nozawa points out that wine was routinely sold to Japanese officials, especially in the second half of the seventeenth century, and that the amount used as official gifts declined at the same time,[26] but it is still the case that as much as several dozens of liters of wine were given away as gifts, some in the formal gifts to the Shogun, but most to local officials in Nagasaki and Edo.

The importance of wine as a gift to Japanese officialdom can be seen in the fact that year in and year out, for hundreds of years, the chief merchants continue to note how much wine was brought, how much of it was sold, how much was used for gifts, and the rituals involved in presenting the gifts. Upon arrival of the year's trading vessels in the autumn, the barrels of wine were removed from the holds and placed in the storage rooms on Deshima. Subsequently, as the small party of Dutchmen were preparing for that year's court journey, the Dutch would remove the barrels and begin to put it into bottles to be parceled out as gifts. It was not uncommon for chief merchants to note how much volume was lost to the removal of sediment, although one wonders just how meticulous the chief merchants were in this regard, or how liberal their definition of "sediment" was! The wine for the more august personages such as the Shogun were often gorgeously and painstakingly packed in decorative bottles and then in cases, while the wine used for Company purposes (and as spontaneous gifts) were simply packed into the crates that were carried to Edo by hired Japanese porters. In April of 1750, in what is a typical notation, we learn that two bottles of Spanish wine, two bottles of tent wine, and four goblets were all packed in a decorative case after the bottles of wine had been "stamped," presumably with the contents and perhaps the date.[27] This ritual was intended for the Nagasaki *bugyō*, who had the duty (and presumably the pleasure) of performing this yearly ritual of tasting the year's shipment of wine. He sent a servant to fetch the bottles, usually equal amounts of Spanish and tent wine, along with Dutch drinking glasses, and then sampled the wares to make sure that they were of suitable quality for the Shogun and his officials in Edo.[28] Once this yearly ritual was complete, the wine was ready for shipment along with the other gifts bound for Edo. Nozawa Joji relates that when high-ranking personages came for wine at Deshima or the Dutch inn in Edo, the servants who fetched the wine insisted on a poison test wherein the Company official who poured out the wine was made to taste it in front of the servant before the transaction could be finalized and the wine sent to the daimyo.[29] Most likely this ritual with the *bugyō* had an element of political calculation to it, but the Dutch often relate in their diaries that the purpose was to ensure that the quality was high enough for the Shogun. Perhaps both things can be true.

The sheer quantity of wine given away both in Nagasaki and in Edo was remarkable. For virtually every year for hundreds of years we read of the Nagasaki *bugyō* or another shogunal official in Edo requesting through a servant a portion of wine, and in a few cases the quantities requested were quite high. This is all the more interesting in light of the fact that, as we've seen earlier, wine was expressly forbidden in an ordinance that was recorded in the Dutch diaries for August 1, 1641. It seems that visitors to the Dutch lodgings were not necessarily restricted by this as we read on August of 1641, just one week after the prohibitions, the Japanese landlords were sharing a drink of wine with the Dutch.[30] Similarly, on October 24, many of the notables in Nagasaki came to the Dutch lodgings on Deshima to bid farewell to the outgoing chief merchant. Not only were these officials treated to wine, but we are told that they asked all manner of questions about the wine in addition to other Dutch foodstuffs, including butter and cheese.[31] Official gifts of wine seemed to have been off limits, however. We are told that in 1644, the Nagasaki *bugyō* was offered a fairly large gift of tent wine on two occasions, and on both occasions he was obliged to refuse.[32] Within a few years this prohibition no longer seems to have been enforced, for we read in January of 1650 that Inoue Masashige, the official specifically assigned to keep eyes on the Dutch and to stamp out Christianity, asked the Dutch to reserve some wine as a gift for a couple of officials.[33] Thereafter, the use of wine as at least semiofficial gifts resumed. In the end, however, the attraction of Spanish wine seemed too much for Japanese officialdom.

Although wine was ubiquitous as a gift for Japanese officialdom, other alcoholic beverages were given as well. In February of 1643, for example, the chief merchant relates that the Company gave two barrels of "good sake" each to two local city officials along with a food gift of *sakana*, which was a dish that was meant to be eaten specifically with *sake* and could consist of a number of small treats, including vegetables, fish, and even sweets.[34] Gifts of sake were not as common as gifts of European wine, but they were given nonetheless with some regularity, especially to more minor Japanese officials. On the same day, the *bugyō* was also given a gift of alcohol, but apparently a person of his rank warranted tent wine rather than the more familiar sake. Sake was a particularly interesting gift in that it was one of the few gifts that served as a routine gift both to the Dutch and to the Japanese. One suspects that much as a fifteen-dollar bottle of wine today, a barrel of sake or two served as a token gift to be given on mundane occasions, a gift of which everyone knew the worldly and symbolic value.

Other types of European alcohol were often given to Japanese officials, although not so much as formal gifts, but certainly at times when the Dutch were entertaining on Deshima. We read of a drink known as "arrack" being given in small samples to Japanese officials upon request or being served to them when they came to visit. Arrack is a liquor that was distilled from sugar cane, most likely grown on Java, and hence is a close relative of rum. It is different from rum because fermented rice is added to the mixture, probably a practice that was learned from Chinese methods of production.[35] Hubert Paul relates an interesting scene from an account of life on Deshima from a Dutch sailor named C. T. van Assendelft de Coningh in which he describes the arrival of Dutch ships and the army of officials who swarmed on board performing the requisite inspections. de Coningh observes that as soon as the official inspections were done, "the police chiefs ('opperbanjoosten') and their assistants headed straight for the captain's cabin, where they knew from experience that wine, liquor and European pastry were awaiting them. This too was standard operating procedure."[36] Given the fact that rituals such as the inspection of incoming ships rarely changed over the decades, one can imagine that a similar situation would have held in the seventeenth and eighteenth centuries as well.

Phillip Franz von Siebold also relates an interesting, if not amusing, scene in which liquor was served to Japanese "guests." Siebold writes that it was not uncommon for the Dutch to bring several prostitutes to Deshima at a time and notes with wry humor that "our stock of confectionary and liqueurs suffered prodigious reductions." He also relates that on such occasions, the prostitutes often rifled through the Dutchmen's belongings and it was more or less obligatory to present them with various articles by way of gifts.[37]

There are many other instances of liquors being shared with the Japanese, but none so regular as wine. We read of several Japanese officials on Deshima being treated to absinthe and Dutch tobacco, after which they left "in a very good mood."[38] We also hear of anisette, brandy, genever, and later, beer.

While the bulk of this chapter has been concerned with gifts that the Dutch routinely presented to various and sundry Japanese, it was also common for Japanese officialdom to provide the Dutch with food and drink, either as a reciprocal gift, a courtesy gift after having been entertained, or as a gift on special occasions, such as upon arrival or departure from Edo on the yearly court journey. It is invariably the case over the course of hundreds of years that when a Japanese official was entertained on Deshima or at the *Nagasaki-ya* in Edo, they sent a return gift by way of thanks. The same is true of Japanese officials who received gifts—no matter how insignificant the gift, the Dutch usually record a reciprocal, token gift delivered through a servant. On these occasions, one of the most common gifts was of food and drink. While not valuable in a financial sense, one can imagine this might have been valuable in the sense that it would have varied the Dutch diet, and it was eminently practical because it could be used even in confinement on Deshima. Of all the food gifts recorded, the most common were various types of birds, fish, and *sake*. Birds were considered a delicacy in Japan, and so the gift, for example, of a crane was quite a prestigious gift. Eric Rath notes that crane was often on the menu when the guest at a banquet was a daimyo, or even an imperial family member.[39] Crane was at times prohibited from being eaten by commoners and was occasionally the target of sumptuary laws, laws like those against wearing silk or living lavishly, that were generally honored, shall we say, in the breach. Other birds offered the Dutch included swan and duck, and these would have been given over to the cook employed on Deshima to prepare for the evening meal.

Another gift given the Dutch was that of fish, most commonly carp. Carp was a common delicacy in Japan and one that was considered auspicious, a fact that can still be observed today in the carp-shaped pennants and kites that are a mainstay of Japanese festivals. Rath notes that carp were especially suited to the ceremonial art of cutting fish and fowl, especially in front of notable dignitaries, but in this case, the carp given the Dutch was certainly meant as a foodstuff for consumption, and the fact that the carp was an auspicious symbol simply heightened the value as a gift. Gifts of fish, which were common among the Japanese aristocracy, was usually accompanied by a gift of wine, and in the case of the Dutch, it was usually the case that the fish was accompanied by rice wine.[40]

Other routine gifts of food to the Dutch were stone bass and boxes of eggs, which came to be a common gift when the Dutch arrived in Edo in the later seventeenth century. Stone bass is what the Japanese call *madai*, which translates into English as "sea bream," still a prized fish in Japanese cuisine today. In fact, these two foodstuffs seem to have become a staple gift to the Dutch as from the seventeenth century we read of the same delicacies year after year. Other foodstuff given as gifts include salmon, both salted and fresh, dried cuttlefish, and so on. While these presents were never very large at any given time, they surely must have served to liven up the Dutch table both in Nagasaki and Edo.

It was often the case that the Dutch were obliged to host the myriad Japanese officials and sometimes their guests on the island of Deshima. On such occasions, it was mandatory that the visiting dignitaries be treated to at least an obligatory round of "sweetmeats" and Japanese pastries, although there were often other treats on offer, such as Japanese fruits. Occasionally, alcohol was served on these visits, but not always. It is not clear if the guests actually ate the sweetmeats on offer, but they were invariably offered. Japanese candies of the time were made more with an eye toward a visual aesthetic rather than the taste, and so it was often the custom to serve these delicacies without the expectation that they would actually be consumed.[41] Occasionally guests would partake of the delicacies, only to hide the sweetmeats in the sleeves of their clothing so as to preserve social niceties.[42] The fruits and alcohol offered, however, were certainly consumed and must have been particularly refreshing on the hot and humid summer days that characterize coastal Kyushu.

One of the more routine offerings both for Dutch visits to officials' residences or Japanese visits to Deshima was what is commonly referred to in the diaries as "wine and *sakana*." This is referred to so many times it's clear that they served as the equivalent of wine and cheese for today's guests. It's not clear from the sources what type of wine was offered, and it may have varied depending on the venue and hosts, but a number of clues suggest that it was probably *sake*, Japanese rice wine. *Sakana* is a word that refers to any number of "snacks" that are served with alcohol. Eric Rath likens *sakana* to the "hors d'oeuvres" that are served with drinks before a main meal. In the case of the Dutch, however, wine and *sakana* were usually served by themselves, not as an appetizer before a larger meal but as a stand-alone treat at times of visits.[43]

While many occasions of entertaining were one-on-one gatherings or small groups that came to visit, other occasions were more formal dinners hosted by the Dutch. One occasion on which the Dutch hosted upward of thirty Japanese officials was the annual New Year banquet. On this holiday, the chief merchant invited all of the officials that played a day-to-day role in facilitating Dutch trade in Japan, including the interpreters (*tsūji*), the minor local officials in Nagasaki (*Otona*), the inspectors (*metsuke*), and the mayors of the city (*machidoshiyori*). Nozawa Joji tells us that from the 1760s onward, the shogunal accountants, men of great influence, joined the dinner party as well.[44] The Dutch do not elaborate in the diaries much about what was served or any of the particulars of the evening, but the chief merchant sometimes includes an epitaph that states the guests went home very satisfied, by which we can assume he meant, among other things, full of drink.

A description of the New Years' banquet is provided by J. F. Van Overmeer Fischer for the year 1813 in which he notes that there was a great variety of dishes, both Western and Japanese, and mainly genever (a drink akin to gin), beer, and arrack to drink. Overmeer writes that the Japanese guests usually took all of the leftovers home with them so that they could share out Western delicacies such as Western-style meat and butter with their friends and family.[45] This is in accordance with what the Dutch report about other types of gifts as well: that the Japanese often ask for gifts from the Dutch partly in order to turn around and "re-gift" to other people, an understandable practice in a society in which gift-giving was all important.[46] On February 4, 1647, the Nagasaki *bugyō* asked the Dutch for a half a cheese and four catties of butter, which the Dutch handed over. In their diary the chief merchant wrote that this foodstuff was almost certainly destined for Edo where it would be used for gifts to other Japanese officials.[47] In a similar vein, we read in an entry for 1654 that the officials to whom the Dutch give "rarities" try, in turn, to garner favor with higher up officials by presenting them with the goods they had received from the Dutch.[48]

Another occasion to share a meal on Deshima presented itself in October when the cargo was all loaded on the ships and the sales were finished for the season. The interpreters arranged a banquet for the Dutch and the minor Japanese officials to which both the Japanese and the Dutch contributed food. De Coningh comments wryly on these gathering by saying that the politically savvy Dutch consciously contributed less than needed to the gathering, knowing they would have to provide more food and drink later in the evening, and by so doing, giving the impression to the Japanese of great largesse and generosity![49]

There seems to have been a fair amount of interest in the manner in which the Dutch ate formal meals as well as in the types of food the Dutch ate. On a few occasions shogunal officials in Edo, during the court journey, asked the Dutch to demonstrate how they dined by preparing a Dutch style meal and then actually sitting down to eat it, all while the Japanese watched. There are a few woodblock prints that demonstrate how the Dutch ate, and, as Marc Gilbert states, these prints were almost always embellished to present the Dutch in exotic if not sometimes grotesque form.[50]

An interesting glimpse of what type of food the Dutch ate on the island can be gained from a memorandum to the junior merchant and steward from the mid-1650s outlining, in somewhat exacting detail, the weekly menu to be served:

> On Sundays: two dishes of fried or braised eel two dishes of fine roast hens or chicken, to wit, in each dish one hen or two chickens; two dishes of two old hens laid in brine; two dishes of braised pork or venison or sausages; two dishes of boiled food of yellow or white lentils or Japanese beans; this makes altogether ten dishes. You should serve this number every day for lunch and dinner, but instead of eel, in the evening, you can serve some other kind of dried or salted fish with a couple of dishes of salad. On Mondays, two dishes of boiled fish; two dishes of roast fish; one dish of small game or a partridge; one dish of salted Dutch or Taiwanese meat or bacon; two dishes of venison or pork stew; two dishes of scrambled, hard-boiled, or peeled eggs. In the evening the same, but because it is not always possible to obtain fresh fish, you can also serve two dishes of salted pike and instead of eggs some crab, shrimp, snails, *awabi*, small oysters, or whatever you can get cheapest.[51]

It should be noted that the given sample menu for two days (he lists a menu for all seven days) is designed to be much cheaper than was usually the case in an effort to cut costs. After listing the menus, he tells the steward: "Instead of fifty to sixty hens which are served every week, you should be able to make do with half the number." This menu was designed that year for eleven people on the island, with a fair amount of leftovers to "properly feed those who come after," meaning of course the servants, often Javanese people who performed all sorts of menial tasks, from cooking and cleaning to playing music. The chief merchant notes that there was a general ban on eating beef from the cattle raised in Nagasaki because "some years ago there was a significant mortality among the cattle here" and that this "has stupidly been attributed to the Dutch alone." Sale of beef was banned on pain of death, and so the Dutch had to make due with fowl and fish and the occasional piece of venison. When this rule was relaxed is not entirely clear. If the above description is of a lean diet, one can imagine the amount of food that would have been served in times of plenty when cost was of no consequence! In addition to the food served, we know from research by Nozawa Joji that the Dutch consumed prodigious amounts of wine with their dinner as evidenced by the number of barrels that were offloaded from the ships when they arrived in the autumn.[52]

Although we may not think of entertainment as a gift in the same way as we do a physical object such as a timepiece or a fine piece of cloth, the Dutch surely thought of the effort and time spent entertaining a whole range of guests as such. The summer of 1652 affords us an opportunity to examine the type of entertaining the Dutch routinely provided on the island. In July, we read of an influential daimyo visiting in order to tour Deshima. The chief merchant writes that the Dutch made it a practice to stock quantities of "sakana and pastries" for important people such as this. He also relates that the daimyo and his considerable retinue was given a tour of the Dutch gardens, as well as allowed to observe the Dutch playing billiards and backgammon.[53] They stayed two hours and left with many expressions of gratitude. Three days later, the Nagasaki *bugyō* came to the island and requested to observe the Dutch singing, playing instruments, and playing billiards. He was treated to almonds and tent wine and left, again, with expressions of gratitude.[54] A couple months later, we read that another influential daimyo's son had come from Edo in order to see the Dutch ships. Accordingly, the ships fired their canons in his honor and the next day he came aboard one of the ships and then was entertained on the island with treats and tent wine. The very next day, the same daimyo's half-brother also visited, toured the factory, and was also treated to wine and *sakana*.[55] The Dutch were visited by so many people that the chief merchant occasionally lashed out in the diaries. On February 8, 1654, for example, he writes, after several sons of daimyos and their entourage were entertained "in this semi-prison, we are being looked at by both large and small, just like strange animals at the fair in our fatherland. It is nonetheless considered a great honor and these heathens undoubtedly satisfy their curiosity."[56] Just a week later, four Dutchmen were invited to Inoue Masashige's house and were entertained with food and drink, but that the real reason they were invited was so that the assembled worthies could gawk at them. A month after that, the chief merchant writes scathingly in his journal that elephants or other fantastical beasts would pale in comparison to the strange Dutchmen and their exotic clothes at the Shogun's court. All of these complaints were from Chief Merchant Happart, who wrote on the latter occasion that the audience with the Shogun was a kind of torture.[57] Here we get a glimpse of the individuality that sometimes shows through in the diaries; on this occasion we notice that the chief merchant complains bitterly about being a spectacle in Japan, as well as the many visits he has to endure on Deshima from a whole host of Japanese, whereas for other chief merchants, one rather gets the impression that they enjoyed the socializing.

While it is certainly true that food and drink are the things of everyday life, they are also the things of day-to-day gifts, much as in our own time we deem it appropriate to give little gifts of wine or beer, chocolates, and cheese on somewhat mundane occasions. This is partly because we know the value of a bottle of wine or a box of chocolates, and, when it's our turn to visit or offer congratulations or condolences, we can easily reciprocate. These also make good gifts because they are ubiquitous and there's little chance of offense or missing the mark with chocolate, say, on Valentine's Day, or with a bottle of wine when arriving at a dinner party. In a sense, gift-giving on Valentine's Day has become a secular version of Pascal's wager: we may not believe in giving gifts on the day, and we may not be shy about expressing our crass cynicism about the commercial nature of the Valentine's industry, but we lose nothing by ponying up for a couple roses and some chocolates (save for a few dollars). On the other hand, woe betide the unfortunate sop who sticks to his principles and comes home with no gift when one is desired or expected. Better to be the poorer by a few bucks rather than be left alone and shunned, a miserable wretch, a byword among men. Gifts of food and drink are also eminently utile in the sense that they not only serve as symbolic markers but also provide real sustenance and enjoyment. And finally, these make particularly fine gifts because food and drink mediate myriad social interactions, whether it be at a formal dinner, a reception after a joyous occasion, or a repast after a somber funeral. Many of the most sacred and solemn, as well as the most celebratory, occasions in life are mediated by food and drink. Food and drink are social lubricants that facilitate day-to-day interactions with other people, and this is the more so when the daily interactions can be tense or when the interactions occur at the intersection of two different cultures. Near daily gifts of food and drink served to maintain a good working relationship with the myriad Japanese officials with whom the Dutch had to work and alongside whom they had to live.

Epilogue:
Gifts and the Coming of the Americans

This book has been concerned primarily with the Dutch East India Company's gift-giving activity in Japan throughout the early modern period, but we should turn, however briefly, to the nineteenth century when other Western countries focused their attention to opening trade relations with Japan in earnest. We will examine three separate attempts to establish trade with Japan, in particular, three attempts by Americans, the last of which was ultimately successful with Commodore Perry's expedition on 1853–54. The reason why these voyages serve as a fitting epilogue to this book is that in all cases, the expeditions included lavish gifts for the Shogun, thus replicating the Dutch practice of the previous two and a half centuries, and indeed, in all three voyages, there is evidence that the Americans used the Dutch experience in Japan to shape their own strategies in approaching their missions.[1]

The first voyage was perhaps the strangest. Because the Dutch were allied to the French (Napoleon had invaded the Republic and installed his brother, Louis Bonaparte, on the throne), the English, in their war against the French, engaged in a comprehensive and effective privateering campaign against Dutch ships. This extended to Dutch ships in Asia, and so from the last years of the eighteenth century to 1807, the Dutch in Batavia were compelled to find an alternative solution to trade with Japan, and they hit upon chartering American ships, captained by American ship captains, to conduct the trade with Deshima.[2] These ships would fly the American flag in open waters so as to avoid capture by British privateers, and just when the ship was about to enter Nagasaki harbor, they would run up the Dutch flag so as to not run afoul of the shogunal authorities.[3]

The first American ship so chartered was the *Eliza* and was captained by an American by the name of William Robert Stewart.[4] Stewart was from New York, and so he felt at home among the Dutch in Batavia, and it seems he even spoke tolerable Dutch. He was instructed on how to behave in Japan and was sent on his way. The Japanese knew that something was up, but allowed the ship to land, conduct trade, and then depart in peace. This mission having been a success,

Stewart was again chartered in the *Eliza* for a second journey to Japan in 1798.[5] This journey was anything but successful, for after a comedy of errors involving serious misjudgments by Stewart, the *Eliza* finally left Deshima but never made it back to Batavia. The authorities assumed the ship had been lost and continued to charter other American ships. Thus the American ship *Massachusetts* was surprised to find another Western ship at Nagasaki when it arrived. It seems that the *Eliza* was probably sold off somewhere and now Stewart was trying to make a buck using his knowledge of the Japan trade. The scheming Stewart was sent back to Batavia to stand trial, but during the investigation, seems to have escaped his captors and fled to Java.

The strangest episode occurred in 1803 when Japanese officials in Nagasaki were surprised by a ship with the American flag sailing into Nagasaki harbor with the name *Nagasaki Maru*.[6] The captain of this ship was, of course, our hero William Robert Stewart. Stewart claimed that he was acting on behalf of the American government and came to establish trade at Nagasaki with the Japanese.[7] Because Stewart had long experience with how the Dutch conducted their business in Japan, he knew that it was a requirement that the Shogun be given gifts every year. Thus, Stewart brought with him on his journey a camel, a water buffalo, and a pair of donkeys for the Shogun's amusement. The authorities in Nagasaki took this request seriously, over Dutch protests, but within a relatively short period of time, decided to reject Stewart's proposal and so he was forced to leave Nagasaki empty-handed.

The Americans aboard these several chartered ships had direct experience of the gifts that were brought to Japan for the Shogun and his officials. William Cleveland includes a relatively detailed description of the gifts brought on the *Massachusetts*, gifts that were of a piece with the variety of gifts we've described in previous chapters. Included were a timepiece, a silver-gilt vase, a telescope, a barrel organ, glasswork, mirrors, and, interestingly, an orangutan.[8] The Americans also had months in which to observe how the Dutch plied Japanese officials with food and drink, and how this largesse was received. William Cleveland, though only a captain's clerk, and only in Japan for a single trading season, was a remarkably observant person whose diary contained quite detailed accounts of interactions with Japanese officialdom. Given the number of Americans who arrived in Japan over these ten years, and given the voyages they shared with Dutch officials going back and forth between Nagasaki and Deshima, it is not surprising that the Americans were well prepared when making preparations for their own voyages to Japan.

The next American voyage never actually reached the islands, but is instructive for our purposes because it affords us a glimpse of the American's early strategy in attempting to open trade.⁹ In 1834, the American ship *Peacock* was charged with concluding diplomatic treaties with the Kingdom of Siam and with Cochin-China, both of which Edmund Roberts, an envoy appointed by President Andrew Jackson, had successfully negotiated on a previous mission and both of which he was returning to with signed treaties from the United States. Attached to the tail end of this mission was a plan to sail to Japan in an attempt to open Japanese trade to the Americans. Already we see the Americans developing a strategy for how to approach the kingdom; the Secretary of State, in a letter to Roberts, advised the diplomat to land at Owari, a port further north on the main island of Japan, so that the Dutch could not interfere with American negotiations.

Many letters went back and forth between Roberts and the Department of State about the proposed mission to Japan, and the most interesting aspect of the letters was the subject of presents for the Shogun. Just like Stewart, Roberts understood that it was imperative to take presents that would impress the Shogun, and yet Washington seems to have been ambivalent about sending gifts to Asian potentates because they thought them too much akin to bribery and, at this early date in the Republic's history were worried about precedent. In the end, Roberts, aware of the Dutch practice, was allowed $2,500 for gifts with which to overawe the Shogun with American power and splendor that would truly set the Americans apart: sheep. And not just any sheep, but Merino sheep. Indeed, one can surmise reading these letters that the future of American-Japanese relations could depend on ten Merino sheep.

According to Andrew Jampoler, officials at the Department of State apparently believed that at some point in the past, the Shogun was extremely interested in obtaining from the Dutch specimens of sheep from which woolen cloth could be made.¹⁰ This would certainly not be too far-fetched, as we've seen several times that Japanese officials often requested what must have seemed like bizarre items, including large animals. The Dutch were apparently not able to fulfill this request, though, because the wool of Dutch sheep was not suitable for wool cloth. And here is where the Secretary of State sensed an opportunity: he reasoned that if the Americans could somehow get the sheep to Japan, the Shogun would be so full of gratitude that he would allow a commercial arrangement to be signed. So preparations to take ten Merino sheep aboard the *Peacock* proceeded, the secretary figuring that if the sheep didn't make it, well, at least the sailors would have a goodly supply of meat. As Jampoler puts it, "Either the [shogun] got the nucleus of a new Japanese fiber and fabric industry in exchange for American access to the home islands, or *Peacock's* people got mutton chops."¹¹ In the end, it proved too difficult to make the voyage work, for sheep are apparently quite delicate creatures that did not take to early modern sea travel all that well. It also turned out that Roberts would die before getting a chance to sail for Japan, and the whole scheme was called off in order for the *Peacock* to sail home with the two signed copies of America's commercial treaties with Siam and Cochin-China. And, perhaps most tragically, the crew of the *Peacock* was forced to forego their lamb chops.

The great sheep debate of the 1830s demonstrates that the Americans were well aware of the use of gifts in procuring the Shogun's favor. The scheming of Roberts also foreshadows Commodore Matthew Perry's attempt twenty years later to open trade with Japan: his fleet would also land not at Nagasaki, but further north in Edo Bay, and, as we will see further, a variety of gifts were brought for the Shogun, carefully selected for their demonstration of American ingenuity.

On July 8, 1853, a squadron of American ships entered Edo Bay in order to ascertain whether the Japanese would agree to open their country to American vessels seeking to obtain coal and provisions, as well as safety for shipwrecked whaling crews.[12] The overall commander of the expedition, Commodore Matthew Calbraith Perry, had prepared himself for this moment with academic precision. He read as many books about Japan as he could, he consulted widely, including with Phillip Franz von Siebold, and he even had his letters to the Shogun translated into Dutch in Shanghai so that the Japanese interpreters would be able to accurately read them and translate them into Japanese. Perry was also prepared to mount a show of force if the Japanese proved reticent about opening relations with the United States, something his predecessors had been loath to do. After several rounds of negotiation, Perry's party was allowed to come ashore and formally hand a letter for the Shogun to two trusted retainers. Perry then departed, promising to return in a year's time.

When Perry again returned on February 13, 1854, he had with him a much larger fleet (ten ships) and well as over a thousand men. After several weeks of negotiations, the Japanese acceded to Perry's demands, and the Treaty of Kanagawa was signed, which opened three ports to American ships for re-provisioning, allowed a consul-general to take up residence, and agreed to provide safety for shipwrecked American sailors.

One of the most iconic images of the Perry expedition was of the various presents carefully selected for the Japanese and presented just before the signing of the treaty. These presents included a one-quarter scale steam engine with coal tender (accounts tell of Japanese officials delightedly riding on top of the train as it circled its track), a telegraph machine with a few miles of wire, agricultural machinery, and several other gifts, including whiskey and firearms, perhaps emblematic of the American wild west! We know that these gifts were carefully chosen, as was the very manner in which Perry chose to engage the Japanese. Perry chose presents for the Japanese with great care, aware that the gifts symbolically represented the United States, for as Steven Lubar also points out, gifts, by their very nature as objects in time and space, make up a "material culture of representation."[13] So, what can we make of Perry's gifts in light of the long history of Dutch gift-giving in Japan?

The main officers of the Perry expedition were well aware of the Dutch experience in Japan as evidenced by the "literature review" provided in S. Wells Williams' narrative of the expedition in which he references Engelbert Kaempfer, J. H. Levyssohn, and Hendrik Doeff.[14] Francis Hawkes, the official chronicler of the Perry Expedition, was familiar with the writings of Phillip Franz von Siebold, Carl Thunberg, and others.[15] And finally, the ten years between 1797 and 1807 provided American ship captains with firsthand experience of Dutch trade at Deshima as their ships were hired to carry out this trade during the Napoleonic Wars. And finally, Lawrence Battistini and Nitobe Inazo point out that in preparation for the expedition, the United States purchased several navigational charts from the Dutch as well as "a wide assortment of books on Japan," including the entirety of von Siebold's archive for the price of $503.00, a large sum in mid-nineteenth century.[16]

In one intriguing passage from Francis Hawkes' *Narrative*, Hawkes recounts a letter that Philipp Franz von Siebold sent to a member of Perry's squadron before its departure in which he gave a great deal of advice on how to deal with the Japanese. Included in the rather long list of advice is the attitude that Perry should adopt: he should come in peace, but use veiled hints of aggression. von Siebold predicted that the Japanese would use every tactic to stall the negotiations in the hope that Perry would simply lose patience and leave; and finally, von Siebold tells Perry to present his petition and then give the Japanese a year to ponder it before demanding an answer. While Hawkes ridicules Siebold, telling the world that the Perry expedition had nothing to do with his advice, and even confirming current rumors that Siebold might have been a Russian spy, in point of fact, the negotiations went exactly as predicted, and Perry seems on the surface to have heeded this advice. The Japanese did try to stall, ad nauseum it seems, for weeks over minor issues of where to anchor the ships, where to erect the buildings for negotiations, who would accept the letter, and so forth. And in fact, Perry did come in peace, but also at several points hinted at his willingness to use force if matters came to a head. And finally, Perry did give the Japanese a year to think about it, although in the event he returned many months sooner than that in order to head off possible Russian negotiations with Japan.

I am struck, reading the various accounts of the Perry expedition, of the similarity between Dutch gift-giving traditions and the American gifts. The most striking similarity is the giving of wine and liquor, and the frequent wining and dining in both formal and informal capacity. The Americans gave the Japanese a barrel of whiskey, a box of champagne, a cherry liqueur, and madeira as formal gifts. On other occasions, the narrators of the expedition make it clear that the Japanese loved American spirits and partook heartily of wine, whiskey, and liqueur.[17] Oliver Statler states that "when entertaining the Japanese, the Commodore was liberal with the ships' store of liquors."[18] The same is true of the Dutch on Deshima. Every year the Dutch brought Spanish wine to Japan, as well as various liqueurs. We read every year of the Nagasaki *bugyō* tasting the wine to see if the quality was good enough for the Shogun, as well as the several requests for wine and other goodies that invariably arrived either on Deshima or in Edo. The Dutch also plied their frequent guests with liberal quantities of wine and Western foods. It probably is a truism that alcohol, then as now, serves as a social lubricant, especially in potentially tense situations where bonds have to be formed relatively quickly.

Another similarity in gift-giving was in the giving of weapons. The Japanese samurai class was, at least in theory, a warrior class, and so it was to be expected that leading officials would be interested in Western weapons. This was certainly true in the seventeenth century, and it remained true in the nineteenth. Dutch merchants would provide the first several Shogun with mortars, grenades, ordnance, personal firearms, and weapons of great artistry.[19] These were always received with great interest, especially in the 1630s and 1640s. Similarly, the Perry expedition gave the Japanese personal firearms, as well as a parting gift of a howitzer cannon from one of Perry's ships.[20]

Another conspicuous similarity in gifts was the mechanical devices that were so popular in the seventeenth through nineteenth centuries at Deshima and the several technological gifts that the Perry expedition brought to Japan. The telegraph and the railroad get the most attention, of course, but Perry also gave clocks, telescopes, stoves, and agricultural implements. The Dutch, while not bringing a railroad, did provide the Japanese with all manner of technological marvels, or "curiosos," as they called them, including navigational equipment, telescopes, viewing boxes, microscopes, clocks, and the like. The journals of the various members of the Perry expedition comment repeatedly on how interested the Japanese were in American technology, from the steam engines on board the two steamships to the telegraph and railroad. Almost exactly the same scene can be found in many of the Dutch diaries as a steady stream of Japanese visitors come to Deshima to be amazed at the Dutch style of life, including the material culture they brought with them.

The Dutch also imported a fair number of books for Japanese scholars to pore over and to translate, especially books on the sciences. It's interesting that the Perry expedition, too, gave the Japanese a large number of books, although these books must have been dense reading at best, especially the riveting *Annals of Congress* and the *Journal of the Senate and Assembly of New York*. The Dutch provided the Japanese with globes and maps, and the Perry expedition, too, brought maps for the Japanese and had a globe on board that they showed the Japanese during the negotiations. In fact, the Americans were impressed that the Japanese immediately knew about Washington, DC, New York City, and the countries of Europe. This was, of course, because of the yearly reports of the Dutch at Deshima as well as the steady stream of books and maps that the Dutch gave the Shogun and his officials.

Needless to say, we could go on in this manner for some time, but just as Martha Chaiklin has shown that the Dutch liberalist tradition was formative in preparing the Japanese to accept an eventual opening of the country to foreign trade, so we can see that the Dutch had an impact, either directly or indirectly, on the actual American attempt to open Japan.[21] Perry's officials were familiar with Dutch writings and experience: Hawkes, for example, states that "limited, however, as have been their sources of information, it is to the Dutch chiefly that the world, until within a very recent period, has been indebted for the knowledge it has had of the Japanese."[22] We know that the Dutch informed the Japanese of Perry's impending visit many months before it happened, but we also know that the Americans were aware of Dutch practices on Deshima. The evidence is too strong. The Americans knew, for example, of the Japanese proclivities for Western food and drink; they knew of Japanese fascination with Western technology, and they knew of the rigid social protocol surrounding diplomatic endeavors in Tokugawa Japan. Just seven years before the Perry expedition, Chaiklin points out that a Dutch ship arrived in Japan with gifts for the Shogun that included "products of industry, art, and science that blossomed under our protection in the Netherlands."[23] In total, the Dutch ship contained seventeen chests of presents, including pistols, a carbine, books, maps, field artillery, and perhaps most importantly, a copy of the recent Treaty of Nanjing. This knowledge helped Perry tailor his expedition to Japanese sensibilities. For example, Perry insisted on a rigid formality when presenting the letter from President Filmore and when signing the Treaty of Kanagawa, but he was also able to break the atmosphere with entertainment from the minstrel troupe he brought with him as well as the fleet's band.[24] And finally, he was able to tailor his gifts to the Japanese so as to strike just the right note of wonder, practical curiosity, and fun.

In all three of these cases, Americans coming to Japan had knowledge of Dutch practices of diplomacy: Stewart through his time in Batavia and in his role as captain of a ship chartered by the Dutch; Roberts through his contacts in the US State Department who had received intelligence about the Dutch trade on Deshima through American sailors such as William Cleveland;[25] and finally, Perry through consultations with von Siebold and others, not to mention the exhaustive research Perry and his officials undertook before leaving the United States. In all three cases the Americans came to Japan bearing exotic, if not somewhat strange, gifts for the Shogun and his officials. While the first two attempts to convince the Japanese to open trade were not successful (and the second never even arrived), Perry's mission was famously successful. While there are many reasons why this might be the case, including changing political and military situations in Japan and in the wider world, there can be no doubt that the American approach was of importance as well. Perry followed a recipe that had been successful for close to two hundred and fifty years for the Dutch: he wined and dined his Japanese hosts with several kinds of Western alcohol and food, he entertained the Japanese with exotic displays of performing arts, and he presented the Japanese with exotic gifts. Such was, apparently, the cost of doing business in Japan, both in the seventeenth and in the nineteenth century.

Notes

Preface

1. Guido Carlo Pugliasco, "Lost in Translation: From Omiyage to Souvenir: Beyond Aesthetics of the Japanese Office Ladies' Gaze in Hawai'i," *Journal of Material Culture* 10, no. 2 (2005): 177–96.
2. Yamamoto Yoshito and Terrence Witkowski, "Omiyage Gift Purchasing by Japanese Travelers in the US," *Advances in Consumer Research* 18 (1991): 123–28.
3. VOC stands for *Verenigde Oost-Indische Compagnie*, chartered in 1602 and dissolved in 1799 with the crisis surrounding the Napoleonic Wars. Hereafter we will refer to what is sometimes called the world's first multinational joint stock company as the VOC, or simply "the Company."
4. Claudia Swan, "Dutch Diplomacy and Trade in *Rariteyten*: Episodes in the History of Material Culture in the Dutch Republic," in *Global Gifts: The Material Culture of Diplomacy in Early Modern Eurasia*, ed. Zoltann Biedermann, Anne Gerritsen and Giorgio Riello (Cambridge: Cambridge University Press, 2018), 184–85.
5. Markus Vink, *Encounters on the Opposite Coast: The Dutch East India Company and the Nayaka State of Madurai in the Seventeenth Century* (Leiden: Brill, 2016), 37–38.
6. Bhawan Ruangsilp, *Dutch East India Company Merchants at the Court of Ayutthaya: Dutch Perceptions of the Thai Kingdom, c. 1604–1765* (Leiden: Brill, 2007).
7. John Wills, *Embassies and Illusions: Dutch and Portuguese Envoys to K'ang Hsi* (Cambridge: Harvard University Asia Center, 1984), 30. See also Jurrien van Goor, *Prelude to Colonialism: The Dutch in Asia* (Hilversum: Verloren, 2004), 42–43.
8. Het Archief van de Nederlandse Factorij in Japan, 1609–1860, 63 (hereafter NFJ): March 20, 1650. The contents of this extensive archive located at the National Archives in the Netherlands have been catalogued by M. P. H. Roessingh, *Het Archief van de Nederlandse Factorij in Japan, 1609–1860* ('s-Gravenhage: Algemeen Rijksarchief, 1964). The diaries for much of the seventeenth century have been partially translated into English by Leonard Blussé and Cynthia Viallé, a source of incalculable aid and comfort to me. See Leonard Blussé and Cynthia Viallé, eds., *The Deshima Dagregisters, Volumes XI–XIII* (Leiden, The Netherlands: Institute for the History of European Expansion, 2001–2010).
9. Gifts play an enormous role in Japanese business culture. Virtually any tutorial on business practices in Japan will include a relatively detailed section on how to select and present a gift, with most of the sites emphasizing that the social obligations

and mores surrounding the gift itself are much more important than the actual gift item itself. Here is just one example, found in an article linked to the popular professional networking site LinkedIn, "Corporate Gift Giving in the Japanese Culture," accessed March 16, 2019, https://www.linkedin.com/pulse/corporate-gift-giving-japanese-culture-nell-king. Although this is but a single example, one can easily find dozens of similar sites offering almost identical information.

10 Donald Keene states emphatically that by the eighteenth century, the sole reason to continue the dwindling trade with Japan was the semiofficial corruption that chief merchants and their higher-ranking colleagues engaged in. Donald Keene, *The Japanese Discovery of Europe, 1720–1830* (Stanford: Stanford University Press, 1969), 6. A fascinating, fictionalized account of such institutionalized corruption can be found in the wonderful historical novel, David Mitchell, *The Thousand Autumns of Jacob de Zoet* (New York: Random House, 2011).

11 For a detailed description of the various officials in Nagasaki, see Itazawa Takeo, *Nihon to Oranda: Kinsei no Gaikō, Bōeki, Gakumon* (Tokyo: Shibundō, 1955), 113–14. In English, see Grant Goodman, *The Dutch Impact on Japan, 1640–1853* (Leiden: Brill, 1967), 20–22. Itazawa writes that the bakufu originally had fully 140 positions devoted to Deshima, although that was later reduced.

Introduction

1 I have chosen to defer to Leonard Blussé and Cynthia Viallé's considerable skill in translation for direct quotes from the diaries kept by the chief merchants on Deshima: Leonard Blussé and Cynthia Viallé, eds., *The Deshima Dagregisters, Volumes XI* (Leiden, The Netherlands: Institute for the History of European Expansion, 2001), 157: July 19, 1654.

2 Ibid., 269: January 11, 1647.

3 An example of the gifts for the Shogun from the late 1630s shows that although a Persian horse was sent for this particular year, the top four types of gifts were of various types of luxury cloth. See Matsui Yoko and Matsukata Fuyuko, eds., *Nihon Kankei Kaigi Shiryō: Dagregisters Gehouden bij de Opperhoofden van het Nederlandsche Factorij in Japan, Volume 3* (Tokyo: Tokyo Daigaku Shiryō Hensanjō, 1975), 148.

4 Marcel Mauss, *The Gift: Forms and Functions of Exchange in Archaic Societies* (London: Cohen and West, 1966). For a critique of Mauss, see Lewis Hyde, *The Gift: Imagination and the Erotic Life of Property* (New York: Random House, 1983).

5 A few of the notable works on various aspects of gift-giving in the early modern world include Martha Chaiklin, ed., *Mediated by Gifts: Politics and Society in Japan, 1350–1850* (Leiden: Brill, 2016); Cynthia Viallé, "In Aid of Trade: Dutch Gift-

Giving in Tokugawa Japan," *Tokyo Daigaku Shiryōhensan-jō Kenkyū Kiyo* 16 (March 2006): 63–64; Cynthia Klekar, "Prisoners in Silken Bonds: Obligation, Trade, and Diplomacy in English Voyages to Japan and China," *Journal of Early Modern Cultural Studies* 6, no.1 (Spring, 2006); Antti Kujala and Mirkka Danielsbacka, *Reciprocity in Human Societies: From Ancient Times to the Modern Welfare State* (London: Palgrave, 2019), Chapter 3: "Moral Obligations in Early Modern Japan"; and for a comparative study, Zoltan Biedermann, Anne Gerritsen, and Giorgio Riello, eds., *Global Gifts: The Material Culture of Diplomacy in Early Modern Eurasia* (Cambridge: Cambridge University Press, 2017).

6 Samuel Purchase, *Hakluytus Posthhumus or Purchase His Pilgrims, Volume 2* (Glasgow: James MacLehose and Sons, 1905), 331–34. This volume contains the original letters and memoirs of William Adams, the English pilot aboard the *Liefde* and the most famous Westerner in Japan in the early modern period, and indeed, perhaps in all of history.

7 The most renowned of these early sailors was Jan Huyghen van Linschoten, a Dutch sailor who wrote a widely read account of his travels with the Portuguese. See Arthur Coke Burnell, ed., *The Voyage of John Huyghen van Linschotten to the East Indies* (London: Hakluyt Society, 1885).

8 There are many works detailing the story of Adams, but perhaps the best and most accessible are Anthony Farrington and Derek Massarella, "William Adams and Early English Enterprise in Japan," LSE STICERD Research Paper No. IS394 (July 2000); and William Corr, *Adams the Pilot: The Life and Times of Captain William Adams: 1564–1620* (London: Curzon Press, 1995).

9 D.W. Davies, *A Primer of Dutch Seventeenth-Century Overseas Trade* (The Hague: Martinus Nijhoff, 1961), 71.

10 Ernest Satow, *The Voyage of Captain John Saris to Japan, 1613* (London: The Hakluyt Society, 1900).

11 Wim Wennekes, *Gouden Handel: De Erste Nederlanders Overzee, en wat zij dar Haalden* (Amsterdam: Atlas, 1996), 229–30.

12 For a record of several envoys arriving at Sunpu requesting Ieyasu's permission to trade with Japan and bearing gifts, see Kawashima Motojirō, *Shuinsen Bōekishi* (Kyoto: Naigai Shuppan Kabushiki Gaisha, 1921); Reinier Hesselink, "A Metal Dealer and Spy from Nagasaki in Manila in the First Quarter of the Seventeenth Century," in *Money in Asia (1200–1900): Small Currencies in Social and Political Contexts*, ed. Jane Kate Leonard and Ulrich Theobald (Leiden: Brill, 2015), 495–99; and Kees Zandfleet, et al., *The Dutch Encounter with Asia, 1600–1950* (Zwolle : Waanders Publishers, 2002).

13 The "Shuinjo" given to the Dutch can be found in Nakamura Tadashi, ed., *Eiinbon Ikoku Nikki*: Konchiin Sūden Gaikō Monjo Shūsei (Tokyo: Tokyo Bijutsu, 1989), 14.

14 T. Volker, *Porcelain and the Dutch East India Company, as Recorded in the Dagh-Registers of Batavia Castle, Those of Hirado and Deshima, and Other Contemporary*

Papers, 1602–1682 (Leiden: E.J. Brill, 1971), 117; Ian Burnett, *East Indies* (Kenthurst, NSW: Rosenberg Publishing, 2013), chapter 11: "Hirado and Deshima."

15 Satow, *The Voyage of Captain John Saris*: September 14, 1613.

16 Kobata Atsushi, *Kingin Bōeki-shi no Kenkyū* (Tokyo: Hōsei Daigaku Shuppankyoku, 1976), 58.

17 Suzuki Yasuko, *Kinsei Nichi-Ran Bōeki-shi no Kenkyū* (Tokyo: Sibunkaku Shuppan, 2004), 40. Suzuki says that in the beginning, the Dutch, unlike others, had no "angle" on the Chinese silk market. Likewise, Massarella quotes an early VOC official to the same effect: "The Trade of Japan, since it subsists upon China goods, and a few European cloths, is not to be entered upon, nor thought of, until we have first a firm grasp of the trade of China." Derek Massarella, *A World Elsewhere: Europe's Encounter with Japan in the Sixteenth and Seventeenth Centuries* (New Haven: Yale University Press, 1990), 82.

18 See Adam Clulow, *The Company and the Shogun: The Dutch Encounter with Tokugawa Japan* (New York: Columbia University Press, 2014), Chapter 4.

19 Suzuki, *Kinsei Nichi-Ran Bōeki-shi no Kenkyū*, 44.

20 In a revealing entry into the Dutch diaries in 1637, the chief merchant writes about the ongoing struggle of the Dutch to procure enough high-quality silk, even with the factory on Taiwan. He complains about the low prices to be had in Japan and that the Portuguese and Chinese can simply import more silk to compensate, but that the Dutch do not enjoy this luxury. See *Dagregisters Gehouden bij de Opperhoofden van het Nederlandsche Factorij in Japan*, 32–41.

21 The numbers, as well as a narrative, can be found in Pieter van Dam, *Beschryvinge van de Oostindische Compagnie*, ed. F. W. Stapel and C. W. Th. Van Boetzelaer, Volume 2, pt. 1 (The Hague: Rijks Geschiedenis Publicatiën, 1977), 367–436.

22 Suzuki Yasuko, *Japan-Netherlands Trade, 1600–1800: The Dutch East India Company and Beyond* (Kyoto: Kyoto University Press, 2012), 13.

23 Robert Innes, *The Door Ajar: Japan's Foreign Trade in the Seventeenth Century* (Ann Arbor, MI: unpublished doctoral dissertation, 1980); Yao Keisuke, *Kinsei Oranda Bōeki to Sakoku* (Tokyo: Yoshikawa Kōbunkan, 1998); Teijirō Yamawaki, *Nagasaki Oranda no Shōkan* (Tokyo: Chūō Kōronsha, 1980); Femme Gaastra, "The Dutch East India Company and the Intra-Asiatic Trade in Precious Metals," in *The Emergence of a World Economy, 1500–1914, Part I (Papers of the XI International Congress of Economic History)*, ed. Wolfram Fischer, Marvin McInnis, and Jürgen Schneider (Stuttgart: F. Steiner Verlag Wiesbaden GmbH, 1986); Watanabe Yogorō, *Kinsei Nihon Bōeki-ron no Tenkai* (Tokyo: Bunka Shobō Hakubun-sha, 1978); Suzuki, *Japan-Netherlands Trade, 1600–1800*, 28–46.

24 For a good sociopolitical history of the Tokugawa period, see Conrad Totman, *Early Modern Japan* (Berkeley: University of California Press, 1995); Mikiso Hane and Louis Perez, *Premodern Japan: A Historical Survey* (Boulder: Westview Press, 2015);

Marius Jansen, *The Making of Modern Japan* (Cambridge, MA: Harvard University Press, 2000).

25 Kobata Atsushi, *Kōzan no Rekishi* (Tokyo: Shibundō, 1956), 66; Tsuji Tatsuya, *Nihon no Rekishi 13: Edo Kaifu* (Tokyo: Chūō Kōronsha, 1966), 161–63.

26 Arano Yasunori, *Edo Bakufu to Higashi Ajia* (Tokyo: Yoshikawa Kōbunkan, 2003), 28.

27 Itazawa, *Nihon to Oranda*, 112.

28 Yao, *Kinsei Oranda Bōeki to Sakoku*, 27.

29 Diego Pacheco, "The Founding of the Port of Nagasaki and it Cession to the Society of Jesus," *Monumenta Nipponica* 2, no. 3–4 (1970): 303–23.

30 Charles Boxer, *The Christian Century in Japan* (Berkeley: University of California Press, 1951), 164–66.

31 For a study of these select merchant families, see Iwao Seiichi, *Shuinsen Bōeki-shi no Kenkyū* (Tokyo: Kyōbundō, 1958).

32 Michael Laver, *The Sakoku Edicts and the Politics of Tokugawa Hegemony* (Amherst, NY: Cambria Press, 2013). The printed version of the original *sakoku* edicts can be found in Ishii Ryōsuke, ed., *Tokugawa Kinrei-Kō/Hōseishi Gakkai Hen, Volume 6* (Tokyo: Sōbunsha, 1959–61), 377–78.

33 Iwao Seiichi, *Shuinsen to Nihonmachi* (Tokyo: Shibundō, 1964).

34 Jurgis Elisonas, "Christianity and the Daimyo," in *The Cambridge History of Japan, Volume 4*, ed. John Hall (Cambridge: Cambridge University Press, 1991).

35 Sukeno Kentarō, *Shimabara no Ran* (Tokyo: Azuma Shuppan, 1967). Boxer, *Christian Century in Japan*, 375–83.

36 The Dutch diaries make for interesting reading at this time because they show that the Japanese had been considering the removal of the Portuguese for some time, as evidenced by interviews in which shogunal officials asked the Dutch if they would be able to take up the slack in imports. The diaries also show that the Dutch were anticipating such an eventuality with some degree of excitement. See, for example, *NKKS: Dagregisters Gehouden bij de Opperhoofden van het Nederlandsche Factorij in Japan, Volume 3*, 152–67.

37 Yamamoto Hirofumi, *Sakoko to Kaikin no Jidai* (Tokyo: Azekura Shobō, 1995), 83.

38 Edward Thompson, ed., *The Diary of Richard Cocks—Cape Merchant in the English Factory in Japan, Volume I* (London: Hakluyt Society, 1883), 186–87.

39 Leonard Blussé, *Visible Cities: Canton, Nagasaki, and Batavia and the Coming of the Americans* (Cambridge, MA: Harvard University Press, 2008), 44–45.

40 For an overview of the different types of interpreters, see Katagiri Kazuo, "The Rise and Development of Dutch Learning in Japan," *Acta Asiatica* 42 (1982): 3.

41 Gary Leupp, *Interracial Intimacy in Japan: Western Men and Japanese Women, 1543–1900* (London: Continuum, 2003), especially chapter 6; Frits Vos, "Forgotten Foibles: Love and the Dutch at Deshima," *East Asian History* 39 (December, 2014): 147–51.

42 Engelbert Kaempfer, *The History of Japan, 3 Volumes* (Glasgow: J. MacLehose, 1906), Volume 1, 185.
43 *NKKS: Dagregisters Gehouden bij de Opperhoofden van het Nederlandsche Factorij in Japan*, Volume 2, 95.
44 Nakamura Tadashi, *Kinsei Nagasaki Bōeki-shi no Kenkyū* (Tokyo: Yoshikawa Kōbunkan, 1988), 118–24.
45 George Bryan Souza, *The Survival of Empire: Portuguese Trade and Society in China and the South China Sea, 1630–1754* (Cambridge: Cambridge University Press, 1986). For the contemporary Dutch account, see *NKKS: Dagregisters Gehouden bij de Opperhoofden van het Nederlandsche Factorij in Japan*, Volume 1, 58–59.
46 Yamamoto, *Sakoku to Kaikin no Jidai*, 83.
47 Dutch diaries indicate that the Nagasaki merchants had been actively and persistently petitioning the Japanese for this move for some time. See, for example, *NKKS: Dagregisters Gehouden bij de Opperhoofden van het Nederlandsche Factorij in Japan*, Volume 3, 48–49.
48 L. M. Cullen, *A History of Japan 1582–1941: Internal and External Worlds* (Cambridge: Cambridge University Press, 2010), 59; Goodman, *The Dutch Impact on Japan*, 35.
49 Katsuya Ōta, *Sakoku Jidai: Nagasaki Bōeki-shi no Kenkyū* (Kyoto: Shibunkaku, 1992), 16. Yanai Kenji says that the main role of the *bugyou* was originally to oversee the trade in raw silk: Yanai Kenji, *Nagasaki* (Tokyo: Shibundō, 1959).
50 See Laver, *Sakoku Edicts*, chapter 3.
51 Tsuruta Kei, "Kinsei Nihon no Yottsu no Kuchi," in *Ajia no naka no Nihonshi 2: Gaikō to Sensō*, ed. Arano Yasunori et al. (Tokyo: Tokyo Daigaku Shuppankai, 1992), 297–316. Arano Yasunori, *Kinsei Nihon to Higashi Ajia* (Tokyo: University of Tokyo Press, 1988); Reinier Hesselink, *Prisoners from Nambu: Reality and Make Believe in Seventeenth-Century Japanese Diplomacy* (Honolulu: University of Hawai'i Press, 2002), 167.
52 Kamiya Nobuyuki and Kimura Naoya, eds., *Kaikin to Sakoku* (Tokyo: Tokyo-dō Shuppan, 2002), 2–4.
53 Katō Eichi, "Deshima Ron," in *Nihon Tsūshi 12: Kinsei 2*, ed. Asao Naohiro (Tokyo: Iwanami Kōza, 1993), 339. Kaempfer describes the Chinese compound as well as the rent they were obliged to pay. He also writes that the Chinese were not allowed a court journey, but seems rather envious of the savings this afforded! See Kaempfer, *History of Japan*, Volume II, 253. Tashiro Kazui and Susan Downing Videen, "Foreign Relations During the Edo Period: Sakoku Reexamined," *Journal of Japanese Studies* 8, no. 2 (Summer, 1982): 288.
54 Nakamura, *Kinsei Nagasaki Bōeki-shi no Kenkyū*, 118–19; A detailed description of these procedures can be found in Katagiri Kazuo, *Hirakareta Sakoku: Nagasaki Dejima no Hito, Mono, Jōhō* (Tokyo: Kōdansha, 1997), 47–71.

55 The Chinese were also required to submit their own version, detailing the political situation in Asia. See Marius Jansen, *China in the Tokugawa World* (Cambridge, MA: Harvard University Press, 2000), 34.
56 See Iwao Seiichi, ed., *Oranda Fūsetsugaki Shūsei* (Tokyo: Japan-Netherlands Institute, 1976).
57 Ōta, *Sakoku Jidai*, 25–27.
58 Ibid., 16–17.
59 Nobuyuki and Naoya, eds., *Kaikin to Sakoku*, 28.
60 Leonard Blussé, "The Grand Inquisitor Inoue Chikugo no Kami Masashige, Spin Doctor of the Tokugawa Bakufu," *Bulletin of Portuguese-Japanese Studies* 7 (2003): 23–43. While Inoue Masashige was his proper name, the Dutch consistently refer to him by his title, Chikugo no Kami. In this book, we shall refer to him by his proper name.
61 Elisonas, "Christianity and the Daimyo," 370.
62 Laver, *The Sakoku Edicts*, chapter 2.
63 Sukeno, *Shimabara no Ran*; George Elison, *Deus Destroyed: The Image of Christianity in Early Modern Japan* (Cambridge, MA: Harvard University Press, 1973), 217–22.
64 Nakamura, *Kinsei Nagasaki Bōeki-shi no Kenkyū*, 170–71.
65 S.J. Hubert Cieslik, "The Case of Christovão Ferreira," *Monumenta Nipponica* 29, no.1 (Spring, 1974): 11–12.
66 An excellent fictionalized account of the torture of priests can be read in Shūsaku Endō, *Silence*, trans. William Johnston (New York: Picador Modern Classics, 2016).
67 Wennekes, *Gouden Handel: De Erste Nederlanders Overzee*, 225–35. See also Willem van Gulik, *Een Verre Hofreis. Nederlanders op weg naar de Shogun van Japan* (Amersterdam: Koninklijk Paleis Amsterdam, 2000). A good Japanese language account of the *hofreis* is found in Katagiri Kazuo, *Oranda Yado Ebiya no Kenkyū* (Kyoto: Shibunkaku Shuppan, 1998) and, by the same author, *Edo no Orandajin: Kapitan no Edo Sanpu* (Tokyo: Chūō Kōron, 2000).
68 Engelbert Kaempfer breaks down the cost of the court journey in his famous description of the journey he made while employed as the Company surgeon. Kaempfer, *The History of Japan*, 236.
69 Timon Screech, *Secret Memoirs of the Shoguns: Isaac Titsingh and Japan, 1799–1822* (London: Routledge, 2006), 10.
70 Van Gulik, *Een Verre Hofreis*, 41.
71 Tom Vermeulen et al., eds., *Deshima Dagregisters, Their Original Table of Contents, Volume VIII: 1760–1780* (Leiden: Center for the History of European Expansion, 1993): September 9–12, 1764.
72 Ronald P. Toby, *State and Diplomacy in Early Modern Japan: Asia in the Development of the Tokugawa Bakufu* (Princeton: Princeton University Press, 1984).

73 Goodman, *The Dutch Impact on Japan*, 34.
74 In October 1644, the Japanese sent a letter to the Dutch requesting specifically that the Company send someone to Edo who could teach the shogun's officials how to use the mortars and grenades previously given as gifts. NFJ 57: October 15, 1644. The Japanese repeated their request on November 10, underscoring the importance of the "pyrotechnist" to the shogun's officials. The next year, no such person arrived, as evidenced by a further request in November of 1645. The requested person eventually did arrive, but not until 1649 with a special embassy to thank the Japanese for releasing several Dutch sailors that had earlier been captured when their ship landed at an unauthorized spot in Japan. In January of 1650, the Shogun requested that the "pyrotechnist," along with the surgeon, should remain in Edo longer than the other Dutch for the shogun's gratification. NFJ 63: January 22, 1650.
75 Grant Goodman states, "Although the knowledge of the west among these seventeenth century Nagasaki interpreters and their associates was often no more than a scrapbook of foreign information, these first efforts at the assimilated Dutch learning laid an important foundation for the evolution of the movement which was to become Rangaku." Goodman, *The Dutch Impact on Japan*, 54.
76 NFJ 82: October 12, 1669.
77 Viallé and Blussé, eds., *The Deshima Dagregisters, Volumes XIII*: August 4, 1770.
78 Ibid., January 7, 1664.
79 These demands have been digitized by the National Library of the Netherlands (Nationaal Archief) and can be found at https://www.geheugenvannederland.nl/en/geheugen/pages/collectie/Japanse+eisen.
80 I am indebted to Martha Chaiklin for this concept: Martha Chaiklin, *Cultural Commerce and Dutch Commercial Culture: The Influence of European Material Culture on Japan, 1700–1850* (Leiden: CNWS Studies in Overseas History 5, 2003), 52.
81 Ibid., 52.
82 Blussé and Viallé, eds., *The Deshima Dagregisters, Volumes XII*, 137: February 20, 1654.
83 There are many good works detailing gift-giving in modern Japan, including Katherine Rupp's magnificent *Gift-Giving in Japan: Cash, Connections, Cosmologies* (Stanford: Stanford University Press, 2003).
84 Arnoldus Montanus, *Gedenkwaerdige gesantschappen der Oost-Indische Maetschappij in't Vereenigde Nederland aen de kaisaren van Japan* (Amsterdam: Jacob Meurs, 1680) has perhaps the earliest firsthand accounts of the Dutch embassy to Edo for general European consumption. Special thanks to the Division of Rare Manuscripts Collection of the Cornell University Library. See also Wolfgang Michel, "Travels of the Dutch East India Company in the Japanese Archipelago," in *Japan—A Cartographic Vision*, ed. Lutz Walter (Munich: Prestel-Verlag, 1993).

Chapter 1

1. Mauss, *The Gift: Forms and Functions of Exchange in Archaic Societies*.
2. Hyde, *The Gift: Imagination and the Erotic Life of Property*.
3. R.W. Belk and G.S. Coon, "Gift-Giving as Agapic Love: An Alternative to the Exchange Paradigm Based on Dating Experiences," *Journal of Consumer Research* 20 (1993): 393–417.
4. Jacques Derrida, *Given Time: 1. Counterfeit Money*, trans. P. Kamul (Chicago: University of Chicago Press, 1991).
5. Chalrles Champetier, "Philosophy of the Gift: Jacques Derrida, Martin Heidegger," *Angelaki: Journal of the Theoretical Humanities* 6, no. 2 (2001): 15.
6. Nathan Miczo, "The Human Condition and the Gift: Toward a Theoretical Perspective on Close Relationships," *Human Studies* 31, no. 2 (2008): 148.
7. Chris Gregory, *Gifts and Commodities* (London, Academic Press, 1982), 190–91; Marshall Sahlins, *Stone Age Economics* (Chicago: Aldine-Atherton, 1972).
8. Rupp, *Gift Giving in Japan: Cash, Connections, Cosmologies*.
9. Klekar, "Prisoners in Silken Bonds," 84. I also include here the wonderful work of Felicity Heal entitled *The Power of Gifts: Gift Exchange in Early Modern England* (London: Oxford University Press, 2014). Though this work deals with late medieval and early modern England, Heal deals masterfully with gifts in the context of early modern political society.
10. While this book focuses on Dutch gift-giving, the Diary of Richard Cocks, the chief merchant of the English factory from 1613–23, is filled with accounts of gift-giving as well, including gifts to local shogunal officials, the Daimyo of Hirado and his family, Nagasaki officials, and Chinese merchants. See Thompson, ed., *The Diary of Richard Cocks—Cape Merchant in the English Factory in Japan*.
11. Christina Brauner, "Connecting Things: Trading Companies and Diplomatic Gift Giving on the Gold and Slave Coasts in the Seventeenth and Eighteenth Centuries," *Journal of Early Modern History* 20 (2016): 408–28; João Melo, "Seeking Prestige and Survival: Gift-Exchange Practices between the Portuguese Estado da India and Asian Rulers," *Journal of the Economic and Social History of the Orient* 56 (2013): 672–95.
12. Hendrick Brouwer wrote in a letter of thanks to the Shogun after a diplomatic stand-off was resolved, "We are your majesty's people." See *NKKS Volume 1 Part 1*, 43–44. When the third Shogun passed away in 1651, the Dutch wrote that "Being faithful vassals and citizens of this empire, we were saddened by the untimely demise of His Majesty. For the comfort of our hearts, we humbly requested His honor to permit one of the interpreters to travel to Edo to convey our condolences." Viallé and Blussé, *The Deshima Dagregisters*, XII, no. 16 (June 24, 1651).
13. See, for example, NFJ July 19, 1654.

14 Viallé and Blussé, *The Deshima Dagregisters, Volumes XIII*: April 19, 1662.
15 Shogo Suzuki, "Europe at the Periphery of the Japanese World Order," in *International Orders in the Early Modern World*, ed. Shogo Suzuki, Yongjin Zhang, and Joel Quirk (New York: Routledge, 2014), 76–93.
16 Both the English and the Dutch visited Sunpu to present gifts to Ieyasu and to receive formal permission to trade. John Saris, *The First Voyage of the English to Japan*, ed. Takanobu Otsuka (Tokyo: Tōyō Bunko, 1941); Corr, *Adams the Pilot*, 96; Pieter Rietbergen, *Japan Verwoord: Nihon Door Nerderlandse Ogen, 1600–1799* (Amsterdam: Hotei Publishing, 2003), 37–38.
17 The official account of the Dutch at Ieyasu's court can be found in Narushima, Motonao, *Kokushi Taikei: Tokugawa Jikki, Volume 1*, ed. Kuroita Katsumi (Tokyo: Yoshikawa Kōbunkan, 1981), 485–90.
18 Murakami Naojirō, ed., *Ikoku Nikki* (Tokyo: Sanshūsha, 1911).
19 Clulow, *The Company and the Shogun*.
20 For a fuller account, see Leonard Blussé, "Bull in a China Shop: Pieter Nuyts in China and Japan," in *Around and About Formosa: Essays in Honor of Professor Ta'ao Yung-ho*, ed. Leonard Blussé (Taipei: Ta'ao Yung-ho Foundation for Culture and Education, 2003), 95–110.
21 An exceptionally well-written and thoroughly researched work on this episode is Hesselink, *Prisoners from Nambu*.
22 NFJ 60: January 22, 1647.
23 The account of the embassy can be found in NFJ 62: September 19 onward.
24 Viallé and Blussé, *The Deshima Dagregisters, Volumes XI*: March 20, 1649.
25 For a discussion of schuit silver, see Suzuki, *Japan-Netherlands Trade, 1600–1800*, 2–3.
26 Perhaps the most accessible, yet rigorous, account of the tribute system is Ji-young Lee, *China's Hegemony: Four Hundred Years of East Asian Domination* (New York: Columbia University Press, 2017).
27 There is a fair amount of scholarly debate about the tribute system, and in particular whether those who chose to send embassies to the Chinese court and performed their ritual submission did so for economic and political expediency or actually subscribed to what has been called the Sino-centric worldview. Yongzin Zhang sums it up well, thus, "It is not clear . . . whether those participating in the Chinese world order actually accept the civilizational assumptions embedded in the tribute system and the Sinocentric conception of superiority and inferiority in their relationship. The centrality and usefulness of the tribute system model as an overarching analytical and explanatory framework in understanding traditional China's foreign relations have therefore been a subject of controversy." See Yongjin Zhang, "The Tribute System," in *Oxford Bibliographies of Chinese Studies*, ed. Tim Wright (New York: Oxford University Press, 2013).

28 Toby, *State and Diplomacy in Early Modern Japan*.
29 Yamawaki, *Nagasaki Oranda no Shōkan*, 38–40.
30 Suzuki, "Europe at the Periphery of the Japanese World Order." For a comprehensive overview of early modern Japanese foreign relations, see Brett Walker, "Foreign Affairs and Frontiers in Early Modern Japan: A Historiographical Essay," *Early Modern Japan* (Fall 2002): 44–128.
31 Jansen, *China in the Tokugawa World*, 1–12.
32 Screech, *The Shogun's Painted Culture*, 84.
33 NFJ 64: November 6, 1650.
34 Chaiklin, ed., *Mediated by Gifts* 7.
35 Timon Screech, ed., *Secret Memoirs of the Shogun*, 6. Screech tells us that the Dutch called this holiday the "Nagasaki Recognition."
36 Yosaburo Takekoshi, *The Economic Aspects of the History of the Civilization of Japan*, Volume II (London: Routledge, 2003), 164–72.
37 Michael Laver, "Butter Diplomacy" *Education About Asia* 17, no. 1 (Spring, 2012): 5–8.
38 NFJ 56: January 17, 1642.
39 F. R. Effert, ed., *The Court Journey to the Shogun of Japan: From a Private Account by Jan Cock Blomhoff* (Leiden: Hotei Publishing, 2000), 9.
40 Ronald Toby states that at least the first three Shogun clearly used embassies for political legitimacy: Toby, *State and Diplomacy in Early Modern Japan*, 77.
41 Adam Clulow, "A Fake Embassy: The Lord of Taiwan and Tokugawa Japan," in *Statecraft and Spectacle in East Asia: Studies in Taiwan-Japan Relations*, ed. Adam Clulow (New York: Routledge, 2011), 37.
42 Leonard Blussé et al., eds., *Deshima Dagregisters, Volumes 2*: August 22, 1770.
43 Ibid.: November 8, 1771.
44 Clulow, *The Company and the Shogun*, 253.
45 Adam Clulow, "The Dutch East India Company, Global Networks, and Tokugawa Japan," in *Global Gifts: The Material Culture of Diplomacy in Early Modern Eurasia*, ed. Zoltann Biedermann, Anne Gerritsen, and Giorgio Riello (Cambridge: Cambridge University Press, 2018), 205; Constantine Vaporis, *Tour of Duty: Samurai, Military Service in Edo, and the Culture of Early Modern Japan* (Honolulu: University of Hawai'i Press, 2008).
46 Christopher Howe goes so far as to say that the court journey was simply an extension of the *sankin-kōtai* system. See Christopher Howe, *The Origins of Japanese Trade Supremacy* (Chicago: University of Chicago Press, 1996), 27.
47 Mikiso Hane, George Tsukahira, Constantine Vaporis, and others state that one of the intended side effects of the alternate attendance system was to force daimyo to expend large sums of cash, mainly on secondary residences and travel expenses. It is estimated that daimyo may have spent up to 2/3 of their total revenues either

directly or indirectly on the system. Mikiso Hane, *Premodern Japan: A Historical Survey* (Boulder: Westview Press, 1991); George Toshio Tsukahira, *Feudal Control in Tokugawa Japan: The Sankin Kōtai System* (Cambridge: Harvard University Press, 1966); Vaporis, *Tour of Duty*.

48 Laver, *The Sakoku Edicts and the Politics of Tokugawa Hegemony*.
49 Tonio Andrade, *The Gunpowder Age, China, Military Innovation, and the Rise of the West in World History* (Princeton: Princeton University Press, 2016); Tonio Andrade, *Lost Colony: The Untold Story of China's First Great Victory over the West* (Princeton: Princeton University Press, 2011); Peter Lorge, *The Asian Military Revolution: From Gunpowder to the Bomb* (Cambridge: Cambridge University Press, 2008); Kenneth Pomeranz, *The Great Divergence: China, Europe, and the Making of the Modern World Economy* (Princeton: Princeton University Press, 2000).
50 Andrade, *Lost Colony*.
51 Jansen, *The Making of Modern Japan*, 82.
52 The requirement was finally relaxed to every two years in 1764, although as the chief merchant notes in his diary, the Company was still obliged to present the gifts even in years when they did not journey to Edo. Instead they gave the gifts to the Nagasaki *bugyō*, and in turn he would also give the Dutch the customary "return gifts." See Leonard Blussé et al., eds., *Deshima Dagregisters Volumes 2*: September 9–12, 1764.
53 Reinier Hesselink, *Prisoners from Nambu: Reality and Make Believe in Seventeenth Century Japanese Diplomacy* (Honolulu: University of Hawai'i Press, 2002), 15.
54 Ibid., 82.
55 Screech, *Secret Memoirs of the Shoguns*, 7.
56 An example of this can be seen in the so-called Breskens Affairs. See Hesselink, *Prisoners from Nambu*, 143–44.
57 A good description of the court journey can be found in Engelbert Kaempfer's original manuscript in English translation, or the helpful edited volume by Beatrice Bodart-Bailey. Kaempfer, *The History of Japan*; Beatrice Bodart-Bailey, ed., *Kaempfer's Japan: Tokugawa Culture Observed* (Honolulu: University of Hawai'i Press, 1999).
58 Bodart-Bailey, *Kaempfer's Japan*, 405.
59 NFJ 74: April 13, 1661.
60 Grant Goodman, *Japan and the Dutch: 1600–1853* (London, Curzon Press, 2000), 29.
61 Brett Walker, *The Conquest of Ainu Lands: Ecology and Culture in Japanese Expansion, 1590–1800* (Berkeley: University of California Press, 2001), 136; Tessa Morris Suzuki, "A Decent into the Past: The Frontier in the Construction of Japanese Identity," in *Multicultural Japan: Paleolithic to Postmodern*, ed. Donald Denoon, Mark Hudson, Gavan McCormack, and Tessa Morris Suzuki (Cambridge: Cambridge University Press, 1996), 83–84.

62 John Wills, *Embassies and Illusions: Dutch and Portuguese Envoys to K'ang Hsi* (Cambridge: Harvard University Asia Center, 1984); John Wills, *Pepper, Guns, and Parleys: The Dutch East India Company and China, 1662–1681* (Cambridge: Harvard University Press, 1974).

63 Beatrice Bodart-Bailey, "A Song for the Shogun: Engelbert Kaempfer and 17th-c. Japan," *IIAS Newsletter Online, 22: 400 Years of Dutch Japanese Relation*, accessed June 6, 2014, http://www.iias.nl/iiasn/22/theme/22T3.html.

64 Clulow, *The Company and the Shogun*, 96–98.

65 Wennekes, *Gouden Handel*, 233–34.

66 Iwao Seiichi, ed., *Oranda Fūsetsugaki Shūsei*.

67 A good English language account of these interviews appears in Reinier Hesselink's *Prisoners from Nambu*. Kaempfer provides a more banal account of the interrogation during the court journey of 1691 when he recounts how the Dutch were asked "a thousand ridiculous and impertinent questions." Kaempfer, *The History of Japan, Volume 2*, 92.

68 Laver, *The Sakoku Edicts and the Politics of Tokugawa Hegemony*.

69 In a letter to the Dutch from the shogunal court in 1652, for example, the Dutch were told that "You Dutchmen are aware that the previous shoguns of Japan have an abhorrence of Christianity and the present ruling shogun, heir to the deceased, has an even greater abhorrence of it than his father." The letter goes on to exhort the Dutch not to bring any Portuguese to the country, nor even to be friends with Portuguese. This follows on the heels of a rumor that there were Portuguese sailors serving on a Dutch ship that had previously come to Japan. The Dutch were told that if they allowed this to happen in the future, it "would not be to your advantage." Blussé and Viallé, eds., *The Deshima Dagregisters, Volumes XII*, 157: May 23, 1652.

70 After 1790, the authorities required a visit only once every four years, although gifts were still forwarded every year. See Katagiri Kazuo, *Oranda Tsūji no Kenkyū* (Tokyo: Yoshikawa Kōbunkan, 1985).

71 Frits Vos, "A Distance of 13,000 Miles: The Dutch through Japanese Eyes," *Delta: A Review of Arts, Life and Thought in the Netherlands* 16, no. 2 (1973): 30.

72 The chief merchant writes in 1651 that a new directive received from Edo stated that personal interactions with the Shogun were henceforth forbidden. This news is followed by an interesting rant in which he writes that this decree, like the other decrees limiting Dutch freedoms, was simply to arbitrarily restrict the Dutch and that the only reason the Dutch were allowed to trade with Japan was because the Japanese feared if they cut the Company off from trade, it would attack Japan with its superior weapons. NFJ 64: March 17, 1651.

73 In 1624 the chief merchant writes that the return gift was offered to the Dutch in the past because of the great efforts they expended to ply the Shogun with extraordinary gifts, but now it was given as a sign of affection, a great honor that was gratefully received by the Dutch, at least according to the florid language in

the diaries. We are also told that the Dutch celebrated this good fortune with the landlords of the Dutch residence in Edo, the interpreters, and the various officials assigned to oversee the Dutch. NFJ 56: January 24, 1642.

74 Chaiklin, *Cultural Commerce and Dutch Commercial Culture*, 41.
75 Tom Vermuelen et al., eds., *Deshima Dagregisters, Volume VIII: 1760–1780*: July 15–17, 1762.
76 In 1643, for example, we are told that Inoue Masashige gave the Dutch five gowns and that twenty other Japanese officials also gave gifts of gowns. NFJ 57: December 18–20, 1643.
77 Chaiklin, *Cultural Commerce and Dutch Commercial Culture*.

Chapter 2

1   Blussé and Viallé, eds., *The Deshima Dagregisters, Volumes XI*, 262: January 6, 1647.
2   Lest we think that megafauna were the only extraordinary gifts, the Dutch also presented a *perspectiefkast* (a "peepshow" box through which the observer would have seen a very detailed three-dimensional diorama) which would no doubt have elicited no small amount of wonderment at court.
3   Noble is an indiscriminate term used by the Dutch to refer to a whole host of people of differing ranks in Japan. The term could be used to refer to members of the imperial court in Miyako, any of the several hundred daimyo that alternated their time between Edo and their home domains, as well as members of the shogunal household.
4   Blussé and Viallé, eds., *The Deshima Dagregisters, Volumes XI*, 269: January 10, 1647.
5   Ibid., 332: November 20, 1648.
6   This episode can be found in NFJ 72: August 26, 1659 to NFJ 73: June 3, 1660.
7   A copy of the woodblock print, the title of which is translated as "The Camels Brought by a Dutchman in 1821," resides in the Philadelphia Museum of Art: http://www.philamuseum.org/collections/permanent/248800.html?mulR=2583 82851%7C43.
8   Martha Chaiklin, "The Merchant's Ark: Live Animal Gifts in Early Modern Dutch-Japanese Relations," *World History Connected* 9, no. 1 (February, 2012).
9   Viallé and Blussé, *The Deshima Dagregisters, Volume XII*, 377: February 1, 1659.
10 Cynthia Viallé, "In Aid of Trade: Dutch Gift-Giving in Tokugawa Japan," *Tokyo Daigaku Shiryōhensan-jō Kenkyū Kiyo* 16 (March, 2006): 63–64.
11 Viallé and Blussé, *The Deshima Dagregisters, Volume XIII*, 243–34: February 3–4, 1668.
12 Ibid., 252: April 15, 1668.

13 Paul van der Velde and Rudolf Backofner, eds., *The Deshima Diaries: Marginalia, 1700–1740* (Tokyo: the Japan-Netherlands Institute, 1992), 303: July 24, 1725.
14 On July 8, the Dutch received a letter on Deshima in which Keijser is described as riding horses in the presence of the Shogun and the shogunal heir, as well as providing instruction in Western horsemanship. Van der Velde and Backofner, eds., *The Deshima Diaries: Marginalia, 1700–1740*, 447: July 8, 1735.
15 Ibid., 452–53. See also Cord Eberspacher, "Johan Georg Keyserling: A German Horseman at Nagasaki and Edo," *Crossroads* 2 (Summer, 1994): 9–26.
16 Grant Goodman, *Japan: The Dutch Experience* (London: Bloomsbury Publishing Company, 2012), 58.
17 Tom Vermeulen et al., *Deshima Dagregisters, Volume II*: October 14, 1773.
18 Timon Screech, *Japan Extolled and Decried: Carl Peter Thunberg's Travels in Japan 1775–1776* (New York: Routledge, 2005), 42. The Dutch note in their diaries that the saddle slipped off the horse, causing the heir to fall off. The cause of death, according to the diary, was loss of blood. Tom Vermeulen et al., *Deshima Dagregisters, Volume II*: April 10, 1779.
19 Leonard Blussé et al., eds., *The Deshima Diaries Marginalia: 1740–1800* (Tokyo: Japan-Netherlands Institute, 2004), xxviii.
20 Thomas Stamford Raffles, *The History of Java, Volume 2* (London: Black, Parbury and Allen, 1817), Appendix B. An interesting account of Raffle's attempt to open trade with Japan can be found in R. Montgomery Martin, *China: Political, Commercial and Social: In an Official Report to Her Majesty's Government* (London: Brewster and West Printers, 1847), 283–85; Screech, *The Shogun's Painted Culture*, 86.
21 Vasili Mikhailovich Golovnin, *Narrative of My Captivity in Japan, during the Years 1811, 1812, and 1813; with Observations on the Country and the People, Volume II* (London: Henry Colburn, 1818), 150–51. It was common at the time for Europeans to refer to the Shogun as the "emperor," including the Dutch in their diaries in which the Shogun is almost always referred to as *Keizer*.
22 Timon Screech, *The Lens Within the Heart: The Western Scientific Gaze and Popular Imagery in Later Edo Japan* (Honolulu: University of Hawai'i Press, 2002), 34.
23 Viallé, "In Aid of Trade," 63.
24 Walker, *The Conquest of Ainu Lands*, 100–109.
25 NFJ 57: December 14, 1643.
26 Viallé and Blussé, eds., *The Deshima Dagregisters, Volume XII*, 153: June 16, 1654.
27 Maria Belozerskaya, *The Medici Giraffe and Other Tales of Exotic Animals and Power* (New York: Hachette, 2009), 199.
28 Viallé and Blussé, eds., *The Deshima Dagregisters, Volume XII*, 282: January 14, 1657.
29 Ibid., 289: February 22, 1657.

30 Kaempfer, *History of Japan*, Volume 3, 6.
31 Martha Chaiklin, "Exotic Bird Collecting in Early Modern Japan," in *JAPANimals: History and Culture in Japan's Animal Life*, ed. Gregory Pflugfelder and Brett Walker (Ann Arbor: Center for Japanese Studies, University of Michigan, 2005), 135.
32 Viallé and Blussé, eds., *The Deshima Dagregisters, Volume XII*, 334: January 29, 1658.
33 Ibid., 353: July 14, 1658.
34 Itazawa, *Nihon to Oranda*, 117.
35 Chaiklin, "Exotic Bird Collecting in Early Modern Japan," 141.
36 Viallé and Blussé, eds., *The Deshima Dagregisters, Volume XII*, 41: January 28, 1652.
37 Alfred Russell Wallace, *The Malay Archipelago: The Land of the Orang-Utan and the Bird of Paradise* (Oxford: John Beaufoy Publishing, 2016).
38 Viallé and Blussé, eds., *The Deshima Dagregisters, Volume XII, 45:* February 9, 1652.
39 Ibid., 126: January 28, 1653.
40 We also read of eleven Persian Partridges intended as gifts for the Shogun in 1641 (October 16), although in November, the chief merchant writes that the Shogun does not want the birds because apparently he had enough (November 11). In the second instance, the diaries refer to Persian "pheasants." On November 19 we read that the birds had been successfully given to two Nagasaki officials, who gladly accepted them.
41 Vermeulen et al., eds., *Deshima Dagregisters, Volume VIII, 1760–1780*, August 9, 1776.
42 NFJ 60: September 2–3, 1647. See also, Ria Winters and Julia Hume, "The Dodo, the Deer, and a 1647 Voyage to Japan," *Historical Biology, An International Journal of Paleobiology* 27, no. 2 (2015): 258–64.
43 Robert Hellyer, *Defining Engagement: Japan and Global Contexts, 1640–1868* (Cambridge, MA: Harvard University Asia Center, 2009), 118. Reinier H. Hesselink, "A Dutch New Year at the Shirandō Academy: 1 January 1795," *Monumenta Nipponica* 50, no. 2 (Summer 1995): 203.
44 The print is entitled "*Oranda-jin kamotsu o kakeru*" (Dutchman Weighing Goods) and is part of an exhibit on the Dutch in Japan called "Red Haired Barbarians" at this International Institute of Social History in Amsterdam, The Netherlands: http://www.iisg.nl/exhibitions/.
45 Viallé and Blussé, eds., *The Deshima Dagregisters, Volume XI*, 328: November 7, 1648.
46 Viallé and Blussé, eds. *The Deshima Dagregisters, Volume XIII*, 235: November 18, 1667.
47 Screech, *Japan Extolled and Decried*.
48 Richard Ellis, *Tiger Bone and Rhino Horn: The Destruction of Wildlife for Traditional Chinese Medicine* (Washington, DC: Island Press, 2005).

49 NFJ 66: January 19, 1653. We read of a great charade being enacted in which the Dutch hide the true value of the horns in order to convince the Japanese that they really are priceless. On this occasion the Dutch even provide their patron with written confirmation that this truly is a unicorn horn.
50 NFJ 66: January 26, 1653.
51 Vermeulen et al., eds., *Deshima Dagregisters, Volume II*: September 5, 1778.
52 The best works on the VOC in Siam are George Vinal Smith, The Dutch in Seventeenth-Century Thailand (Northern IL: Center for Southeast Asian Studies Special Report, 1977) and Dhiravat Pombejra, *Court, Company, and Campong: Essays on the VOC Preserce in Ayutthaya* (Phra Nakhon Sri Ayutthaya: Ayutthaya Historical Study Center, 1992).
53 W. Ph. Coolhaas, ed., Generale Missiven *van Gouverneurs-Generaal en Raden aan Heren XVII der Verenigde Oostindische Compagnie*, Deel II: 1610–1638 ('s-Gravenhage: Martinus Nijhoff, 1960), 358.
54 Asta Bredsdorff, *The Trials and Travels of Willem Leyel: An Account of the Danish East India Company in Tranquebar, 1639–1648* (Copenhagen: Museum Tusculanum Press, 2009), 120. Robert Parthesius, *Dutch Ships in Tropical Waters: The Development of the Dutch East India Company Shipping Network in Asia, 1595–1660* (Amsterdam: Amsterdam University Press, 2010), 137.
55 Anne Gerritsen and Giorgio Riello, eds., *The Global Lives of Things: The Material Culture of Connections in the Early Modern World* (New York: Routledge, 2016), 62–80.
56 Viallé and Blussé, eds., *The Deshima Dagregisters, Volume XIII*, 256: May 25, 1668.
57 NFJ 59: January 26–28, 1646.
58 NFJ 65: May 24, 1652. Among the many requested items were samples of mermaid's teeth.
59 NFJ 67: July 19, 1654. Brett Walker outlines other strange animal products from Ezo also given as gifts by the Ainu, such as fur seal penis and bear gall bladder. Walker, *The Conquest of Ainu Lands*, 203.

Chapter 3

1 Chaiklin, *Cultural Commerce and Dutch Commercial Culture.*
2 Cullen, *A History of Japan, 1582–1941*, 45.
3 Blussé and Viallé, eds., *The Deshima Dagregisters, Volumes XIII*, 277: October 7, 1668.
4 Narushima, *Kokushi Taikei: Tokugawa Jikki, Volume 41*, 135.
5 The account of this exchange can be found in van der Velde et al., eds., *Deshima Dagregisters, Volume I*: October 1–3, 1740 and Blussé et al., eds., *Deshima Dagregisters, Volume II*: October 4–5, 1741.

6   NFJ 62: October, 6, 1649. This episode also reveals a bit about the care taken in ordering goods for the Shogun. The Dutch relate that a few years before, the Nagasaki *bugyō* came to the Dutch with samples of a rug that the Shogun desired. The Dutch, presumably using these samples as a guide, then ordered the rug, which arrived three years later.
7   Blussé and Viallé, eds., *The Deshima Dagregisters, Volumes XI*, 308: November 30, 1647.
8   Alexandra Curvelo, "Nagasaki/Deshima after the Portuguese in Dutch Accounts of the Seventeenth Century," *Bulletin of Portuguese/Japanese Studies* 6 (June, 2003): 152.
9   Blussé and Viallé, eds., *The Deshima Dagregisters Volumes XII*, 376: January 10, 1659.
10 NFJ 61: November 15, 1648.
11 Cieslik, "The Case of Christovão Ferreira," 1–54.
12 Blussé and Viallé, eds, *The Deshima Dagregisters, Volumes XI*, 302: September 18, 1647.
13 Blussé and Viallé, eds., *The Deshima Dagregisters, Volume XIII*, 372–73: April 15–28, 1663.
14 On June 24, the Dutch call themselves faithful vassals and citizens of the Japanese empire: NFJ 64: June 24, 1651.
15 Blussé and Viallé, eds., *The Deshima Dagregisters, Volume XI*, 103: June 29, 1643.
16 The following details can be found in Blussé and Viallé, eds., *The Deshima Dagregisters, Volumes XII*, 239–48: February and March, 1656.
17 For a good overview of the career of Inoue and his relationship with the Dutch, see Blussé, "The Grand Inquisitor Inoue Chikugo no Kami Masashige," 23–43.
18 NFJ 83: January 12, 1670.
19 NFJ 61: November 30, 1647.
20 Blussé and Viallé, eds., *The Deshima Dagregisters, Volumes XIII*, 93–98: January 6–February 11.
21 Inoue Masashige expressly asked the Company to bring "paintings of battles on land and sea" as gifts for the Shogun on February 28, 1658. Blussé and Viallé, eds., *The Deshima Dagregisters, Volume XII*, 343: February 27, 1658. Accordingly, the two paintings were brought in 1664.
22 Charles Boxer, *Jan Compagnie in Japan, 1600–1850: An Essay on the Cultural Artistic and Scientific Influence Exercised by the Hollanders in Japan from the Seventeenth to the Nineteenth Centuries* (Den Haag: Martinus Nijhoff, 1950), 3.
23 Christopher Duffy, *Siege Warfare: The Fortress in the Early Modern World, 1494–1660* (London: Routledge, 1996), 242.
24 Blussé and Viallé, eds., *The Deshima Dagregisters, Volume XII*, 343: February 27, 1658.

25 *NKKS*, 34–37; 116.
26 Timon Screech, *The Shogun's Painted Culture: Fear and Creativity in the Japanese States, 1760–1829* (London: Reaktion Books, 2000), 202.
27 *NKKS* Volume 1, 34: November 11, 1633.
28 NFJ 61: September 27, 1648.
29 NFJ 77: March 27, 1664.
30 Screech, *The Shogun's Painted Culture*, 262.
31 A detailed account of the negotiations over the fate of Nuyts can be found in Clulow, *The Company and the Shogun*, 24–49.
32 Nuyts' journal can be found in Japanese in Nagazumi Yōko (ed), *Hirado Oranda Shōkan no Nikki, Volume 1* (Tokyo: Iwanami Shoten, 1969). For a comprehensive treatment of this episode, see Clulow, *The Company and the Shogun*, 225–28; Tonio Andrade, *How Taiwan Became Chinese: Dutch, Spanish, and Han Colonization in the Seventeenth Century* (New York: Columbia University Press, 2008), 40–62; Michael Laver, *Japan's Economy by Proxy in the Seventeenth Century: China, The Netherlands, and the Bakufu* (Amherst, NY: Cambria Press, 2008), 147–55.
33 Iwao Seiichi, *Nihon no Rekishi 14: Sakoku* (Tokyo: Chūō Kōronsha, 1973), 258–68.
34 F. Dekker, *Betrekkingen Tuschen de Oost-Indische Compagnie en Japan* ('s-Gravenhage: L. J. C. Boucher, 1941), 30.
35 Nuyts seems to have ignored advice that he received from Neijenroode a couple years before that the Japanese must be treated with a certain amount of discretion. See Watanabe, *Kinsei Nihon Bōeki Ron no Tenkai*, 64.
36 Leonard Blussé, et al. eds., *De Daghregister Van Het Kasteel Zeelandia, Taiwan, Deel I (1625–1640)* (Den Haag: Instituut Voor Nederlandse Geschiedenis, 1994), 26.
37 Ōishi Shinzaburō, *Shuinsen to Miname e no Senkisha* (Tokyo: Gyōsei, 1986), 132.
38 For a good overview of the suspension, see Cheng Shaogang, *De VOC en Formosa, 1624–1662: Een Vergeten Geschiedenis* (Amsterdam: Bataafsche Leeuw, 1997), 76–80.
39 The whole of the "Nuyts Affair" can be traced in the diaries kept in the Dutch factory at Taiwan and make for fascinating reading: Blussé et al., eds., *De Daghregister Van Het Kasteel Zeelandia, Taiwan, Deel I*, 45–48. Nagazumi Yōko, *Shuinsen*, 195–96; Maehira, Fusaaki, "'Sakoku:' Nihon no Kaigai Bōeki," in *Nihon no Kinsei: Seikaishi no naka no Kinsei*, ed. Asao Naohiro (Tokyo: Chūō Kōronsha, 1991), 136–37.
40 Blussé et al., eds., *De Daghregister Van Het Kasteel Zeelandia, Taiwan, Deel I*, 84. Asao Naohiro, *Nihon no Kinsei 1:Seikai Shi no naka no Kinsei* (Tokyo: Chūō Kōronsha, 1991), 137.
41 Dekker, *Betrekkingen Tuschen de Oost-Indische Compagnie en Japan*, 35.
42 For an example of a petition presented to the authorities in Edo for the release of Nuyts, see, *NKKS Volume 1*, 30–31.

43 *NKKS Volume 2*, 82: July 5, 1636.
44 The diary entry for April 18, 1665 tells us that the Shogun was very pleased and that he had the two lanterns sent to Nikkō to join its counterpart from twenty years earlier. NFJ 78: April 18, 1665.
45 Kaempfer, *The History of Japan, Volume II*, 224.
46 The Dutch analysis of the new strictness and its possible cause is found in NFJ 80: January 24–27, 1667.
47 Viallé and Blussé, *The Deshima Dagregisters Volume XIII*, February 22, 1667.
48 Ibid., May 8, 1668.
49 Ibid., September 23, 1668.
50 NFJ 82: April 17, 1669. Here again we catch a glimpse of a "quasi-gift." The chief merchant notes that the twenty Koban is actually 220 gulden less than what it really cost.
51 Yamawaki, *Nagasaki Oranda no Shōkan*, 9–13.
52 Blussé and Viallé, eds., *The Deshima Dagregisters, Volumes XIII*, 44: February 13–15, 1668.
53 NFJ 61: January 18, 1648.
54 M. E. van Opstall, "Dutchmen and Japanese in the Eighteenth Century," in *Trading Companies in Asia: 1600–1830*, ed. J. van Goor (Utrecht: Hes Uitgevers, 1986), 117.
55 All records of the silver ship can be found in Blussé and Viallé, eds., *The Deshima Dagregisters, Volumes XII*, 1648–50.
56 Screech, *Secret Memoirs of the Shoguns*, 47. Screech tells us that a second model was requested in 1718, but because one did not come from Batavia, a model from the chief merchant's own belongings was given the next year instead.
57 Ryusaku Tsunoda, Wm. Theodore De Barry, and Donald Keene, eds., *Sources of Japanese Tradition, Volume 1* (New York: Columbia University Press, 1958), 27–29.
58 Walter Edwards, "In Pursuit of Himiko. Postwar Archaeology and the Location of Yamatai," *Monumenta Nipponica* 51, no. 1 (Spring 1996): 53–79.
59 NFJ 61: January 18, 1648.
60 Viallé and Blussé, eds., *The Deshima Dagregisters, Volumes XII*, 152: May 5, 1654.
61 NFJ 69: February 6, 1656.
62 NFJ 69: February 13, 1656.
63 Viallé and Blussé, eds., *The Deshima Dagregisters, Volumes XII*, 287: February 17, 1657.
64 Viallé and Blussé, eds., *The Deshima Dagregisters, Volumes XIII*, 322: January 3, 1670.
65 NFJ 74: April 14, 1661.
66 Viallé and Blussé, eds., *The Deshima Dagregisters, Volumes XII*, 255: July 1, 1656.
67 Screech, *The Shogun's Painted Culture*, 38.
68 NFJ 68: February 4, 1655.

69 Viallé and Blussé, eds., *The Deshima Dagregisters, Volumes XIII*, April 29, 1666.
70 Kaempfer, *The History of Japan*, Volume 2, 171.

Chapter 4

1 NFJ 69: February 21, 1656; Blussé and Viallé, eds., *The Deshima Dagregisters, Volume XII*, 247.
2 NFJ 69: February 5, 1658. Blussé and Viallé, eds., *The Deshima Dagregisters, Volume XII*, 335.
3 Peter Kornicki, "Narrative of a Catastrophe: *Musashi Abumi* and the Meireki Fire," *Japan Forum* 21 no. 3 (2010), 347–61.
4 Roman Cybriwsky, *Historical Dictionary of Tokyo* (Plymouth: The Scarecrow Press, 2011), 140.
5 Matsukata Fuyuko, "Fires and Recoveries Witnessed by the Dutch in Edo and Nagasaki: The Great Fire of Meireki in 1657 and the Great Fire of Kanbun in 1633," *Itinerario* 37, no. 3 (December 2013): 172–87.
6 NFJ 71: February 12, 1658.
7 NFJ 62: October 8, 1649.
8 For an interesting, if enigmatic, source on telescopes in Japan, see Peter Abraham, "The History of the Telescope in Japan," http://home.europa.com/~telscope/tsjapan.txt.
9 Henk Zoomers, "The Netherlands, Siam, and the Telescope. The First Asian Encounter with a Dutch Invention," in *The Origins of the Telescope*, ed. Albert van Helden et al. (Amsterdam: KNAW Press, 2010), 305–6. On the occasion of the 400th anniversary of Dutch-Japanese relations, a new telescope, constructed according to traditional methods, was given to the Japanese: Sean Curtin, "The Return of Japan's Long Lost Telescope," accessed April 2, 2019, https://www.japansociety.org.uk/34439/the-return-telescope/.
10 NFJ 57: May 7, 1644.
11 Viallé and Blussé, eds., *The Deshima Dagregisters, Volume XI*, 42: October 28, 1641; 143: December 14, 1641.
12 Ibid., 268: January 9, 1647.
13 The following exchanges can all be found in Viallé and Blussé, eds., *The Deshima Dagregisters, Volumes XI and XII*.
14 Ibid., 245: February 19, 1656.
15 Ibid., 162: September 27, 1654.
16 See, for example, Cecilia Segawa Seigle, "Tokugawa Tsunayoshi and the Formation of Edo Castle Rituals of Gift-Giving," in *Mediated by Gifts: Politics and Society in Japan, 1350–1850*, ed. Martha Chaiklin (Leiden: Brill, 2016).

17 Ibid., 245: February 19, 1656.
18 Viallé and Blussé, eds., *The Deshima Dagregisters, Volume XII*, 287–88: February 18, 1657.
19 Ibid, 381: April 7, 1659.
20 MIT Visualizing Culture, "Black Ships and Samurai," accessed April 4, 2019, https://visualizingcultures.mit.edu/black_ships_and_samurai/gallery/pages/02_016a_Dejima.htm.
21 The original painting is housed in the Peabody Essex Museum.
22 Vermuelen et al., eds., *Deshima Dagregisters, Volume VIII: 1760–1780*, 10.
23 Viallé and Blussé, eds., *The Deshima Dagregisters, Volume XI*, 272–73: January 15, 1647.
24 Ibid., XII, 368–69: October 8, 1649.
25 Ibid., *XII*, 42–43: January 31, 1652.
26 Ibid., 64–65: May 24, 1652; 88–89: October 28, 1652.
27 Ibid., *XIII*, 256: April 25, 1668.
28 Ibid., 238: February 6, 1656.
29 NFJ 65: February 1–21, 1652.
30 Viallé and Blussé, eds., *The Deshima Dagregisters, Volume XIII*, 218: April 14, 1667.
31 Ibid., *XI*, 325: October 7, 1648.
32 Ibid, 282: April 10, 1647. This type of comment is made several times in the diaries. On December 7, for example, the chief merchant relates that because their old patron cannot accept gifts, the chief merchant sets the price very low. NFJ 57: December 7, 1643.
33 NFJ 69: October 27, 1655.
34 NFJ 69: February 11, 1656.
35 Viallé and Blussé, eds., *The Deshima Dagregisters, Volume XII*, 6: January 9, 1651.
36 NFJ 57: May 7, 1644.
37 NFJ 60: November 23, 1646.
38 Viallé and Blussé, eds., *The Deshima Dagregisters, Volume XIII*, 296: April 17, 1669.
39 Ibid., *XI*, 248. November 23, 1646.
40 Peter Borschberg, "The Euro-Asian Trade in Bezoar Stones (approx. 1500–1700)," in *Artistic and Cultural Exchanges between Europe and Asia, 1400–1900: Rethinking Markets, Workshops and Collections*, ed. Thomas Kaufmann and M. North (Aldershot: Ashgate, 2010), 29–43.
41 A complete, and fascinating, description of bezoar stones in Asia can be found in Philip Baldaeus, *A Description of the East Indian Coast of Malabar and Coromandel and also of the Isle of Ceylon with Their Adjacent Kingdoms and Provinces* (London: A. and J. Churchill, 1672), 658.
42 Viallé and Blussé, eds., *The Deshima Dagregisters, Volume XI*, 393: April 10, 1650.
43 Ibid., 197: February 21, 1655.

44 Ibid., *XI*, 396: July 10, 1650. We are told that the pyrotechnist also built a redoubt for the Shogun and was going to attack it with the mortars, once ordnance could be sent from Nagasaki for the purpose. See NFJ 63: October 4, 1650. Christopher Joby tells us a bit about the pyrotechnist: "The Swede, Juriaen Schedel . . . remained . . . in Edo for a considerable period of time after the audience with the Shogun. Schedel gave the Japanese lessons in mathematics, surgery and mortar shooting. He is described as a vuerwercker, or low-ranking artilleryman (referred to as a corporal in English texts), and so doubt must necessarily be cast on the effectiveness of his lessons in the first two subjects mentioned. Nevertheless, he is also said to have taught the skills of geometry and surveying to Hōjō Ujinaga (1610–1670), who would become a celebrated cartographer." Christopher Richard Joby, "Dutch in Seventeenth-Century Japan: A Social History," *Dutch Crossing* 42 no. 2 (2018): 175–96.

45 Goodman, *Japan and the Dutch*, 25–26 and Hesselink, *Prisoners from Nambu*.

46 Viallé and Blussé, eds., *The Deshima Dagregisters, Volume XII*, 191: February 2, 1655.

47 Stephen Gudeman, "Postmodern Gifts," in *Postmodernism, Economics, and Knowledge*, ed. Stephen Cullenberg, Jack Amariglio, and David Ruccio (London: Routledge, 2001) as quoted in Margarita Winkel, "Gift Exchange and Reciprocity: Understanding Antiquarian/Ethnographic Communities Within and Beyond Tokugawa Borders," in *Mediated by Gifts: Politics and Society in Japan*, ed. Martha Chaiklin (Leiden: Brill, 2016), 220.

48 Suzuki, *Japan-Netherlands Trade, 1600–1800*, 191.

49 As quoted in Suzuki, *Japan-Netherlands Trade, 1600–1800*, 192.

50 NFJ 61: September 4–9, 1648.

51 NFJ 65: December 6, 1651.

52 Jayant S. Joshi and Rajesh Kumar, "The Dutch Physicians at Dejima or Deshima and the Rise of Western Medicine in Japan," *Proceedings of the Indian History Congress* 63 (2002): 1062–72.

53 Beatrice Bodart-Bailey, "Kaempfer Restor'd," *Monumenta Nipponica* 43, no. 1 (Spring, 1988): 10.

54 Christopher Joby tells us, "In 1650 Schamberger visited Edo on the hofreis. He was required to spend an extended period in Edo due to the poor health of Shogun Iemitsu. It would be Schamberger's success in treating 'a member of Iemitsu's court' that first led the Japanese to believe that there was some value in Western learning. Schamberger spent ten months at Edo instructing the court physicians in medicine and became the founder of the Kasuparuryū (Caspar School), which continued to function until the end of the Tokugawa period (1603–1868)." Joby, "Dutch in Seventeenth-Century Japan: A Social History."

55 Wolfgang Michel, "Medicine and Allied Sciences in the Cultural Exchange between Japan and Europe in the Seventeenth Century," in *Theories and Methods in Japanese*

Studies: Current State & Future Developments—Papers in Honor of Josef Kreiner, ed. Hans Dieter Ölschleger (Göttingen: Vandenhoeck & Ruprecht Unipress, 2007): 285–302. Goodman states that Schamberger's visit set a precedent for the surgeon going on the court journey to Edo. Goodman, *Dutch Impact on Japan*, 29.

56 Richard Rubinger, *Private Academies of the Tokugawa Period* (Princeton: Princeton University Press, 1988), 113.

57 Vermeulen et al., eds., *Deshima Dagregisters, Volume 2*: April 7–9, 1760. The visiting physicians were also treated to anisette and sweetmeats.

58 Mukai Gensho, for example, came to the Deshima specifically to train with the Dutch surgeon in 1656. See Blussé and Viallé, eds., *The Deshima Dagregisters, Volumes XII*, 252: May 7, 1656.

59 Ibid., *Volumes XII*, 278: December 13, 1656.

60 Terrance Jackson, *Network of Knowledge: Western Science and the Tokugawa Information Revolution* (Honolulu: University of Hawai'i Press, 2016).

61 Mina Ishizu and Simona Valeriani, "Botanical Knowledge in Early Modern Japan and Europe: Transformations and Parallel Developments," in *Transformations of Knowledge in Dutch Expansion*, ed. Susanne Friedrich, Arndt Brendecke, and Stefan Ehrenpreis (Berlin: de Gruyter, 2015); Joby, "Dutch in Seventeenth-Century Japan: A Social History," 175–96.

62 An important study of this subject is W. J. Boot, "The Transfer of Learning: The Import of Chinese and Dutch Books in Tokugawa Japan," *Itinerario* 37, no. 3 (2013): 188–206.

63 Peter Kornicki, *The Book in Japan: A Cultural History from the Beginnings to the Nineteenth Century* (Leiden: Brill, 1998), 302.

64 Ibid., 303.

65 Viallé and Blussé, eds., *The Deshima Dagregisters, Volume XIII*; April 24, 1659.

66 For a thorough discussion of clocks as gifts, see Chaiklin, *Cultural Commerce and Dutch Commercial Culture*, 89–101.

67 NFJ 83: August 3–November 1, 1670. Viallé and Blussé, eds., *The Deshima Dagregisters, Volume XIII*, 347–67.

68 Geoffrey Gunn, *Asia without Borders: The Making of an Asian World Region, 1000–1800* (Hong Kong: Hong Kong University Press, 2011), 255–62; Kate Wildman Nakai, *Shogunal Politics: Arai Hakuseki and the Premise of Tokugawa Rule* (Cambridge, MA: Harvard University Asia Center, 1988), chapter 5.

69 Keene, *The Japanese Discovery of Europe, 1720–1830*, 6.

70 Chaiklin, *Cultural Commerce and Dutch Commercial Culture*, 2.

71 Nagazumi, Yōko, "From Company to Individual Company Servants: Dutch Trade in Eighteenth Century Japan," in *On the Eighteenth Century as a Category of Asian History: Van Leur in Retrospect*, ed. Leonard Blussé and Femme Gaastra (Aldershot: Ashgate, 1998), 148.

72 The chief merchant in 1752 complained that the Japanese were asking for microscopes as if the Dutch had them just laying about! Blussé et al., eds., *Deshima Diaries Volume 2*: October 8, 1752.

Chapter 5

1 Amy Shuman, "Food Gifts: Ritual Exchange and the Production of Excess Meaning," *The Journal of American Folklore* 113, no. 450 (Autumn, 2000): 495–508.
2 Harumi Befu, "Gift Giving in a Modernizing Japan," *Monumenta Nipponica* 23, no. 3/4 (1968): 447.
3 Eirik Furubotn and Rudolf Richter, *Institutions and Economic Theory: The Contribution of the New Institutional Economics* (Ann Arbor: University of Michigan Press, 2005), 175.
4 For a theoretical perspective on gift-giving and utilitarianism, see Aafte Komter, "Gifts and Social Relations: The Mechanisms of Reciprocity," *International Sociology* 22, no. 1 (2007): 93–107.
5 Befu, "Gift Giving in a Modernizing Japan," 445.
6 Yonemori Keizo, "Japanese Pomological Magic: Producing Fruits for Gifts," *Chronica Horticulturae* 49, no. 3 (2009): 15–18.
7 As noted in the introduction, this is a prime consideration of the *omiyage* that are purchased by tourists for friends, families, and co-workers. Lin Lin and Pei-chuan Mao, "Content Analysis Study of Food Specialties and Souvenirs," *Journal of Hospitality and tourism Management* 22 (March, 2015): 19–29.
8 Blussé and Viallé, eds., *The Deshima Dagregisters*, XII, 306–07: May 10–11, 1657.
9 Grant Goodman estimates that there were well over two hundred officials directly related to the Dutch on Deshima, although he also notes that "many . . . were nothing more than hangers-on and all of whom were listed on the Dutch expense account." Goodman, *Japan and the Dutch, 1600–1853*, 20–21.
10 Kailin Wooley and Ayelet Fishbach, "A Recipe for Friendship: Similar Food Consumption Promotes Trust and Cooperation," *Journal of Consumer Psychology* 27, no. 1 (2017): 1–10. "We find that strangers who are assigned to eat similar (vs. dissimilar) foods are more trusting of each other in a trust game (Study 1). Food consumption further influences conflict resolution, with strangers who are assigned to eat similar foods cooperating more in a labor negotiation, and therefore earning more money (Study 2)."
11 Blussé and Viallé, eds., *The Deshima Dagregisters, Volume XI*, 252–53: February 4, 13, 1647.
12 Michael Kinski, "*Materia Medica* in Edo Period Japan: The Case of Mummy," *Japonica Humboldtiana* 9 (2005): 120.

13 Dirk Barreveld, *From New Amsterdam to New York: The Founding of New York by the Dutch in July 1625* (San Jose: Writers Club Press, 2001), 205.
14 Goodman, *Japan: The Dutch Experience*, 61. For the aesthetics of gift presentation, see Joy Hendry, *Wrapping Culture: Politeness, Presentation, and Power in Japan and Other Societies* (Oxford: Oxford University Press, 1993).
15 The chief merchant writes in 1778 that because of the death of the heir to the shogunate, they may have to stay in Edo for longer than usual. He requested "250 bottles of red wine, one cellaret of jenever, and one cask of butter." See Vermeulen et al., eds., *Deshima Dagregisters, Volume VIII: 1760–1780*: April 28, 1778. Olive oil is not mentioned nearly as much as wine, but, especially in the later seventeenth century onward, it becomes a source of small gift-giving.
16 Blussé and Viallé, eds., *The Deshima Dagregisters, Volume XII*, 186: December 21, 1654.
17 NFJ 57: May 7, 1644.
18 Blussé and Viallé, eds., *The Deshima Dagregisters, Volume XI*, 288: July 2, 1647.
19 Ibid, 41: October 24, 1641.
20 The English factory head, Richard Cocks, recorded the shogunal decree in his diary: Thompson, *Diary of Richard Cocks*, 191.
21 NFJ: February 29, 1660.
22 Blussé and Viallé, eds., *The Deshima Dagregisters, Volume XI*, 14: August 1, 1641.
23 Joji Nozawa, "Wine as a Luxury at the Dutch Factory at Japan During the Second Half of the 18th Century," in *Luxury in the Low Countries: Miscellaneous Reflections on Netherlandish Material Culture, 1500 to the Present*, ed. Rengenier Rittersma (Brussels: Pharo Publishing, 2010), 98–99.
24 Joji Nozawa, "Wine Drinking Culture in Seventeenth Century Japan: The Role of Dutch Merchants," in *Japanese Foodways, Past and Present*, ed. Eric Rath and Stephanie Assmann (Urbana: University of Illinois Press, 2010), 110.
25 Ibid., 109.
26 Ibid., 113–14.
27 Blussé et al., eds., *The Deshima Diaries Marginalia: 1740–1800*: April 6, 1750.
28 Vermeulen et al., eds., *Deshima Dagregisters, Volume VIII: 1760–1780*: January 30: 1771.
29 Nozawa, "Wine Drinking Culture in Seventeenth Century Japan," 115.
30 Blussé and Viallé, eds., *The Deshima Dagregisters, Volume XI*, 19: August 8, 1641.
31 Ibid., 41: October 24, 1641.
32 Ibid., 155: December 23, 1643; 158: February 14, 1644.
33 Ibid., 382: January 17, 1650.
34 Ibid., 19: February 14, 1643; Michael Kinski, "Table Manners in the Edo Period," in *Japanese Foodways Past and Present*, ed. Eric Rath and Stephanie Assmann (Urbana: University of Illinois Press, 2010), 48. Eric Rath writes that *osakana* often consisted

of "konbu seaweed, dried chestnuts, and dried abalone." See Eric Rath, "Banquets against Boredom: Towards Understanding (Samurai) Cuisine in Early Modern Japan," *Early Modern Japan: An Interdisciplinary Journal* XVI (2008), 47.

35 David Wondrich, "Recovering the World's First Luxury Spirit: Batavia Arrack," accessed April 10, 2019, https://www.thedailybeast.com/rediscovering-the-worlds-first-luxury-spirit-batavia-arrack. Kerry Marjorie Knerr, "In Search of a Good Drink: Punches, Cocktails, and Imperial Consumption," Master's Thesis, University of Texas, 2015.

36 Hubert Paul, "De Coningh on Deshima: Mijn Verblijf in Japan, 1856," *Monumenta Nipponica* 32, no. 3 (Autumn, 1977): 351.

37 Quoted in Leupp, *Interracial Intimacy in Japan*, 112–13.

38 Leonard Blussé et al., eds., *Deshima Dagregisters, Volume 2*: March 22, 1743.

39 Eric Rath, *Food and Fantasy in Early Modern Japan* (Berkeley: University of California Press, 2010), 39, 115.

40 Michael Cooper, *Joao Rodrigues's Account of Sixteenth-Century Japan* (London: The Hakluyt Society, 2002), 206. While in modern Japanese *sakana* is the word for fish, in this context the word refers to any number of small foodstuffs that were meant to be eaten with rice wine. This could have included fish, but could also have been vegetables or even sweets.

41 The Dutch were also treated to "sweetmeats" when they visited officials such as the Nagasaki *bugyō*'s residence in Nagasaki. An interesting account of such a visit can be found in James Duncan Phillips, "The Voyage of the Margaret in 1801: The First Salem Voyage to Japan," *Proceedings of the American Antiquarian Society* 54, no. 2 (October, 1944): 321. This account is of an American ship that was chartered by the Dutch in Batavia to get around English naval blockades of Dutch shipping during the Napoleonic Wars. The author goes on to relate that the whole party was lavishly wined and dined after this round of appetizers, and the entertainment for the evening included "tumblers."

42 Rath, "Banquets Against Boredom," 47.

43 Eric Rath, "Honzen Dining: The Poetry of Formal Meals in Late Medieval and Early Modern Japan," in *Japanese Foodways, Past and Present*, ed. Eric Rath and Stephanie Assmann (Urbana: University of Illinois Press, 2010), 25.

44 Nozawa, "Wine as a Luxury at the Dutch Factory in Japan during the Second Half of the Eighteenth Century," 102.

45 J. F. Van Overmeer Fischer, *Bijdrage tot de Kennis von het Japansche Rijk* (Amsterdam: J. Mueller and Co., 1833); Vos, "A Distance of Thirteen Thousand Miles," 133.

46 In May 1644, a daimyo to whom the Dutch gave the gift of a dog told the Company explicitly that he wanted to use it as a gift for the Shogun. NFJ 57: May 16, 1644. Adam Clulow writes that when the Dutch were based at Hirado, the gifts they gave

to the local daimyo family, the Matsuura, were resold for a tidy profit. See Adam Clulow, "From Global Entrepot to Early Modern Domain: Hirado, 1609–1641," *Monumenta Nipponica* 65, no. 1 (Spring, 2010): 8.
47 NFJ 60: February 4, 1657.
48 NFJ 67: August 27, 1654.
49 Paul, "De Coningh on Deshima: Mijn Verblijf in Japan, 1856," 359.
50 Marc Jason Gilbert, "Paper Trails: Deshima Island: A Stepping Stone between Civilizations," *World History Connected* 3, no. 3 (July, 2006). http://worldhistoryconnected.press.uillinois.edu/3.3/gilbert.html.
51 Blussé and Viallé, eds., *The Deshima Dagregisters, Volume XII*, 373–74: December 20, 1658.
52 Nozawa, "Wine Drinking Culture in Seventeenth Century Japan,"109.
53 NFJ 65: July 21, 1652.
54 NFJ 65: August 2, 1652.
55 NFJ 65: October 22–26, 1652.
56 Blussé and Viallé, eds., *The Deshima Dagregisters, Volume XII*, 134: February 8, 1654.
57 NFJ 67: March 16, 1654.

Epilogue

1 The best comprehensive synopsis of this era in US-Japanese relations is found in Sakamaki Shunzo, *Japan and the US, 1790–1853* (Tokyo: Asiatic Society of Japan, 1939).
2 Suzuki, *Japan-Netherlands Trade, 1600–1800*, 153–54.
3 For a good, relatively recent, summary of this period, as well as a description of Hendrick Doeff, see Blussé, *Visible Cities*, 91–99.
4 A comprehensive review of Stewart's voyages to Japan can be found in Walter Gourlay, "A Camel for the Shogun: William Robert Stewart and the Deshima Connection," ASPAC (2008), Centre for Asia-Pacific Initiatives, University of Victoria, British Columbia.
5 Screech, *The Shogun's Painted Culture, 1600–1800*, 85–86.
6 Hendrik Doeff, the chief merchant at the time, relates much of these events in Hendrick Doeff, *Recollections of Japan*, trans. and annotated Annick Doeff (Victoria, B.C: Trafford, 2003).
7 Bob Tadashi Wakabayaki, *Anti-Foreignism and Western Learning in in Early Modern Japan: The New Theses of 1825* (Cambridge, MA: Harvard University Asia Center, 1986), 91.
8 Kanai Madoka, ed., *A Diary of William Cleveland, Captain's Clerk aboard the Massachusetts* (Quezon City, Philippines: Institute of Asian Studies, University of the Philippines, 1965), 380.

9. For a thoroughly researched account of Roberts' two journeys to Asia, see Andrew Jampoler, *Embassy to the Eastern Courts: America's Secret First Pivot Towards Asia, 1832–37* (Annapolis: Naval Institute Press, 2015).
10. According to Martha Chaiklin, the sheep appear in the demands of the Shogun in the mid-eighteenth century, but the Dutch refused to import sheep that were suitable for the production of woolen cloth in order not to jeopardize their own production. See Chaiklin, *Cultural Commerce and Dutch Commercial Culture*, 52.
11. Ibid., 115.
12. For an overview of the Perry expedition, see James Huffman, *Japan in World History* (New York: Oxford University Press, 2010), 73.
13. Steven Lubar, "In the Footsteps of Perry: The Smithsonian Goes to Japan," *The Public Historian* 17, no. 3 (Summer, 1995): 26.
14. S. Wells Williams, *A Journal of the Perry Expedition (1853–1854)*, ed. F. W. Williams (Yokohama: Kelly and Walsh, 1910).
15. Francis Hawks, *Narrative of the Expedition of an American Squadron to the China Seas and Japan: Performed in the Years 1852, 1853, and 1854, under the Command of Commodore M. C. Perry, United States Navy, by Order of the Government of the United States* (Washington: Beverly Tucker, 1856).
16. Nitobe Inazo, *The Intercourse between the US and Japan* (Baltimore: John Hopkins Press, 1891).
17. Matthew Calbraith Perry, *The Japan Expedition, 1852–1854; The Personal Journal of Commodore Matthew C. Perry*, ed. Roger Pineau with an Introduction by Samuel Eliot Morison (Washington, DC: Smithsonian Institution Press, 1968), 233.
18. Oliver Statler, *The Black Ship Scrolls* (Rutland, VT: Charles Tuttle Company, 1964).
19. On December 25, 1641, the Dutch gave the Shogun gifts of two pieces of ordnance, grenades, and balls, among other things. The Dutch handed these weapons over to the Japanese "armorer" to await instructions from the court. NFJ 56: December 25, 1641.
20. Perry, *Narrative of the Expedition*, 458. The Library of congress contains a brilliant digital collection surrounding Perry's voyage to Japan, including a concise timeline of events, "Timeline of the 1852 to 1855 Voyage of the U. S. Steam Frigate Mississippi, Part 3," accessed April 16, 2019, https://www.loc.gov/collections/william-speiden-journals/articles-and-essays/voyage-of-mississippi-to-china-seas-and-japan/january-1854-to-july-2-1854/.
21. Martha Chaiklin, "Monopolists to Middlemen: Dutch Liberalism and American Imperialism in the Opening of Japan," *The Journal of World History* 21, no. 2 (June 2010): 249–69.
22. Hawks, *Narrative of the Expedition*, 4.
23. Chaiklin, "Monopolists to Middlemen," 255.
24. George Henry Preble, *The Opening of Japan: A Diary of Discovery in the Far East, 1853–1856*, ed. Boleslaw Szczesniak (Norman: University of Oklahoma Press,

1962), 126. Victor Fell Yellin, "Mrs. Belmont, Matthew Perry, and the 'Japanese Minstrels,'" *American Music* 14, no. 3 (Autumn, 1996): 257–75. Perry's use of music as well as food and drink are, of course, reminiscent of successful Dutch strategies on Deshima.

25 Kanai, ed., *A Diary of William Cleveland.*

Bibliography

Primary Sources

The major archival source used in this book is entitled *Het Archief van de Nederlandse Facorij in Japan*, 1609–1860 and is located at the Nationaal Archief in the Hague, The Netherlands (Nationaal Archief, Den Haag, Nederlandse Factorij in Japan, nummer toegang 1.04.21). An inventory of the contents of this archive can be found online at http://www.gahetna.nl/collectie/archief/ead/index/eadid/1.04.21 and in book form: Roessingh, M. P. H. *Het Archief van de Nederlandse Facorij in Japan, 1609–1860*. The Hague: Algemeen Rijksarchief, 1964. Most of the sources for this book come from edited versions of these archives, most notably:

Blussé, Leonard and Cynthia Viallé, eds. *The Deshima Dagregisters, Volumes XI–XIII*. Leiden, The Netherlands: Institute for the History of European Expansion, 2001–2010.

Blussé, Leonard, M. E. van Opstall, and Ts'ao Yung-ho, eds. *De Daghregister Van Het Kasteel Zeelandia, Taiwan, Deel I (1625–1640)*. Den Haag: Instituut Voor Nederlandse Geschiedenis, 1994.

Coolhaas, W. Ph., ed. *Generale Missiven van Gouverneurs-Generaal en Raden aan Heren XVII der Verenigde Oostindische Compagnie*. 's-Gravenhage: Martinus Nijhoff, 1960.

Narushima, Motonao. *Kokushi Taikei: Tokugawa Jikki*. Edited by Kuroita Katsumi. Tokyo: Yoshikawa Kōbunkan, 1982.

Matsui Yoko and Matsukata Fuyuko, eds. *Dagregisters Gehouden bij de Opperhoofden van het Nederlandsche Factorij in Japan*. Tokyo: Historiographical Institute, 1974.

Remelink, Willem, et al., eds. *The Deshima Diaries Marginalia: 1740–1800*. Tokyo: Japan-Netherlands Institute, 2004.

Velde, Paul van der and Rudolf Backofner, eds. *The Deshima Diaries: Marginalia, 1700–1740*. Tokyo: The Japan-Netherlands Institute, 1992.

Vermuelen, Tom, et al., eds. *Deshima Dagregisters, Their Original Table of Contents, Volume VIII: 1760–1780*. Leiden: Leiden Centre for the History of European Expansion, 1986.

Secondary Sources (English, Dutch, and Japanese)

Abraham, Peter. "The History of the Telescope in Japan." http://home.europa.com/~telscope/tsjapan.txt.

Andrade, Tonio. *How Taiwan Became Chinese: Dutch, Spanish, and Han Colonization in the Seventeenth Century*. New York: Columbia University Press, 2008.

Andrade, Tonio. *Lost Colony: The Untold Story of China's First Great Victory over the West*. Princeton: Princeton University Press, 2013.

Andrade, Tonio. *The Gunpowder Age, China, Military Innovation, and the Rise of the West in World History*. Princeton: Princeton University Press, 2016.

Arano, Yasunori. *Kinsei Nihon to Higashi Ajia*. Tokyo: University of Tokyo Press, 1988.

Asao, Naohiro. *Nihon no Kinsei 1: Seikai Shi no naka no Kinsei*. Tokyo: Chūō Kōronsha, 1991.

Baldaeus, Phillip. *A Description of the East Indian Coast of Malabar and Coromandel and also of the Isle of Ceylon with Their Adjacent Kingdoms and Provinces*. London: A. and J. Churchill, 1672.

Barreveld, Dirk. *From New Amsterdam to New York: The Founding of New York by the Dutch in July 1625*. San Jose: Writers Club Press, 2001.

Befu, Harumi. "Gift Giving in a Modernizing Japan." *Monumenta Nipponica* 23, no. 3/4 (1968): 445–56.

Belk, R. W. and G. S. Coon. "Gift-Giving as Agapic Love: An Alternative to the Exchange Paradigm Based on Dating Experiences." *Journal of Consumer Research* 20 (1993): 393–417.

Belozerskaya, Maria. *The Medici Giraffe: And Other Tales of Exotic Animals and Power*. New York: Hachette, 2009.

Biedermann, Zoltan, Anne Gerritsen, and Giorgio Riello, eds. *Global Gifts: The Material Culture of Diplomacy in Early Modern Eurasia*. Cambridge: Cambridge University Press, 2017.

Blussé, Leonard. "Bull in a China Shop: Pieter Nuyts in China and Japan." In *Around and About Formosa: Essays in Honor of Professor Ta'ao Yung-ho*, edited by Leonard Blussé. Taipei: Ta'ao Yung-ho Foundation for Culture and Education, 2003.

Blussé, Leonard. *Visible Cities: Canton, Nagasaki, and Batavia and the Coming of the Americans*. Cambridge, MA: Harvard University Press, 2008.

Blussé, Leonard. "The Grand Inquisitor Inoue Chikugo no Kami Masashige, Spin Doctor of the Tokugawa Bakufu." *Bulletin of Portuguese-Japanese Studies* 7 (2003): 23–43.

Bodart-Bailey, Beatrice. "A Song for the Shogun: Engelbert Kaempfer and 17th-c. Japan." *IIAS Newsletter Online, 22: 400 Years of Dutch Japanese Relations* (2009), http://www.iias.nl/iiasn/22/theme/22T3.html.

Bodart-Bailey, Beatrice. "Kaempfer Restor'd." *Monumenta Nipponica* 43, no. 1 (Spring, 1988): 1–33.

Bodart-Bailey, Beatrice, ed. *Kaempfer's Japan: Tokugawa Culture Observed*. Honolulu: University of Hawai'i Press, 1999.

Boot, W. J. "The Transfer of Learning: The Import of Chinese and Dutch Books in Tokugawa Japan." *Itinerario* 37, no. 3 (2013): 188–206.

Borschberg, Peter. "The Euro-Asian Trade in Bezoar Stones (approx. 1500–1700)." In *Artistic and Cultural Exchanges between Europe and Asia, 1400–1900: Rethinking*

Markets, Workshops and Collections, edited by Thomas Kaufmann and M. North. Aldershot: Ashgate, 2010: 29–43.

Boxer, Charles. *Jan Compagnie in Japan, 1600–1850: An Essay on the Cultural Artistic and Scientific Influence Exercised by the Hollanders in Japan from the Seventeenth to the Nineteenth Centuries.* Den Haag: Martinus Nijhoff, 1950.

Boxer, Charles. *The Christian Century in Japan.* Berkeley: University of California Press, 1951.

Brauner, Christina. "Connecting Things: Trading Companies and Diplomatic Gift Giving on the Gold and Slave Coasts in the seventeenth and Eighteenth Centuries." *Journal of Early Modern History* 20 (2016): 408–28.

Bredsdorff, Asta. *The Trials and Travels of Willem Leyel: An Account of the Danish East India Company in Tranquebar, 1639–1648.* Copenhagen: Museum Tusculanum Press, 2009.

Burnell, Arthur Coke, ed. *The Voyage of John Huyghen van Linschotten to the East Indies.* London: Hakluyt Society, 1885.

Burnett, Ian. *East Indies.* Kenthurst, NSW: Rosenberg Publishing, 2013.

Chaiklin, Martha. *Cultural Commerce and Dutch Commercial Culture: The Influence of European Material Culture on Japan, 1700–1850.* Leiden: CNWS Studies in Overseas History 5, 2003.

Chaiklin, Martha. "Exotic Bird Collecting in Early Modern Japan." In *JAPANimals: History and Culture in Japan's Animal Life*, edited by Gregory Pflugfelder and Brett Walker. Ann Arbor: Center for Japanese Studies, University of Michigan, 2005.

Chaiklin, Martha. "Monopolists to Middlemen: Dutch Liberalism and American Imperialism in the Opening of Japan." *The Journal of World History* 21, no. 2 (June, 2010): 249–69.

Chaiklin, Martha. "The Merchant's Ark: Live Animal Gifts in Early Modern Dutch-Japanese Relations." *World History Connected* 9, no. 1 (February, 2012), http://worldhistoryconnected.press.uillinois.edu/9.1/chaiklin.html.

Chaiklin, Martha. *Mediated by Gifts: Politics and Society in Japan, 1350–1850.* Leiden: Brill, 2016.

Champetier, Charles. "Philosophy of the Gift: Jacques Derrida, Martin Heidegger." *Angelaki: Journal of the Theoretical Humanities* 6, no. 2 (2001): 15–22.

Cheng, Shaogang. *De VOC en Formosa, 1624–1662: Een Vergeten Geschiedenis.* Amsterdam: Bataafsche Leeuw, 1997.

Cieslik, Hubert, SJ. "The Case of Christovão Ferreira." *Monumenta Nipponica* 29, no. 1 (Spring, 1974): 1–54.

Clulow, Adam. "From Global Entrepot to Early Modern Domain: Hirado, 1609–1641." *Monumenta Nipponica* 65, no. 1 (Spring, 2010): 1–35.

Clulow, Adam. "A Fake Embassy: The Lord of Taiwan and Tokugawa Japan." In *Statecraft and Spectacle in East Asia: Studies in Taiwan-Japan Relations*, edited by Adam Clulow. New York: Routledge, 2011.

Clulow, Adam. *The Company and the Shogun: The Dutch Encounter with Tokugawa Japan*. New York: Columbia University Press, 2014.

Clulow, Adam. "The Dutch East India Company, Global Networks, and Tokugawa Japan." In *Global Gifts: The Material Culture of Diplomacy in Early Modern Eurasia*, edited by Zoltann Biedermann, Anne Gerritsen, and Giorgio Riello. Cambridge: Cambridge University Press, 2018.

Cooper, Michael. "The Mechanics of the Macau-Nagasaki Silk Trade." *Monumenta Nipponica* 27, no. 4 (Winter, 1972): 423–33.

Cooper, Michael. *Joao Rodrigues's Account of Sixteenth-Century Japan*. London: The Hakluyt Society, 2002.

Corr, William. *Adams the Pilot: The Life and Times of Captain William Adams: 1564–1620*. London: Curzon Press, 1995.

Cullen, L. M. *A History of Japan, 1582–1941: Internal and External Worlds*. Cambridge: Cambridge University Press, 2003.

Curvelo, Alexandra. "Nagasaki/Deshima after the Portuguese in Dutch Accounts of the Seventeenth Century." *Bulletin of Portuguese/Japanese Studies* 6 (June, 2003): 147–57.

Cybriwsky, Roman. *Historical Dictionary of Tokyo*. Plymouth: The Scarecrow Press, 2011.

Dam, Pieter van. *Beschryvinge van de Oostindische Compagnie*. Edited by F. W. Stapel and C. W. Th. Van Boetzelaer. The Hague: Rijks Geschiedenis Publicatiën, 1977.

Davies, D. W. *A Primer of Dutch Seventeenth-Century Overseas Trade*. The Hague: Martinus Nijhoff, 1961.

Dekker, F. *Betrekkingen Tuschen de Oost-Indische Compagnie en Japan*. 's-Gravenhage: L. J. C. Boucher, 1941.

Derrida, Jacques. *Given Time: 1. Counterfeit Money*. Translated by P. Kamul. Chicago: University of Chicago Press, 1991.

Doeff, Hendrick. *Recollections of Japan*. Translated and annotated by Annick Doeff. Victoria, BC: Trafford, 2003.

Duffy, Christopher. *Siege Warfare: The Fortress in the Early Modern World, 1494–1660*. London: Routledge, 1996.

Eberspacher, Cord. "Johan Georg Keyserling: A German Horseman at Nagasaki and Edo." *Crossroads* 2 (Summer, 1994): 9–26.

Edwards, Walter. "In Pursuit of Himiko. Postwar Archaeology and the Location of Yamatai." *Monumenta Nipponica* 51, no. 1 (Spring, 1996): 53–79.

Effert, F. R., ed. *The Court Journey to the shogun of Japan: From a Private Account by Jan Cock Blomhoff*. Leiden: Hotei Publishing, 2000.

Elison, George. *Deus Destroyed: The Image of Christianity in Early Modern Japan*. Cambridge, MA: Harvard University Press, 1973.

Elisonas, Jurgis. "Christianity and the Daimyo." In *The Cambridge History of Japan, Volume 4*, edited by John Hall. Cambridge: Cambridge University Press, 1991.

Ellis, Richard. *Tiger Bone and Rhino Horn: The Destruction of Wildlife for Traditional Chinese Medicine*. Washington, DC: Island Press, 2005.

Endō, Shūsaku. *Silence*. Translated by William Johnston. New York: Picador Modern Classics, 2016.

Farrington, Anthony and Derek Massarella. "William Adams and Early English Enterprise in Japan." LSE STICERD Research Paper No. IS/2000/394. July, 2000.

Furubotn, Eirik and Rudolf Richter. *Institutions and Economic Theory: The Contribution of the New Institutional Economics*. Ann Arbor: University of Michigan Press, 2005.

Gaastra, Femme. "The Dutch East India Company and the Intra-Asiatic Trade in Precious Metals." In *The Emergence of a World Economy, 1500–1914*, Part I (Papers of the XI International Congress of Economic History), edited by Wolfram Fischer, Marvin McInnis, and Jürgen Schneider. Stuttgart: F. Steiner Verlag Wiesbaden GmbH, 1986.

Gerritsen, Anne and Giorgio Riello, eds. *The Global Lives of Things: The Material Culture of Connections in the Early Modern World*. New York: Routledge, 2016.

Gilbert, Marc Jason. "Paper Trails: Deshima Island: A Stepping Stone between Civilizations." *World History Connected* 3, no. 3 (July, 2006), http://worldhistoryconnected.press.uillinois.edu/3.3/gilbert.html.

Golovnin, Vasili Mikhailovich. *Narrative of My Captivity in Japan, During the Years 1811, 1812, and 1813; With Observations on the Country and the People, Volume II*. London: Henry Colburn, 1818.

Goodman, Grant. *The Dutch Impact on Japan, 1640–1853*. Leiden: Brill, 1967.

Goodman, Grant. *Japan and the Dutch: 1600–1853*. London: Curzon Press, 2000.

Goodman, Grant. *Japan: The Dutch Experience*. London: Bloomsbury Publishing Company, 2012.

Goor, Jurrien van. *Prelude to Colonialism: The Dutch in Asia*. Hilversum: Verloren, 2004.

Gourlay, Walter. "A Camel for the Shogun: William Robert Stewart and the Deshima Connection." ASPAC 2008. Centre for Asia-Pacific Initiatives, University of Victoria, British Columbia, 2008.

Gregory, Chris. *Gifts and Commodities*. London, Academic Press, 1982.

Gudeman, Stephen. "Postmodern Gifts." In *Postmodernism, Economics, and Knowledge*, edited by Stephen Cullenberg, Jack Amariglio, and David Ruccio. London: Routledge, 2001.

Gulik, Willem van. *Een Verre Hofreis. Nederlanders op weg naar de Shogun van Japan*. Amersterdam: Koninklijk Paleis Amsterdam, 2000.

Gunn, Geoffrey. *Asia without Borders: The Making of an Asian World Region, 1000–1800*. Hong Kong: Hong Kong University Press, 2011.

Hane, Mikiso and Louis Perez. *Premodern Japan: A Historical Survey*. Boulder: Westview Press, 2015 [Originally published 1991].

Hawks, Francis. *Narrative of the Expedition of an American Squadron to the China Seas and Japan: Performed in the Years 1852, 1853, and 1854, Under the Command of Commodore M. C. Perry, United States Navy, by Order of the Government of the United States*. Washington: Beverly Tucker, 1856.

Heal, Felicity. *The Power of Gifts: Gift Exchange in Early Modern England*. London: Oxford University Press, 2014.
Hellyer, Robert. *Defining Engagement: Japan and Global Contexts, 1640–1868*. Cambridge, MA: Harvard University Asia Center, 2009.
Hendry, Joy. *Wrapping Culture: Politeness, Presentation, and Power in Japan and Other Societies*. Oxford: Oxford University Press, 1993.
Hesselink, Reinier. "A Metal Dealer and Spy from Nagasaki in Manila in the First Quarter of the Seventeenth Century." In *Money in Asia (1200–1900): Small Currencies in Social and Political Contexts*, edited by Jane Kate Leonard and Ulrich Theobald. Leiden: Brill, 2015.
Hesselink, Reinier. "A Dutch New Year at the Shirandō Academy: 1 January 1795." *Monumenta Nipponica* 50, no. 2 (Summer, 1995): 189–234.
Hesselink, Reinier. *Prisoners from Nambu: Reality and Make Believe in Seventeenth Century Japanese Diplomacy*. Honolulu: University of Hawai'i Press, 2001.
Hyde, Lewis. *The Gift: Imagination and the Erotic Life of Property*. New York: Random House, 1983.
Huffman, James. *Japan in World History*. New York: Oxford University Press, 2010.
Innes, Robert. *The Door Ajar: Japan's Foreign Trade in the Seventeenth Century*. Unpublished doctoral dissertation, Ann Arbor, MI, 1980.
Ishii Ryōsuke, ed. *Tokugawa Kinrei-Kō/Hōseishi Gakkai Hen.* vol. 6. Tokyo: Sōbunsha, 1959–61.
Ishizu, Mina and Simona Valeriani. "Botanical Knowledge in Early Modern Japan and Europe: Transformations and Parallel Developments." In *Transformations of Knowledge in Dutch Expansion*, edited by Susanne Friedrich, Arndt Brendecke, and Stefan Ehrenpreis. Berlin: de Gruyter, 2015.
Iwao, Seiichi. *Shuinsen Bōeki-shi no Kenkyū*. Tokyo: Kyōbundō, 1958.
Iwao, Seiichi. *Nihon no Rekishi 14: Sakoku*. Tokyo: Chūō Kōronsha, 1973.
Itazawa, Takeo. *Nihon to Oranda: Kinsei no Gaikō, Bōeki, Gakumon*. Tokyo: Shibundō, 1955.
Iwao, Seiichi. *Shuinsen to Nihonmachi*. Tokyo: Shibundō, 1964.
Iwao, Seiichi, ed. *Oranda Fūsetsugaki Shūsei*. Tokyo: Japan-Netherlands Institute, 1976.
Jackson, Terrance. *Network of Knowledge: Western Science and the Tokugawa Information Revolution*. Honolulu: University of Hawai'i Press, 2016.
Jampoler, Andrew. *Embassy to the Eastern Courts: America's Secret First Pivot Towards Asia, 1832–37*. Annapolis: Naval Institute Press, 2015.
Jansen, Marius. *China in the Tokugawa World*. Cambridge, MA: Harvard University Press, 2000a.
Jansen, Marius. *The Making of Modern Japan*. Cambridge, MA: Harvard University Press, 2000b.
Joshi, Jayant S. and Rajesh Kumar. "The Dutch Physicians at Dejima or Deshima and the Rise of Western Medicine in Japan." *Proceedings of the Indian History Congress* 63 (2002).

Kaempfer, Engelbert. *The History of Japan, along with a Description of Siam*. Translated by J. G. Scheuchzer. Glasgow: James MacLehose and Sons, 1906.

Kamiya, Nobuyuki and Kimura Naoya, eds. *Kaikin to Sakoku*. Tokyo: Tokyo-dō Shuppan, 2002.

Kanai, Madoka, ed. *A Diary of William Cleveland, Captain's Clerk Aboard the Massachusetts*. Quezon City, Philippines: Institute of Asian Studies, University of the Philippines, 1965.

Katagiri, Kazuo. "The Rise and Development of Dutch Learning in Japan." *Acta Asiatica* 42 (1982): 1–17.

Katagiri, Kazuo. *Oranda Tsūji no Kenkyū*. Tokyo: Yoshikawa Kōbunkan, 1985.

Katagiri, Kazuo. *Hirakareta Sakoku: Nagasaki Dejima no Hito, Mono, Jōhō*. Tokyo: Kōdansha, 1997.

Katagiri, Kazuo. *Oranda Yado Ebiya no Kenkyuu*. Kyoto: Shibunkaku Shuppan, 1998.

Katagiri, Kazuo. *Edo no Orandajin: Kapitan no Edo Sanpu*. Tokyo: Chūō Kōron, 2000.

Katō, Eichi. "Deshima Ron." In *Nihon Tsūshi 12: Kinsei 2*, edited by Asao Naohiro. Tokyo: Iwanami Kōza, 1993.

Kawashima, Motojirō. *Shuinsen Bōekishi*. Kyoto: Naigai Shuppan Kabushiki Gaisha, 1921.

Kazui, Tashiro and Susan Downing Videen. "Foreign Relations During the Edo Period: Sakoku Reexamined." *Journal of Japanese Studies* 8, no. 2 (Summer, 1982): 283–306.

Keene, Donald. *The Japanese Discovery of Europe, 1720–1830*. Stanford: Stanford University Press, 1969.

Kinski, Michael. "*Materia Medica* in Edo Period Japan: The Case of Mummy. Takai Ranzan's *Shokuji kai*, Part Two." *Japonica Humboldtiana* 9 (2005): 55–170.

Kinski, Michael. "Table Manners in the Edo Period." In *Japanese Foodways Past and Present*, edited by Eric Rath and Stephanie Assmann. Urbana: University of Illinois Press, 2010.

Klelar, Cynthia. "Prisoners in Silken Bonds: Obligation, Trade, and Diplomacy in English Voyages to Japan and China." *Journal of Early Modern Cultural Studies* 6, no. 1 (Spring, 2006): 84–105.

Knerr, Kerry Marjorie. "In Search of a Good Drink: Punches, Cocktails, and Imperial Consumption." Master's Thesis, University of Texas, 2015.

Kobata, Atsushi. *Kōzan no Rekishi*. Tokyo: Shibundō, 1956.

Kobata, Atsushi. *Kingin Bōeki-shi no Kenkyū*. Tokyo: Hōsei Daigaku Shuppankyoku, 1976.

Komter, Aafte. "Gifts and Social Relations: The Mechanisms of Reciprocity." *International Sociology* 22, no. 1 (2007): 93–107.

Kornicki, Peter. *The Book in Japan: A Cultural History from the Beginnings to the Nineteenth Century*. Leiden: Brill, 1998.

Kornicki, Peter. "Narrative of a Catastrophe: *Musashi Abumi* and the Meireki Fire." *Japan Forum* 21, no. 3 (2010): 347–61.

Kujala, Antti and Mirkka Danielsbacka. *Reciprocity in Human Societies: From Ancient Times to the Modern Welfare State*. London: Palgrave, 2019.

Laver, Michael. *Japan's Economy by Proxy in the Seventeenth Century: China, The Netherlands, and the Bakufu*. Amherst, NY: Cambria Press, 2008.

Laver, Michael. "Butter Diplomacy." *Education About Asia* 17 no. 1 (Spring, 2012): 5–8.

Laver, Michael. *The Sakoku Edicts and the Politics of Tokugawa Hegemony*. Amherst, NY: Cambria Press, 2013.

Lee, Ji-young. *China's Hegemony: Four Hundred Years of East Asian Domination*. New York: Columbia University Press, 2017.

Leupp, Gary. *Interracial Intimacy in Japan: Western Men and Japanese Women, 1543–1900*. London: Continuum, 2003.

Library of Congress. William Speiden Journals, https://www.loc.gov/collections/william-speiden-journals/articles-and-essays/voyage-of-mississippi-to-china-seas-and-japan/january-1854-to-july-2-1854/.

Lin, Lin and Pei-chuan Mao. "Content Analysis Study of Food Specialties and Souvenirs." *Journal of Hospitality and tourism Management* 22 (March, 2015): 19–29.

Lorge, Peter. *The Asian Military Revolution: From Gunpowder to the Bomb*. Cambridge: Cambridge University Press, 2008.

Lubar, Steven. "In the Footsteps of Perry: The Smithsonian Goes to Japan." *The Public Historian* 17, no. 3 (Summer, 1995): 25–59.

Maehira, Fusaaki. "'Sakoku:' Nihon no Kaigai Bōeki." In *Nihon no Kinsei: Seikaishi no naka no Kinsei*, edited by Asao Naohiro. Tokyo: Chūō Kōronsha, 1991.

Massarella, Derek. *A World Elsewhere: Europe's Encounter with Japan in the Sixteenth and Seventeenth Centuries*. New Haven: Yale University Press, 1990.

Matsui, Yoko and Matsukata Fuyuko, eds. *Nihon Kankei Kaigai Shiryō* (Diaries Kept by the Heads of the Dutch Factory in Japan) *Volume 1* Part 1. Tokyo: Shiryō Hensanjō, 1976.

Matsukata, Fuyuko. "Fires and Recoveries Witnessed by the Dutch in Edo and Nagasaki: The Great Fire of Meireki in 1657 and the Great Fire of Kanbun in 1633." *Itinerario* 37, no. 3 (December, 2013): 172–87.

Mauss, Marcel. *The Gift: Forms and Functions of Exchange in Archaic Societies*. London: Cohen and West, 1966.

Melo, João. "Seeking Prestige and Survival: Gift-Exchange Practices between the Portuguese Estado da India and Asian Rulers." *Journal of the Economic and Social History of the Orient* 56 (2013): 672–95.

Michel, Wolfgang. "Medicine and Allied Sciences in the Cultural Exchange between Japan and Europe in the Seventeenth Century." In *Theories and Methods in Japanese Studies: Current State & Future Developments—Papers in Honor of Josef Kreiner*, edited by Hans Dieter Ölschleger. Göttingen: Vandenhoeck & Ruprecht Unipress, 2007.

Michel, Wolfgang. "Travels of the Dutch East India Company in the Japanese Archipelago." In *Japan—A Cartographic Vision*, edited by Lutz Walter. Munich: Prestel-Verlag, 1993.

Miczo, Nathan. "The Human Condition and the Gift: Toward a Theoretical Perspective on Close Relationships." *Human Studies* 31, no. 2 (2008): 133–55.

Mitchell, David. *The Thousand Autumns of Jacob de Zoet*. New York: Random House, 2011.

MIT Visualizing Culture: "Black Ships and Samurai," https://visualizingcultures.mit.edu/black_ships_and_samurai/gallery/pages/02_016a_Dejima.htm.

Montanus, Arnoldus. *Gedenkwaerdige Gesantschappen der Oost-Indische Maetschappij in't Vereenigde Nederland aen de Kaisaren van Japan*. Amsterdam: Jacob Meurs, 1680.

Morris Suzuki, Tessa. "A Descent into the Past: The Frontier in the Construction of Japanese Identity." In *Multicultural Japan: Paleolithic to Postmodern*, edited by Donald Denoon, Mark Hudson, Gavan McCormack, and Tessa Morris Suzuki. Cambridge: Cambridge University Press, 1996.

Murakami, Naojirō, ed. *Ikoko Nikki*. Tokyo: Sanshūsha, 1911.

Nagazumi, Yōko. "From Company to Individual Company Servants: Dutch Trade in Eighteenth Century Japan." In *On the Eighteenth Century as a Category of Asian History: Van Leur in Retrospect*, edited by Leonard Blussé and Femme Gaastra. Aldershot: Ashgate, 1998.

Nakai, Kate Wildman. *Shogunal Politics: Arai Hakuseki and the Premise of Tokugawa Rule*. Cambridge, MA: Harvard University Asia Center, 1988.

Nakamura, Tadashi, ed. *Eiinbon Ikoku Nikki: Konchiin Sūden Gaikō Monjō Shūsei*. Tokyo: Tokyo Bijutsu, 1989.

Narushima, Motonao. *Kokushi Taikei: Tokugawa Jikki*. Edited by Kuroita Katsumi. Tokyo: Yoshikawa Kōbunkan, 1982.

Nakamura, Tadashi. *Kinsei Nagasaki Bōeki-shi no Kenkyū*. Tokyo: Yoshikawa Kōbunkan, 1988.

Nationaal Archief. "Japanese Demands: Digitization," https://www.geheugenvannederland.nl/en/geheugen/pages/collectie/Japanse+eisen/Digitalisering.

Nitobe, Inazo. *The Intercourse between the US and Japan*. Baltimore: John Hopkins Press, 1891.

Nozawa, Joji. "Wine as a Luxury at the Dutch Factory at Japan During the Second Half of the 18th Century." In *Luxury in the Low Countries: Miscellaneous Reflections on Netherlandish Material Culture, 1500 to the Present*, edited by Rengenier Rittersma. Brussels: Pharo Publishing, 2010.

Nozawa, Joji. "Wine Drinking Culture in Seventeenth Century Japan: The Role of Dutch Merchants." *Japanese Foodways, Past and Present*, edited by Eric Rath and Stephanie Assmann. Urbana: University of Illinois Press, 2010.

Ōishi, Shinzaburō. *Shuinsen to Miname e no Senkisha*. Tokyo: Gyōsei, 1986.

Opstall, M. E. van. "Dutchmen and Japanese in the Eighteenth Century." In *Trading Companies in Asia: 1600–1830*, edited by J. van Goor. Utrecht: Hes Uitgevers, 1986.

Ōta, Katsuya. *Sakoku Jidai: Nagasaki Bōeki-shi no Kenkyū*. Kyoto: Shibunkaku, 1992.

Overmeer Fischer, J. F. Van. "Bijdrage tot de Kennis von het Japansche Rijk." Amsterdam: J. Mueller and Co., 1833.

Pacheco, Diego. "The Founding of the Port of Nagasaki and Its Cession to the Society of Jesus." *Monumenta Nipponica* 25, no. 3/4 (1970): 303–23.

Parthesius, Robert. *Dutch Ships in Tropical Waters: The Development of the Dutch East India Company Shipping Network in Asia, 1595–1660*. Amsterdam: Amsterdam University Press, 2010.

Paul, Hubert. "De Coningh on Deshima: Mijn Verblijf in Japan, 1856." *Monumenta Nipponica* 32, no. 3 (Autumn, 1977): 347–64.

Perry, Matthew Calbraith. *The Japan Expedition, 1852–1854; The Personal Journal of Commodore Matthew C. Perry*. Edited by Roger Pineau with an Introduction by Samuel Eliot Morison. Washington, DC: Smithsonian Institution Press, 1968.

Phillips, James Duncan. "The Voyage of the *Margaret* in 1801: The First Salem Voyage to Japan." *Proceedings of the American Antiquarian Society* 54, no. 2 (October, 1944): 313–39.

Pombejra, Dhiravat. *Court, Company, and Campong: Essays on the VOC Presence in Ayutthaya*. Phra Nakhon Sri Ayutthaya: Ayutthaya Historical Study Center, 1992.

Pomeranz, Kenneth. *The Great Divergence: China, Europe, and the Making of the Modern World Economy*. Princeton: Princeton University Press, 2000.

Preble, George Henry. *The Opening of Japan: A Diary of Discovery in the Far East, 1853–1856*. Edited by Boleslaw Szczesniak. Norman: University of Oklahoma Press, 1962.

Pugliasco, Guido Carlo. "Lost in Translation: From Omiyage to Souvenir: Beyond Aesthetics of the Japanese Office Ladies' Gaze in Hawai'i." *Journal of Material Culture* 10, no. 2 (2005): 177–96.

Purchase, Samuel. *Hakluytus Posthhumus or Purchase his Pilgrims, Volume 2*. Glasgow: James MacLehose and Sons, 1905.

Raffles, Thomas Stamford. *The History of Java, Volume 2*. London: Black, Parbury and Allen, 1817.

Rath, Eric. "Banquets against Boredom: Towards Understanding (Samurai) Cuisine in Early Modern Japan." *Early Modern Japan: An Interdisciplinary Journal* XVI (2008): 43–55.

Rath, Eric. *Food and Fantasy in Early Modern Japan*. Berkeley: University of California Press, 2010a.

Rath, Eric. "Honzen Dining: The Poetry of Formal Meals in Late Medieval and Early Modern Japan." In *Japanese Foodways, Past and Present*, edited by Eric Rath and Stephanie Assmann. Urbana: University of Illinois Press, 2010b.

Remelink, Willem, et al., eds. *The Deshima Diaries Marginalia: 1740–1800*. Tokyo: Japan-Netherlands Institute, 2004.

Rietbergen, Pieter. *Japan Verwoord: Nihon Door Nerderlandse Ogen, 1600–1799*. Amsterdam: Hotei Publishing, 2003.

Ruangsilp, Bhawan. *Dutch East India Company Merchants at the Court of Ayutthaya: Dutch Perceptions of the Thai Kingdom, c. 1604–1765*. Leiden: Brill, 2007.

Rubinger, Richard. *Private Academies of the Tokugawa Period*. Princeton: Princeton University Press, 1988.

Rupp, Katherine. *Gift-Giving in Japan: Cash, Connections, Cosmologies*. Stanford: Stanford University Press, 2003.

Sahlins, Marshall. *Stone Age Economics*. Chicago: Aldine-Atherton, 1972.

Sakamaki, Shunzo. *Japan and the US, 1790–1853*. Tokyo: Asiatic Society of Japan, 1939.

Saris, John. *The First Voyage of the English to Japan*. Edited by Takanobu Otsuka. Tokyo: Tōyō Bunko, 1941.

Satow, Ernest. *The Voyage of Captain John Saris to Japan, 1613*. London: The Hakluyt Society, 1900.

Screech, Timon. *The Shogun's Painted Culture: Fear and Creativity in the Japanese States, 1760–1829*. London: Reaktion Books, 2000.

Screech, Timon. *The Lens Within the Heart: The Western Scientific Gaze and Popular Imagery in Later Edo Japan*. Honolulu: University of Hawai'i Press, 2002.

Screech, Timon. *Japan Extolled and Decried: Carl Peter Thunberg's Travels in Japan 1775–1776*. New York: Routledge, 2005.

Screech, Timon. *Secret Memoirs of the Shoguns: Isaac Titsingh and Japan, 1799–1822*. London: Routledge, 2006.

Seigle, Cecilia Segawa. "Tokugawa Tsunayoshi and the Formation of Edo Castle Rituals of Gift-Giving." In *Mediated by Gifts: Politics and Society in Japan, 1350–1850*, edited by Martha Chaiklin. Leiden: Brill, 2016.

Shuman, Amy. "Food Gifts: Ritual Exchange and the Production of Excess Meaning." *The Journal of American Folklore* 113, no. 450 (Autumn, 2000): 495–508.

Smith, George Vinal. *The Dutch in Seventeenth-Century Thailand*. Northern Illinois: Center for Southeast Asian Studies Special Report, 1977.

Souza, George Bryan. *The Survival of Empire: Portuguese Trade and Society in China and the South China Sea, 1630–1754*. Cambridge: Cambridge University Press, 1986.

Statler, Oliver. *The Black Ship Scrolls*. Rutland, VT: Charles Tuttle Company, 1964.

Sukeno, Kentarō. *Shimabara no Ran*. Tokyo: Azuma Shuppan, 1967.

Suzuki, Shogo. "Europe at the Periphery of the Japanese World Order." In *International Orders in the Early Modern World*, edited by Shogo Suzuki, Yongjin Zhang, and Joel Quirk. New York: Routledge, 2014.

Suzuki, Yasuko. *Kinsei Nichi-Ran Bōeki-shi no Kenkyū*. Tokyo: Sibunkaku Shuppan, 2004.

Suzuki, Yasuko. *Japan-Netherlands Trade, 1600–1800: The Dutch East India Company and Beyond*. Kyoto: Kyoto University Press, 2012.

Swan, Claudia. "Dutch Diplomacy and Trade in *Rariteyten*: Episodes in the History of Material Culture in the Dutch Republic." In *Global Gifts: The Material Culture of Diplomacy in Early Modern Eurasia*, edited by Zoltann Biedermann, Anne Gerritsen, and Giorgio Riello. Cambridge: Cambridge University Press, 2018.

Takekoshi, Yosaburo. *The Economic Aspects of the History of the Civilization of Japan, Volume II*. London: Routledge, 2003.

Toby, Ronald P. *State and Diplomacy in Early Modern Japan: Asia in the Development of the Tokugawa Bakufu*. Princeton: Princeton University Press, 1984.

Thompson, Edward, ed. *The Diary of Richard Cocks—Cape Merchant in the English Factory in Japan, Volume I*. London: Hakluyt Society, 1883.

Totman, Conrad. *Early Modern Japan*. Berkeley: University of California Press, 1995.

Tsuji, Tatsuya. *Nihon no Rekishi 13: Edo Kaifu*. Tokyo: Chūō Kōronsha, 1966.

Tsunoda, Ryusaku, Wm. Theodore De Barry, and Donald Keene, eds. *Sources of Japanese Tradition, Volume 1*. New York: Columbia University Press, 1958.

Tsukahira, George Toshio. *Feudal Control in Tokugawa Japan: The Sankin Kōtai System*. Cambridge: Harvard University Press, 1966.

Tsuruta, Kei. "Kinsei Nihon no Yottsu no Kuchi." In *Ajia no naka no Nihonshi 2: Gaikō to Sensō*, edited by Arano Yasunori, et al. Tokyo: Tokyo Daigaku Shuppankai, 1992.

Vaporis, Constantine. *Tour of Duty: Samurai, Military Service in Edo, and the Culture of Early Modern Japan*. Honolulu: University of Hawai'i Press, 2008.

Velde, Paul van der and Rudolf Backofner, eds. *The Deshima Diaries: Marginalia, 1700–1740*. Tokyo: The Japan-Netherlands Institute, 1992.

Vermuelen, Tom et al., eds. *Deshima Dagregisters, Their Original Table of Contents, Volume VIII: 1760–1780*. Leiden: Leiden Centre for the History of European Expansion, 1986.

Viallé, Cynthia. "In Aid of Trade: Dutch Gift-Giving in Tokugawa Japan." *Tokyo Daigaku Shiryōhensan-jō Kenkyū Kiyō* 16 (March, 2006): 57–78.

Vink, Markus. *Encounters on the Opposite Coast: The Dutch East India Company and the Nayaka State of Madurai in the Seventeenth Century*. Leiden: Brill, 2016.

Volker, T. *Porcelain and the Dutch East India Company, as Recorded in the Dagh-Registers of Batavia Castle, Those of Hirado and Deshima, and Other Contemporary Papers, 1602–1682*. Leiden: E. J. Brill, 1971.

Vos, Frits. "A Distance of 13,000 Miles: The Dutch through Japanese Eyes." *Delta: A Review of Arts, Life and Thought in the Netherlands* 16, no. 2 (1973): 29–46.

Vos, Frits. "Forgotten Foibles: Love and the Dutch at Deshima." *East Asian History* 39 (December, 2014): 139–52.

Wakabayaki, Bob Tadashi. *Anti-Foreignism and Western Learning in in Early Modern Japan: The New Theses of 1825*. Cambridge, MA: Harvard University Asia Center, 1986.

Walker, Brett. *The Conquest of Ainu Lands: Ecology and Culture in Japanese Expansion, 1590–1800*. Berkeley: University of California Press, 2001.

Walker, Brett. "Foreign Affairs and Frontiers in Early Modern Japan: A Historiographical Essay." *Early Modern Japan* (Fall, 2002): 44–128.

Wallace, Alfred Russell. *The Malay Archipelago: The Land of the Orang-Utan and the Bird of Paradise*. Oxford: John Beaufoy Publishing, 2016.

Watanabe, Yogorō. *Kinsei Nihon Bōeiki-ron no Tenkai*. Tokyo: Bunka Shobō Hakubunsha, 1978.

Wennekes, Wim. *Gouden Handel: De Erste Nederlanders Overzee, en wat zij dar Haalden*. Amsterdam: Atlas, 1996.

Williams, S. Wells. *A Journal of the Perry Expedition (1853-1854)*. Edited by F. W. Williams. Yokohama: Kelly and Walsh, 1910.

Wills, John. *Pepper, Guns, and Parleys: The Dutch East India Company and China, 1662-1681*. Cambridge: Harvard University Press, 1974.

Wills, John. *Embassies and Illusions: Dutch and Portuguese Envoys to K'ang Hsi*. Cambridge: Harvard University Asia Center, 1984.

Winkel, Margarita. "Gift Exchange and Reciprocity: Understanding Antiquarian/Ethnographic Communities Within and Beyond Tokugawa Borders." In *Mediated by Gifts: Politics and Society in Japan*, edited by Martha Chaiklin. Leiden: Brill, 2016.

Winters, Ria and Julia Hume. "The Dodo, the Deer, and a 1647 Voyage to Japan." *Historical Biology, An International Journal of Paleobiology* 27, no. 2 (2015): 258-64.

Wondrich, David. "Recovering the World's First Luxury Spirit: Batavia Arrack," https://www.thedailybeast.com/rediscovering-the-worlds-first-luxury-spirit-batavia-arrack.

Wooley, Kailin and Ayelet Fishbach. "A Recipe for Friendship: Similar Food Consumption Promotes Trust and Cooperation." *Journal of Consumer Psychology* 27, no. 1 (2017): 1-10.

Yamamoto, Hirofumi. *Sakoko to Kaikin no Jidai*. Tokyo: Azekura Shobō, 1995.

Yamamoto, Yoshito and Terrence Witkowski. "Omiyage Gift Purchasing by Japanese Travelers in the US." *Advances in Consumer Research* 18 (1991): 123-28.

Yamawaki, Teijirō, *Nagasaki Oranda no Shōkan: Seikai no naka no Sakoku Nihon*, (Tokyo: Chūō Kōronsha, 1980).

Yao, Keisuke. *Kinsei Oranda Bōeki to Sakoku*. Tokyo: Yoshikawa Kōbunkan, 1998.

Yellin, Victor Fell. "Mrs. Belmont, Matthew Perry, and the 'Japanese Minstrels.'" *American Music* 14, no. 3 (Autumn, 1996): 257-75.

Yonemori, Keizo. "Japanese Pomological Magic: Producing Fruits for Gifts." *Chronica Horticulturae* 49, no. 3 (2009): 15-18.

Zandfleet, Kees, et al. *The Dutch Encounter with Asia, 1600-1950*. Zwolle: Waanders Publishers, 2002.

Zhang, Yongjin. "The Tribute System." In *Oxford Bibliographies of Chinese Studies*, edited by Tim Wright. New York: Oxford University Press, 2013.

Zoomers, Henk. "The Netherlands, Siam, and the Telescope. The First Asian Encounter with a Dutch Invention." In *The Origins of the Telescope*, edited by Albert van Helden, et al. Amsterdam: KNAW Press, 2010.

Index

Adams, William   3, 4, 62
alcatieven. *See* carpets, as gift
almonds, as gift   102–3
Amaterasu   72
Americans
   with Cochin-China   117–18
   gifts for Shogun   116–22
   in Japan   115–22
   with Siam   117–18
   technology   121
ana-tsurushi (pit torture)   12
Andrade, Tonio   29
animal products, as gift   51–4
animal skins, as gift   52
Anno Domini   11
anti-Christian edicts   9
Arai, Hakuseki   95
arrack, as gift   108
Arrival of a Dutch Ship (Kawahara)   83
artistic works, as gifts   55–76
   candelabras   63–4, 66–71
   carpets   56–8
   clocks   71
   decorative containers   59–61
   engravings   61, 62–3
   glassware   75–6
   globes   58–9
   harmonica   63
   maps   59
   metalworking   63–76
   mirrors   72–4
   paintings   61–2
   silver ship   71
   tapestries   61, 63
asses, as gift   46
astrolabes, as gifts   93
Atlas Japonnensi (Montanus)   72
audience   13

bakufu   10, 11, 12, 23, 25, 27–8
Barreveld, Dirk   101
Battistini, Lawrence   119

beer   111
Befu, Harumi   98
Belozerskaya, Maria   47
Bengali carpets   57
bezoar stones   90
birds, as gift   46–51, 109
Blokhovius, Petrus   23
Blomhoff, Jan Cock   26
Boxer, Charles   62
Brauner, Christina   21
Breskens   91
Brouwer, Hendrick   131 n.12
buffaloes, as gift   39–40
bugyō   9, 13, 26
burning glasses. *See* reading glasses
butter, as gift   101–2

camels, as gift   37–42
candelabras, as gift   63–4, 66–71
Caron, Francois   65
carp   109
carpets, as gift   56–8
cassowaries   46–8
Catholicism   11
Chaiklin, Martha   16, 34, 41, 49, 55, 121, 151 n.10
Chamberlain, Richard   3
cheese, as gifts   103–4
China
   dynasties   24
   English voyages to   20
   European invasion of   29
   silk   4, 7, 9
Choson dynasty   25
Christianity   9–12, 63, 83
Clavell, James   3
Cleveland, William   116, 122
clocks, as gift   71
Clulow, Adam   23, 26–7, 31, 69
Cocks, Richard   62
compasses, as gifts   93–4
Couckebacker, Nicholas   62, 65–6

Coxinga 53. *See also* Zheng Chenggong
Cruijdeboeck (Dodonaeus) 93
Cullen, L. M. 55
curiosos 1, 15, 30, 34, 45, 76, 77, 101, 120

Daigaku-Sama, Tōdō 46
de Coningh, C. T. van Assendelft 108, 111
decorative containers, as gift 59–61
deerskins, as gift 53
De Liefde 2–3
de Roij, Nicholaes 78
Derrida, Jacques 20
Deshima 8–9, 10, 26, 35, 100
dodo 50
Dodonaeus, Rembert 93
Doeff, Hendrik 119
Duffy, Christopher 62
Dutch 126 n.20, 127 n.36, 135 n.69, 135 n.72
  in Asia 39, 115
  to Deshima 9
  as foreign 31–2
  gifts to Shogun 4, 12–17, 21–5 (*see also specific gifts*)
  in Japan 2–5, 11, 17, 25–33, 34, 64–76
  medical knowledge 14–15
  to Nagasaki 9
  obedience 26
  Portuguese and 2–3
  restrictions on 8
  role as vassals 32
  silk cartel 9
  submission 26
  trading 2–5, 9, 11, 17, 25–33, 34, 63–76
  visits to Edo 12–17, 27, 28–9, 28–48, 51–4, 55–76, 77–95, 97–114, 117, 118

East India Company 3, 21–2, 25, 97, 115
Edo
  Dutch visits to 12–17, 27, 28–48, 51–4, 55–76, 77–95, 97–114, 117, 118
  knowledge to 14
  medical knowledge to 14–15

  as political, economic, and military center of East Asia 24
eggs, as gift 110
eisboek (registry of requests) 49
elephants, as gift 45
engravings, as gift 61, 62–3
entertainment 113
"Estado da India" 21
European
  military technology 29
  scientific technology 79
exotic animals, as gifts 37–54
  animal products 51–4
  birds 46–51
  megafauna 40–6

Ferreira, Cristovão 58
fire engines, as gifts 77–9
Fischer, J. F. Van Overmeer 111
fish 109
food and drink, as gifts
  almonds 102–3
  butter 101–2
  carp 109
  cheese 103–4
  in early modern Japanese-Dutch interactions 97–114
  eggs 110
  fish 109
  role in rituals 97–8
  as social lubricant 99–114
  stone bass 110
  as symbolic gifts 97
  wine 103–10
foreign trade 6–12
Forer, Matthi 26
Fort Zeelandia 64
Frisius, Andries 23–4
fūsetsugaki 10, 32
Fuyuko, Matsukata 78

genever 111
gift-giving 15–17, 19–35, 120
  celebratory occasions for 25
  Derrida's views on 20
  economy 19, 96
  with expectation of reciprocity 19–20, 21
  as expression of love 19–20
  Gregory's views on 20

in Japan 21–35, 98
Miczo's views on 20
model 19–20
in pre-modern Japan 80–1
in relationships building 19, 20
Rupp's study of 20
and social obligations 20
for society binding 19
as symbolism 20
works of art as 55–76
gifts 1–2, 123n.9, 124 n.3
almonds 102–3
animal products 51–4
animal skins 52
arrack 108
asses as 46
birds 46–51
buffaloes 39–40
butter 101–2
candelabras 63–4, 66–71
carpets 56–8
cheese 103–4
clocks 71
compasses 93–4
for cordial relations with Japanese officialdom 1–2, 14–17
decorative containers 59–61
Dutch to Shogun 4, 12–17, 21–5
(*see also specific gifts*)
eggs 110
elephants as 45
engravings 61, 62–3
exotic animals as 37–54
fire engines 77–9
food and drink 97–114
glassware 75–6
globes 58–9
harmonica 63
Hassaku 25
horses 42–5
institutionalized 16
intangible 98–9
maps 59
medicines 88–91
megafauna 40–6
mirrors 72–4
navigational tools 93–4
official 16
oxen 41–2
paintings 61–2

for political/economic gain 1
quasi 16, 32–4, 40, 49, 53, 55, 79, 85, 88–9, 93, 95
role in trade and diplomacy 1
sake 106–7
scientific paraphernalia as 77–96
silver ship 71
spectacles 84–8
stone bass 110
tapestries 61, 63
telescope/spyglasses 79–84
transactional 21–2
unicorn horns 52
wine 103–10
works of art as 55–76
Gilbert, Marc 112
glassware, as gifts 75–6
globes, as gift 58–9
gold pocket watch 44
Goldsmith, Oliver 31
Goodman, Grant 14, 130 n.75
Great Meireki Fire 78
Gregory, Chris 20
Gudeman, Stephen 91

Hamarda, Yahyōe 64–5
harbor tax 64
harmonica, as gift 63
Hassaku 25
Hawkes, Francis 119, 121
herbalist 14–15
Hideyoshi, Toyotomi 5
Himiko 72–3
Hirado 3, 6, 7–8, 9, 11
History of Japan (Kaempfer) 95
Hofreis (Court journey) 12–17, 28–30
Hokkaido 10
horses, as gift 42–5
housekeepers 8
Hyde, Lewis 19

Ikoku Nikki 22
Inazo, Nitobe 119
institutionalized gifts 16
intangible gifts 98–9
Itowappa Nakama 9

Jackson, Andrew 117
Jackson, Terry 93
Jampoler, Andrew 117

Jansen, Marius   30
Japan
   American in   115–22
   dodo in   50
   Dutch in   2–5, 11, 17, 25–8, 25–33, 34, 64–76
   foreign trade in   6–12
   gift-giving in   21–35
   networks of reciprocity in   20
   Nuyts, Pieter and   64–7
   Portuguese trade with   2, 7–8
   silks   2, 4, 7, 9
   Tokugawa   5–12
   VOC factory in   4
Japanese Discovery of Europe (Keene)   95
Joby, Christopher   145 n.44, 145 n.54
Joji, Nozawa   105–7, 111

Kaempfer, Engelbert   8, 68, 76, 92, 119, 128 n.53, 129 n.68
kasuparu-ryū geka   92
Keene, Donald   70, 95, 123 n.10
Keiga, Kawahara   83
Keijser, H. J.   43
kimono   33
Kingdom of Ryūkaya   10, 12, 24–5
Klekar, Cynthia   20, 21
koban, as gift   89
Konchi-in Sūden   22
Korean trade   95
Kyushu   6

The Land of the Orang-utan and the Bird of Paradise (Wallace)   49
Levyssohn, J. H.   119
Lubar, Steven   119

madai   110
The Making of Modern Japan (Jansen)   30
The Malay Archipelago (Wallace)   49
maps, as gift   59
Masashige, Inoue   38, 49, 53, 59–60, 63, 69, 71, 74, 77–8, 80–6, 88–91, 101, 105, 107, 113, 129 n.60
Mastsumae family   10, 46
material wealth   19
Matsura family   9
Mauss, Marcel   19
medicines, as gifts   88–91

megafauna   40–6
Melo, João   21
Merino sheep   117
metalworking, as gift   63–76
Miczo, Nathan   20
military technology   29
Ming dynasty   24–5
mirrors, as gift   72–4
Mitsunari, Ishida   5
Montanus, Arnoldus   72
moon island. *See* Deshima

Nagasaki city   1, 6–11, 7–8, 10, 13, 15–16, 23, 25–6, 32–5, 48–51
   prostitutes in   8
   Tokugawa and   9, 25
naorai   98
Narrative (Hawkes)   119
navigational tools, as gifts   93–4
New Years' banquet   110–11
noble   136 n.3
Nuyts, Pieter   23, 64–7

obedience   26
objets d'art   56
official gifts   16
Okinawa   10
ōmetsuke   11
Oosterwijk, Quirijn   71
Oranda Kapitan   13
Oranda Kapitan. See ostriches
ornamental cases   59–60
ostriches   46, 48–50
oxen, as gift   41–2

paintings, as gifts   61–2
Patani   3
Paul, Hubert   108
Perry, Matthew   118, 119–21
Persian carpets   57
Philippines   7
Portuguese   32
   Dutch and   2–3
   silk trade   4
   trade with Japan   2, 7–8
private trade   95
prostitutes   8
Puyck, Nicholaas   3
pyrotechnics   14
pyrotechnist   24, 91, 130 n.74

Qing dynasty   24–5, 29
Quackernaeck, Jacob   3
quasi-gifts   16, 32–4, 40, 49, 53, 55, 79, 85, 88–9, 93, 95

rangaku   14–15, 93
rariteyten   1
Rath, Eric   109, 110
ray skins, gift   53
reading glasses   87
renaissance fort   29
return gifts   13, 33–4, 60, 79, 89, 97, 100, 135 n.73. *See also* gift-giving
Roberts, Edmund   117
rug   57
Rupp, Katherine   20

sakana   110, 113
sake, as gift   106–7
sakoku edicts   7–9
sankin kotai system   12, 28
Saris, John   3, 21, 79
Schamberger, Caspar   92
scientific paraphernalia, as gifts   77–96, 120–1
    fire engines   77–9
    medicines   88–91
    navigational tools   93–4
    reading glasses   87
    spectacles   84–8
    telescope/spyglasses   79–84
Screech, Timon   25, 30, 62, 63, 75
Shimazu family   6, 10
Shogun   2–4, 12–17, 21–5, 30, 56
    almonds as gift for   102–3
    animal skins as gift for   53
    asses as gift for   46
    birds as gift for   46–51
    buffaloes as gift for   39–40
    butter as gift for   101–2
    camels as gift for   37–42
    candelabras as gift for   63–4, 66–71
    carpets as gift for   56–8
    cheese as gift for   103–4
    compasses as gifts for   93–4
    court   2–3, 5, 10, 12, 15, 23, 30, 35, 42, 66, 80
    decorative containers as gift for   59–61
    elephants as gift for   45
    engravings as gift for   61, 62–3
    globes as gift for   58–9
    harmonica as gift for   63
    Hidetada   66
    horses as gift for   42–5
    Iemitsu   11, 66–7
    maps as gift for   59
    medicines as gifts for   88–91
    navigational tools as gifts for   93–4
    oxen as gift for   41–2
    paintings as gift for   61–2
    spectacles as gifts for   84–8
    telescope/spyglasses as gifts for   79–84
    unicorn horns as gift for   52–3
    wine as gift for   103–10
    Yoshimune   43, 62, 71, 93, 102, 105
Shogun (Clavell)   3
shuinjo   3
Shumon Aratame Yaku   11
silks   2
    cartel   9
    China   4, 7, 9
silver ship, as gift   71
Sino-centric world order   24–5
Six, Daniel   89
Spanish wine   105, 107, 120
spectacles, as gifts   84–8
State and Diplomacy in Early Modern Japan (Toby)   24
Statler, Oliver   120
steam engines   121
Stewart, William Robert   115–16
stone bass, as gift   110
submission   26
surgeon   14
Suzuki, Shogo   22
Suzuki, Yasuko   91, 126 n.17
symbolism   20, 55, 98

Tang dynasty   24
tapestries, as gift   61, 63
telescope/spyglasses, as gifts   79–84
temporary marriages   8
tent wine   105, 107
Thunberg, Carl Peter   52, 92, 119
timepieces, as gifts   93, 94
Toby, Ronald   14, 24
Tojin Yashiki   10
Tokugawa
    family   5–12, 24
    Ieyasu   3–4, 5–6, 11, 22, 57, 66, 79

Tokugawa Japan 5–12
    foreign affairs, control of 6–12
    regulations 6
    restrictions 7–8
Tokugawa Jikki 57
Treaty of Kanagawa 118, 122
Treaty of Nanjing 121
tribute system 24
Tsukahira, George 28
tsukijima. *See* Deshima
Tsushima 10
Turkish carpets 57

unicorn horns, gift 52
Utagawa Kuniyasu 41

Valentine's Day 114
van den Broeck, Abraham 3
van Linschoten, Jan Huyghen 125 n.7
van Loodensteyn, Jan Joosten 3
van Nijenroode, Cornelus 67
van Opstall, M. E. 71
van Royen, Willem 62
van Santvoort, Melchior 3
Vaporis, Constantine 28
Verenigde Oost-Indische Compagnie
    (VOC) 4–5, 31, 34–5, 82, 123n.3
    challenge 4
    factory in Japan 4–5
    factory in Taiwan 64
    gift-giving activity in Japan 22, 24
        (*see also* gift-giving; gifts; return gifts)
    Inaba incident 67–76
    in island of Taiwan 4
    merchants 1–2, 3
    Nuyts incident 64–7
Vertseeghen, Willem 37
Viallé, Cynthia 46
Volger, Willem 89
von Siebold, Phillip Franz 83, 92, 108, 118, 119
Vos, Frits 33

Wagenaer, Zacarias 58
Walker, Brett 46
Wallace, Alfred Russell 49
Wei dynasty 72–3
Werner, Jan Jephart 43
Williams, S. Wells 119
wine, as gifts 103–10

Yamatai 72
Yamawaki, Teijirō 24–5
Yōko, Nagazumi 91
Yoshimune 43, 62, 71, 93, 102, 105

Zhang, Yongzin 132 n.27
Zheng Chenggong 69

www.ingramcontent.com/pod-product-compliance
Lightning Source LLC
Chambersburg PA
CBHW052047300426
44117CB00012B/2013